A Straitened Stage

For Tom Conneelly, Tawnaghbawn,
in memory of his parents

A Straitened Stage
A Study of the Theatre of
J. Saunders Lewis

Ioan Williams

SEREN BOOKS

SEREN BOOKS is the book imprint of
Poetry Wales Press Ltd
Andmar House, Tondu Road, Bridgend, Mid Glamorgan

© Ioan Williams, 1991

A British Library Cataloguing in Publication Data
Record is available from the CIP office

ℛ   ISBN   1-85411-043-8

*The publisher acknowledges the financial support ot the
Welsh Arts Council*

Typeset in 10.5 point Plantin
Printed in Wales by WBC Print Ltd, Bridgend

Contents

Preface

I have written this book in the belief that Saunders Lewis's drama deserves to attract the widest interest. In the first place, it provides a way of approaching modern Welsh literature and culture, which is a uniquely valuable field of study. Then, from a European viewpoint, his Theatre provides a fascinating perspective on modern sensibility. It is not only that as a poet and dramatist he challenges comparison with major artists in other countries. His contribution has amounted to a recognisably distinct development of mainstream European culture.

In writing the book it was difficult not to take for granted some acquaintance with the outline of Saunders Lewis's career as a scholar, artist and politician. Readers to whom the subject is quite new may find a general account of his remarkable career in *The Oxford Companion to the Literature of Wales,* compiled and edited by Meic Stephens (1986). The following is a brief resumé.

J. Saunders Lewis was born in 1893 in Wallesey, Cheshire, to parents who both belonged to families prominent in the history of the Calvinist Methodist Church. Educated in a private school and in Liverpool University, he fought as an infantryman during the First World War, experienced a 'conversion' to nationalism and began to write in Welsh. Subsequently he published a number of critical studies, of novels and poems and some twenty plays, which remain the most significant body of literature produced by any modern Welsh writer. His political career is also of great importance. He was one of the founders of the party since known as Plaid Cymru, the Party of Wales, and was active for years in politics and political journalism. Together with Lewis Valentine and D.J.Williams, he initiated the strategy of resistance to the indifference or hostility to Welsh opinion of British Governments and the British Establishment by setting fire to materials collected on the site of a projected bombing school at Penyberth in the Llyn Peninsula. For this offence against British law he served a term of imprisonment after a jury at Caernarfon had failed to find him and his companions guilty and the trial had been removed to London to secure conviction. Subsequently, although widely recognized as a scholar of striking originality and verve, he lost his job as a lecturer in University College, Swansea and was reduced for years to teaching at a Catholic private school. In 1962 his radio lecture on the 'Fate of the Language' initiated a new wave of activity which expressed itself through the newly formed Welsh Language Society, who adopted non-violent methods modelled on those of the Penyberth protesters.

During his life Saunders Lewis was a controversial figure, not least because he wrote as a Catholic in Non-Conformist Wales. At this distance he remains controversial, as a scholar and critic, as a political thinker and even as a dramatist, though to a lesser extent.This book assumes that difficulties of interpretation and assessment exist, but that he is a figure of considerable interest and importance in the history of Twentieth Century Theatre, not merely in Wales.

Throughout the book I have translated freely from Saunders Lewis's works myself because it seemed best to present my understanding of the texts in the run of my argument. The problems of translating from Welsh to English are very considerable and I have to confess that I despair of ever being able to present anything resembling a proper English equivalent of the dignified, muscular yet familiar dialogue which runs throughout his later plays. The difficulty is not merely linguistic, of course, but arises from the fact that the literary and cultural registers of the two countries are so very different, so different as to seem at times even mutually hostile. The problem of translation is similar to that which arises in the case of Racine.

Short quotations in the body of the text are given only in English. Longer quotations are provided first in the original, followed by a translation. I have not indicated in the text whether quotations from his works are given in the original language or not. References in the notes show whether the original was written in English or Welsh.

I have used the proper titles of Saunders Lewis's plays in the text, but provide English versions in the Appendix. I hope that one reference will be all that is needed and that after a while non-Welsh speaking readers will be able to accept the Welsh phrase quite naturally. The Bibliography contains a short list of translations and books which provide information about Saunders Lewis. This study does no more than show the hem of the garment and I hope that it may stimulate interest in other aspects of the work and the career of this most remarkable man.

In concluding I should confess a highly personal debt to the writings of Saunders Lewis. It is also a great pleasure to acknowledge my gratitude for what I have gained from others while working in this field and for the experience of working within an intellectual community of which until so recently Saunders Lewis himself was a member. They include Professors Geraint Gruffudd and Bobi Jones of Aberystwyth, the National Librarian, Dr. Brinley Roberts. Professor Bedwyr Lewis Jones of Bangor and Dr Emyr Humphreys have very kindly tried to keep me from mistakes and errors of judgement. I am sure that everyone who has worked on the theatre of Saunders Lewis will share my gratitude to Dafydd Glyn Jones, whose work on the dramatist provides a constant standard and point of reference.

Finally, I would like to thank Mrs Mair Jones for her kind permision to quote from her father's works throughout the volume.

Introduction

The traditionalism of Saunders Lewis's Theatre, which is immediately noticeable in his constrictive use of the stage, seems to set him apart from the mainstream of Twentieth Century Theatre. The major trends in European Theatre since 1918 have been a series of reactions against the conventions and methods of Naturalism. The Naturalist assumes the firmness and substantiality of the material world and makes his theatre approximate to it as closely as possible. To achieve this end he restricts the range of movements and structures his stage reflects to those available in the world around him.[1] In the main, modern practitioners of Theatre have sought to challenge categories of reason, social forms and moral and material certainties. Their stage has been open and flexible, permitting sharp contrast and wide varieties of movement. Though in different ways, Expressionist Theatre, the practical experiments of Meyerhold in Russia, the plays of Pirandello and Brecht and, more recently, of writers as diverse in method and aim as Beckett, Durrenmat and Ionesco, all exploit Theatre's insubstantiality and its dependance on convention to show how the forms of human experience and even the apparent solidities of the human world may melt and merge into one another.

However, the conventions on which Saunders Lewis's theatre are based derive immediately from Naturalism. Like Ibsen's, his stage is narrow and clearly defined and his plays develop through dialogue and debate. His is not a theatre of movement and action, but of reaction. His particular strengths and limitations appear clearly in contrast with those of the French Catholic playwright, Paul Claudel (1868-1955). Like Claudel, he presented an existential vision of life in which mankind struggled to define the terms of their own being in the light of their painful and bitter awareness of the need for God. His theatre, however, lacks the imaginative freedom and bold movement characteristic of the modernist, Claudel, whose audience will be swept away from themselves, threatened perhaps, and certainly shaken out of the possibility of repose. By contrast Saunders Lewis's plays are clear and concentrated in focus, limited in scope. Their characteristic three Act structure, developing through dialogue, inescapably logical, sustains an unremitting drive to demonstrate the relatedness of the spiritual and the human world. His is a theatre of irony, celebrating success and recording failure indifferently, but a theatre in which the audience is uniquely involved and ultimately responsible.

The analysis of the German critic, Peter Szondi,[2] provides a context in which this theatrical traditionalism may be fully understood as a positive and progressive contribution to the development of European Theatre. Szondi identified a common European tradition of drama, which emerged in the Renaissance and sustained itself throughout the following two centuries. The characteristics of this drama, he maintained, were: that it presented actions which arose from the relationships between individuals and was consequently mainly dependent on dialogue; that it was free standing, self-sufficient and self-explanatory, requiring neither narrator nor commentary; and that, unlike the novel, which permitted the reader to be simultaneously aware of different places and time scales, it sought to narrow and concentrate the audience's awareness, achieving its themes in terms of their immediate, sensuous apprehension of the theatrical event.

By the middle of the Nineteenth Century, Szondi argued, the Drama was in crisis. People began to think of individual experience as in essence an experience of isolation and lost confidence in personal and social relations. As this tendency increased, playwrights found it increasingly difficult to work in terms of inter-personal actions and the foundations of the traditional Drama were consequently weakened. Signs of the crisis were clearly evident long before. The hero of Romantic drama suffers agonies of uncertainty and self reproach in proportion as he feels that he has lost the ability to relate to the human world. His creator, the dramatist, insisted that unity and meaning were there to be discovered by the hero, but he failed completely in the attempt to devise an action which would permit his characters to experience them. The great achievement of the Realist novelists of the mid-century consisted in their success in bridging the gulf between the inner, personal experience of their characters and their experience as social beings. This was possible in the novel by virtue of the range of strategies of control and comment which what Szondi called the "autonomy" of drama prohibited. Moreover, as the sense of disconnectedness increased, even the novelist became less able to cope with it effectively.

Naturalism, which developed as a self-conscious movement in the novel before it affected Theatre, reflects bitter disillusion with the certainties of Realist art. In Naturalist drama, exemplified in the plays of Gerhard Hauptmann and Maxim Gorky[3], the solid material world presses in on individuals, who lose their grasp on their own experience in the struggle to cope with it. Contemporary Symbolist drama, as in the later plays of Strindberg, Maurice Maeterlinck and W.B. Yeats[4], embodied an awareness of the same crisis of sensibility, though in a different mode. The Symbolist dramatist had no more faith than his Naturalist counterpart in the individual's ability to relate the different aspects of his own experience. The action of his drama presents the movements of the unseen oceans in which human and non-human forms of life helplessly wash to and fro.

That both these tendencies are so fully and honestly developed in Ibsen's work explains his dominant position on the threshhold of the modern period. The greatness of Ibsen's achievement was that he was able to adapt the themes and conventions of the traditional Drama to express the problematic consciousness which threatened to overwhelm it. However, as Peter Szondi's analysis of his work reveals, this achievement was based on a fragile compromise which Ibsen himself was unable to sustain beyond his middle years. In his most famous and successful plays the inter-personal action presented immediately before us on stage is sustained by another, past, action, which is presented only indirectly. In a very real sense the dramatic focus in these plays is not what we see before us but its relation to other events which we do not see. So Ibsen's audience must understand not simply the relations and reactions presented immediately on stage, but the way they relate to past action, which is simultaneously presented to them and kept in their minds by means of various literary and dramatic devices. One of these is the symbolism which intrudes even into the most 'Naturalist' plays; another is the supernumary character, like Ulrik Bremen in *Rosmersholm,* who is employed to give depth and general import to the behaviour of other characters through whose movements the action is supposed to develop.

The bitter mistrust of society and, increasingly as his life wore on, of human experience itself, is a prominent part of Ibsen's legacy to European dramatists. What they have chosen for the most part to abandon, however, is his continuing struggle against the fear of failure and meaninglessness. Characters like Solness, his Master Builder, and John Gabriel Borkman, blasted by their own self-deceit and failure, nevertheless retain heroic stature. Far more widely representative of the modern period is Eugne Ionesco's *Rhinocéros* (1960), which dramatises precisely that loss of faith in personal relations that Szondi identifies as the root cause of the crisis in modern drama. Ionesco's hero, Bérenger, is a solitary, comic figure, whose insubstantial humanity deprives him even of the freedom to choose to become a rhinoceros. Friedrich Durrenmatt's *The Physicists* (1962), from a quite different viewpoint, presents us with a powerful image of social life as a form of madness. His hero, shamming madness, is locked away for ever from a world dominated by the genuinely insane psychiatrist.

Absurdist Theatre cannibalizes the themes and structures of traditional drama so as to create a new comedy, which gives us a way of living in a world which, sooner or later, in spite of ourselves, we must recognize as impossible. In this respect Absurdist dramatists may be said to be typical of Twentieth Century dramatists in general, even those whose political or social commitment dictates quite different aims and methods. The two great masters of Twentieth century European drama, Pirandello and Brecht, are equally committed to the deconstruction of traditional drama and its reconstruction in a way which will suggest a fundamentally critical view of the world it represented.

Saunders Lewis shared both Pirandello's sense of the fragility of human reality and Brecht's suspicion of the individual's capacity to exploit the material and social world in pursuit of self-definition. In spite of this, however, he refused to follow the path of deconstruction. For him drama continued to offer opportunities to work out the problematic elements in contemporary experience through the medium of action based on personal relations. The world of his drama is the world in which we live, a world in which consciousness is necessarily a consciousness of relatedness, a world of yesterday and tomorrow, of action and consequence. This is because for him the idea of character as it had developed in traditional drama remained essential. The dreadful loneliness and despair endured by some of his central characters never displaces the firm conviction that there is a spiritual dimension to the merely human. The world of Saunders Lewis's drama is not permeated by Spirit — he differs clearly from Claudel and from Eliot in this respect. His central characters face the difficult task of overcoming the world without abandoning it. To achieve this they have to master the devouring weakness of fear: and when they have done this they are free of the world and free to love. In Saunders Lewis's view this is to achieve humanity, which begins in an honest acknowledgement of isolation, but which can only fulfil itself in relation to others, in the world.

His great achievement and his contribution to history of European drama arises from the fact that he conceded nothing in the honesty and sharpness of his criticism and yet was able to hold on to and even greatly to strengthen the values which elsewhere similar criticism had swept away and with them the themes and structures of traditional drama. This is why he was able to maintain his grasp on the classic form of drama which Brecht had insisted impeded our understanding of reality. Saunders Lewis did not accept the Marxist view that the reality of human character derives from society. On the other hand, unlike Ionesco and Durrenmatt, he did insist that the individual could only be fully himself through relatedness, even though he carried with him everywhere the inner experience of isolation.

Saunders Lewis's theatre gives formal validation to this view because he had learnt to create his drama on the basis of the crisis of relatedness rather than by tracing its development or decline. From this it followed naturally that his plays remain what Szondi calls "inter personal" and that they are constructed in terms of traditional patterns of dialogue and debate. This also enables him to maintain the unity of time and place inherited from traditional Drama, though at the price of occasional strain, which leaves its mark clearly on individual plays. His economy and relative brevity as a dramatist, and the exceptionally narrow definition of his stage, though no doubt partly affected by the fact that he wrote so often for radio and television, also derive from the same source.

In many respects Saunders Lewis's theatre closely resembles that of the Seventeenth Century dramatist, Jean Racine (1639-99), especially in the way in which his plays develop around a point of crisis. Saunders Lewis's drama inclines constantly towards tragedy. The major characters of his plays are heroic, exceptional in their ability to suffer and their willingness to choose suffering rather than avoid it. As a dramatist Saunders Lewis has no interest in those who prefer the various kinds of death which may be achieved without that particular kind of active suffering. At the centre of his world is the Minotaur, fear, which his characters must overcome and are willing to overcome, in the only way possible, by accepting their weakness. Because of this many of his most impressive and memorable characters are women, whose sensitivity and vulnerability condition their all-important courage to endure fear and failure. Beyond success or failure they experience fragility and desolation and in spite of this they fight to preserve what they have discovered themselves to be. Their faith, beyond any possiblity of substantiation, is sharpened by the loneliness they discover in love and betrayal alike. And it is a faith in the values which inform human relations even beyond the point when relatedness has broken down.

In technical terms the achievement of this dramatic vision was based on two related factors. These were the economy and discipline with which he defined the playing space in his plays and the irony through which he developed a dual awareness in his audience. The focal centre in Saunders Lewis's theatre is not on what is done but rather how it is understood and that only partly by the characters themselves. Saunders Lewis depends more heavily than almost any other modern dramatist on the fact that meaning in the theatre derives from the audience's awareness of aspects of the situation which are understood only partially by those involved in them, or differently understood. Even his most heroic characters know only their own truth; there is always irony and the larger truth of the artist's vision.The function of irony and anachronism in his plays and also, to a considerable extent, of poetry, is to reinforce the audience's sense of their own social and cultural reality. At the same time the privacy of the stage space and the immediacy of the moments of passionate conflict and interchange which absorb it reinforce our sense of the tension between isolation and relatedness which informs all our experience.

Speaking in terms of a distinctive Theatre implies a considerable body of work sharing clearly definable characteristics and we have this in the latest group of plays which Saunders Lewis wrote in the decade from 1956 to 1966: *Gymerwch Chi Sigaret?*, *Brad*, *Esther*, and *Cymru Fydd*. All these plays reflect directly on the condition of modern life and particularly on circumstances in Wales. They embody the same mature vision of life and demonstrate the same technical mastery. They do not mark an end to Saunders Lewis's career as a dramatist: he went on almost to the very last, working out particular problems through the medium of drama and his last play, *Branwen*, a return to a theme taken from the Mabinogi,[5] represents a new departure which was taking him beyond the confines of the theatre as he had previously defined it. However, his particular contribution to Theatre is fully achieved with the completion of this group of plays.

The aim of this study is to trace his development as a dramatist and to describe the characteristics of his theatre as it is defined in his major plays.[6.] Consequently it falls naturally into three parts. The first concerns two groups of plays which correspond roughly to the two major 'conversions' which took place in his early life. The first of these was the conversion to Wales and to the idea of community; the second was the conversion to the Roman Catholic Church. The four early plays *The Eve of Saint John*, (1921) and *Gwaed Yr Uchelwyr* (1922); *Buchedd Garmon* (1937) and *Amlyn ac Amig* (1940) tell us a great deal about the ideals and conventions on which his Theatre was built.

Part II concerns a second group of plays written in verse which have been enormously influential in Wales. *Blodeuwedd* (1948) and *Siwan* (1956), are unforgettable plays; separately and together they have great poetic beauty and imaginative strength. It is impossible to say how they may appear to foreign readers through the veil of translation and across the barriers of cultural trans-notation, but from this side of the Severn at least, they seem to constitute a quite distinctive contribution to the tradition of European drama. Indeed, it would not be difficult to argue that they both reveal a degree of dramatic energy and intensity which Saunders Lewis never attained again. On the other hand, considered as Theatre, they do stand apart, showing a degree of tension and awkwardness later resolved. In the plays of the later group the dramatic focus is clearer, more rigorously developed and more firmly held. Considered together, these plays represent a remarkably coherent and positive response to that crisis in European drama which Peter Szondi described. This response is distinctively Welsh but is also important in a wider dimension; it is not too much to say that it throws light over the whole field of modern European drama. This is a different kind of Modernism,[7] a different kind of criticism, which may alter the perspective in which we see European drama in general.

Part I

1. Slow and Piecemeal

The first phase of Saunders Lewis's development as a dramatist covers two astonishingly active years, from 1921 to 1922, when he struggled to implement in drama the consequences of his dramatic war time conversion from aestheticism to cultural nationalism. This involved finding a way of experiencing the individual's urge for self-definition in relation to the social world, rather than in opposition to it. The process took many years — Saunders Lewis himself called it "slow and piecemeal" and even with *Blodeuwedd* (1948), he still faced difficult technical problems in adapting his mature vision to the medium of Theatre. It was begun even with his first play, *The Eve of Saint John* (1921) but was taken very much further with his second, *Gwaed yr Uchelwyr* (1922). In technical terms this second step involved a drastic shift from Anglo-Celtic quaintness to the rigorous structure of the Naturalist problem play. Even while Saunders Lewis was busy elaborating the Symbolist aesthetic he had derived from Yeats and welcoming the new anti-Naturalism of Gordon Craig[1] and contemporary French practitioners, he was preparing for this decisive move in another direction. To some extent it was a false move. The dramatic patchwork of *Gwaed yr Uchelwyr,* betrays immaturity and uncertainty. That a deeper, imaginative certainty awaited development even then is indicated by the fact that Saunders Lewis began the first version of *Blodeuwedd* immediately after finishing *Gwaed yr Uchelwyr,* but in 1923 he failed to finish it. Before that could be done there were other uncertain steps and piecemeal experiments.

* * *

Born in Wallasey in 1893, the descendant of two families prominent in the history of Calvinistic Methodism, educated at Liscard High School and in the English Department of Liverpool University,

Saunders Lewis went off to the trenches of Flanders with his head full
of the aestheticism of Walter Pater, whose advice to the young was
that their lives should burn "with a hard, gemlike flame"[2]:

> Daeth y rhyfel. Dyna'r dyddiau yr oeddwn i wedi meddwi ar Walter
> Pater, ac yn ceisio deall ac arfer ei athrawiaeth ef. Dysgais mai profiad ei
> hun, er ei fwyn ei hun, ac nid ffrwyth profiad, oedd amcan bywyd.
> Llwyddiant mewn bywyd oedd disgyblu'r synhwyrau fel y profent cy-
> flawnder bywyd yn helaethach beunydd: 'To be present always at the
> focus where the greatest number of vital forces unite in their purest
> energy.' Ac er fy mwyn fy hun, yn unig fel y caffwn i fwynhau'r profiad
> hwn o egni byw ar ei eithaf, mi ymdaflais innau i'r fyddin, a chael blas
> wrth gwrs ar glywed canmol fy newrder a'm hunan aberth.

> The war came. Those were the days when I was drunk on Walter Pater,
> trying to understand and practice his philosophy. He taught me that
> experience in itself, for its own sake and not the fruit of experience, was
> the end of life. Success in life was attained by disciplining the senses so
> that they could experience life more fully day by day: 'To be present
> always at the focal point where the greatest number of vital forces unite
> in the purest energy.' And for my own sake, only so as to be able to enjoy
> this experience of the energy of life at its fullest, I threw myself into the
> army and, of course, took pleasure in hearing myself praised for my
> bravery and self-sacrifice.[3]

Some eighteen months later, in a book shop in Abbeville, he came
across the three volumes of Maurice Barrès' *Le Culte du Moi*.[4] In Barrès
he thought at first he had found another Pater, who would confirm
him in the struggle to free himself from "every responsibility and
tradition". Unlike Wilfred Owen and Siegfried Sassoon and the artist
David Jones, Saunders Lewis was delighted with the life of an infantryman: "Because to live from hour to hour, savouring the sweetness
of each passing minute, careless of what might come, was the essence
of that life." As he read on through the three volumes of Barrès' work,
however, he discovered a new world. Barrès traces the history of his
young hero, painfully self-aware in a world of strangers, a world
organized on principles which seem to deny his essential being. At first
he seeks freedom in isolation from this world of Philistines. This "free
man", as Saunders Lewis describes him, "was he who could live in
himself and for himself, in the face of every tradition and every society
which would bind him with ideals or responsibilities which did not
arise from his own heart." This is the life which he sought for himself,

even in the unlikely context of the trenches.The charm it held for him
is preserved in his description even now:

> ...disgrifia Barrès ei arwr yn ymdrechu byw yn gwbl anfoesol (hynny yw,
> heb gyfrifoldeb cymdeithasol), yn tyfu'n syth o'i wreiddyn...heb ymbly-
> gu dan un awel nac o'r gorffenol, nac o'i amgylchedd; bywyd annibyn-
> nol,aristocrataidd, unig, bywyd yn gelf, a'r Philistiaid neu'r barbariaid y
> tu allan. A swyn ei arddull! Hyd heddiw mi gofiaf ddarllen y penodau
> hynny yn ffosydd Loos, a'r haul uwchben yn yr awyr eglur, a'r gelynion
> ganol dydd — y barbariaid — yn dawel, a minnau mewn gwynfyd pur.
> Dyddiau dedwydd Loos.

> Barrès describes his hero struggling to live completely immorally (that is
> without social responsibility), growing straight from his own root...with-
> out bending before any breeze, either from the past or from his own
> environment; an independent, aristocratic, lonely life, life as an art, and
> the Philistines or the barbarians outside. And the charm of his style! Even
> now I remember reading those chapters in the trenches of Loos, with the
> sun up above in the clear sky and the enemy — the barbarians — quiet
> at mid-day, and myself in my seventh heaven. Happy days at Loos.[5]

As he read on, however, he encountered new ideas and acquired a
new philosophy. For the free man of Barrès' early volumes gives way
to the active politician, who encounters in the garden of Bérénice, the
soul of his nation and the essence of his own being. With Barrès' hero
Saunders Lewis also learnt that freedom cannot be attained in isolation:

> ...bod ei wreiddiau yn y ddaear honno ac yn gymysg â gwreiddiau ei
> phobl, yn un bleth â hwythau; mai munud yw bywyd dyn yn nhreigl
> bywyd hir a thawel ei wlad a'i genedl; nid oes i funud ddechrau na
> diwedd, canys ar ei phen ei hun nid oes iddo fod nac ystyr; a thrwy
> ymdaflu i fywyd ei wlad a'i genedl y gall dyn ei adnabod ei hun, a meithrin
> ei enaid yn llawn ac yn gyfoethog, a byw yn artist hyd at eithaf ei
> ymwybod.

> ...that his roots are in that earth, and entwined with the roots of his
> people; that a man's life is a moment in the long and slow progress his
> nation's life; that a moment has no beginning and no end because it has
> no being nor meaning in itself and that by throwing himself into the life
> of his country and his people a man comes to know himself, to nurture
> his own soul fully and richly, and lives as an artist to the full extent of his
> consciousness.[6]

On his way to France as a young infantry officer in 1914 he had
thought, like Joyce's Stephen Dedalus, that "nationality, language,
religion" were nets to hold back the artist's soul in flight[7] Barrès taught
him that the artist may never be independent of circumstances and
that language, tradition and culture are actually the only means by
which the individual may achieve fulfilment. After this experience
Saunders Lewis tells us, he was inevitably a nationalist in literature:
"Barrès had convinced me that Wales for me was not a net but a root".[8]
That he returned from France to Liverpool still hoping to write in
English rather than in Welsh is explained by the fact that he interpreted
Barrès' cultural nationalism as a part of a wide European current of
thought and feeling. He saw the "search for places and communities
where the spring-time of the local life flourished" as a link between
Barrès, the Anglo-Irish writers, Yeats and Synge and the contemporary
English dramatists, like Lascelles Abercrombie and Gordon Bottomley, whose influence he had already felt.[9] Even Eliot's *The Waste Land*
(1922), he thought a "restatement and culmination" of this movement, rather than a new departure. Cultural primitivism was not,
however, what Barrès meant at all and the experience of writing *The
Eve of Saint John* quickly brought Saunders Lewis to realize this.
Barrès' novels, which Saunders Lewis had gone on to read after the
initial shock of *Le Culte du Moi,* concentrate intense attention on the
individual's practical involvement in social life. In contrast to Joyce,
whose mastery of the novel is so much greater, Barrès' achievement
was in combining the Naturalist's vision of man as a helpless object in
a brutally physical world with a conviction that he is immediately
responsible for the way he bears himself in relation to those around
him. A similar combination is to be found in Ibsen's plays, in *Hedda
Gabler,* for example, or *The Wild Duck* and it could only have been
through a revision of the mistrust of Ibsen's analytic method which he
had derived from Yeats' *Plays and Controversies* (1923) that Saunders
Lewis was to implement in drama what he had learned from Barrès.
His earliest essays on the Theatre urge the abandonment of the
combination of Naturalism and melodrama found in contemporary
Welsh 'pamphlet plays' and argue for a fresh acceptance of the
possibilities which Theatre offers as a conscious art form. He wrote
very critically in 1920 about the imaginative poverty of Ibsen's *Ghosts*
(1881). The thematic strength and coherence of Ibsen's plays, he
argued, echoing Yeats, undermined their effectiveness as drama:

Drama gref yw Dychweledigion. Soniwyd llawer am ei chrefft a pherffeithrwydd ei datblygiad. Ond y gwir yw mai dyna ei gwendid. Cytunwn fod ei chynllun yn ddifwlch megis problem mewn Euclid; o'r act gyntaf hyd yr olaf y mae'r cysylltiadau mor gadarn, y rhesymeg mor sicr, fel y gwelwn y terfyn yn glir o'n blaen a dim i'w waredu. Ie, ac felly y dylai fod mewn Euclid, ond nid yn foel felly y gweithia bywyd. Y mae Dychweledigion yn fethiant celfyddydol, oblegid mai ar wyddoniaeth y'i seiliwyd, ar ddeddfau allanol ac nid ar gymeriad.

Ghosts is a strong play. Much has been made of its craftsmanship and the perfection of its organization. But in fact that is its weakness. Let us agree that its construction is as complete as a Euclidean formula: from the first act to the last the connections are so strong, the reasoning so clear, that we see the conclusion clearly before us with no means of escaping it. Yes, and so it should be with Euclid, but life doesn't work so mechanically. *Ghosts* is an artistic failure because it is based on Science, on external laws and not on character.[10]

Ibsen's characters, Saunders Lewis argued, were as simple and consistent as arithmetic, lacking the abundant life of Molière's Harpagon and Shakespeare's Anthony, who were "varied and inconsistent and so alive." In 1920, in a series of essays on dramatic art, he attacked the Naturalist assumption that Theatre should aim at creating the illusion of reality:

Rhoi awgrym i'r ysbryd yw amcan golygfa mewn drama, nid diwallu chwant y llygaid; ac ar ris yr awgrym fe hed yr ysbryd i fan gweledigaeth y celfwr. Nid oes gan dwyll ran mewn celf. Nid twyllo cynulleidfa i gredu mai fferm fach yw'r llwyfan yw amcan y dramodydd pan ddangoso olygfa felly, eithr awgrymu fferm fel y gallo'r ysbryd esgyn i gydymdeimlo ag awyrgylch ac bywyd y fferm — dyna'r cwbl o'i amcan, os yw gelfwr.

The aim of the set is to suggest rather than satisfy the desire of the eye; on the level of suggestion the spirit will swiftly capture the artist's vision. Illusion has no part in art. To deceive an audience into believing that the stage is a small farm is not the dramatist's aim when that is what the setting reveals, but to suggest such a farm in such a way that the spirit may attain to sympathy with its life and atmosphere — that is his sole aim if he be an artist[11]

He calls on Goethe to prove "that art must be 'unnatural'" and on Gordon Craig to support his insistence on the importance of colour and lighting as means of creating the beauty on which theatrical art is entirely dependant. Shakespeare, however, is an authority to whom he returns again and again. The first Act of *Hamlet*, for example, reveals a mastery of the dramatist's whole art:

> Sut i greu awyrgylch, sut i bortreadu cymeriad a'i ddatblygu, sut i drin iaith at bwrpas drama, a'r modd i ddangos y chwedl, chwi gwech y cwbl yno o law meistr nad oes un Ibsen yn y byd a'i rydd i'w fedd fyth.

> How to create atmosphere, how to portray character and develop it, how to adapt language to the aims of drama and the way to set out the action — there you have them all at the hands of a master whom no Ibsen the world may see will ever bury.[12]

Within a few months after this, by July 1921, he had found further support for these ideas in the practice of Jacques Copeau at his Théâtre du Vieux Colombiers and in the writings of the director, Firmin Gémier [13]

> Myn Gémier mai'r modd ebrwyddaf i ddychwelyd at symledd y Groegiaid gynt yw tynnu tô ôddiar y chwaraedy, a mynd yn l at ddrama'r awyr agored. Ar amnaid felly, dyna ddiwedd ar oleuadau llawr, dyna derfyn ar amlder a drysni celfi a dodrefn a holl betheuach y chwaraedai. Dyna'r chwaraewyr a'r gynulleidfa ochr yn ochr dan oleu dydd, a dibynna'r ddrama bellach yn gwbl ar fawredd creadigaeth y dramodydd ac ar allu'r actiwr i'w dehongli yn syml ac yn urddasol drwy gyfrwng llais ac ystum. Canlyniad hynny a fyddai galw'r bardd yn ôl at ddrama; canys pan fo lliaws pobl ynghyd, yr unig iaith sy'n ddigon nerthol i'w symud oll i gydymdeimlad yw barddoniaeth.

> Gémier insists that the quickest way to return to the simplicity of the Ancient Greeks is to take the roof off the playhouse and go back to open air drama. Thus you put an end at once to floor lighting, the proliferation of stage furnishings and the whole paraphenalia of the theatre. There you have the players and the audience side by side in broad daylight, with the play thenceforth entirely dependent on the greatness of the dramatist's creation and the actor's ability to convey it simply and with dignity by means of voice and gesture. The result of this would be to summon the poet back to the theatre; because when many are brought together the only language sufficiently powerful to move them all to sympathy is poetry.[14]

Even at this time, however, he was willing to recognize the poet in Ibsen and acknowledge *Rosmersholm* (1885-86) and *The Master Builder* (1891-92) as masterpieces of imaginative art.[15] Here Ibsen, he thought, had given up the attempt to reform society and returned to the dramatist's true task of portraying the dreams and confusion he found within himself. By 1922 Saunders Lewis' prejudice against the intellectual had largely disappeared, leaving the way free for his own experience with the 'pamphlet play' he had previously attacked as out-dated and untrue. When Yeats published his *FourPlaysforDancers* (1916 & 1917) Saunders Lewis said if it were put in the hands of Welsh dramatists, it would save them, "from many misconceptions about the methods of producing plays", but beyond that he had nothing to say about Yeats' dramatic technique. Instead he praises "the intellectual beauty" and music of Yeats' verse and the "subtlety and intellectuality" of his work.[16]

Twenty five years later, on the verge of completing the second version of *Blodeuwedd*, he took the occasion of the appearance of a study of the Abbey Theatre to praise Yeats' insistence on integrity and intellectual consistency.[17] By now Saunders Lewis is prepared to argue, "Logic is plot in drama". Aeschylus and Sophocles, Racine, Corneille and Molière are all brought forward to assist his argument that everything in a play, including its characterisation, must follow on the consistent elaboration of one central idea. Passion itself, he argues, can only exist in art when the accidental and inessential are banished, in obedience to the logic and necessity of art. Studying Yeats' example at the Abbey, he thought, might go a long way to eradicating the weakness of contemporary drama. In the year that he wrote *Gwaed yr Uchelwyr* he praised above all the Irish dramatist's treatment of the theme of war in *The Dreaming of the Bones* .[18] Many years later, in *Cymru Fydd* (1967), perhaps his greatest play, he depicted a hero similar to Yeats' young soldier in *The Dreaming of the Bones*, confused, on the run from a lost battle, but it was not from Yeats' example that he had learnt how to exercise intellectual and imaginative consistency in his own drama. The spiritual father of *Cymru Fydd*'s young hero was the creator of Johannes Rosmer and Halvard Solness.

2. *The Eve of Saint John*

Looking back at *The Eve of Saint John* along the perspective created by *Cymru Fydd* would suggest that this first play was very much a false start to his career. This 'Anglo-Celtic' experiment, however, was an important first step in the process of realizing what Saunders Lewis had learnt from Maurice Barrès. His starting point as an artist was precisely that accentuated self-awareness which had drawn him to Barrès in the first place. This implied a problematic relationship between the individual and the world. Even Pater's preoccupation with 'experience' implied a world of phenomena from which the artist could never be entirely free. The only recourse of the contemporary artist who had fallen under Pater's charm seemed to be the various forms of the Symbolist aesthetic, which offered a communion between the individual and the colourful, joyful world which lay beyond the one in which he lived. Few of the artists who survived for long during the 1914-1918 war held on to an aesthetic which relegated the horrific world in which they lived and died to a secondary grade of reality. That Saunders Lewis avoided the trauma and bitterness of contemporary English War poets was because Barrès offered a view of the world in which immediate self-awareness and imaginative vision could be reconciled through a willing acceptance of relatedness in the concrete world of beauty and bombs. What Barrès did not offer, however, was any clear guidance as to the form of that commitment should take.

In the meantime the achievement of the Abbey Theatre, which Saunders Lewis had visited as early as 1914, and particularly the plays of J.M.Synge, seemed to suggest a possible alternative. Synge's comedy arises from a violent clash between the demands of the romantic passionate individual and the mundane reality of the social world, which is resolved on the level of romantic myth. His stage represents a cramped, inhibited and sordid world, from which those few individuals who preserve the integrity of the imagination may escape, to wander freely in a wider world. The reality of this freedom, which is

certainly not to be found in the world outside the theatre, is validated
by the poetic richness and passion of the language he gives to his
characters.

Like Yeats, Synge himself believed that this language represented the
speech of the society he was representing, which was "fiery and
magnificent and tender".[19] If it did exist, the beauty of this natural
speech could be taken to guarentee the reality of the choice between
mundaneity and passion which Synge's plays celebrate, as did the
continuance of romantic myths and legends preserved in rural societies. In 1921 Saunders Lewis accepted this belief. Writing on
Anglo-Irish drama in general, the year after he published *The Eve of
Saint John,* he commented on the way in which the Irish, having lost
their own language, took up English, "gave it a new and utterly distinct
accent and idiom, and made it the reflection of their own minds and
aspiration". [20] He also seems to have believed that with rich and
beautiful poetic language a poet may open a door on a colourful, inner
world and that when we enter this world through the theatre it sustains
our freedom to achieve beauty and consistency in the world outside.
What Saunders Lewis did not allow for when he determined to emulate
Synge is that even poetic dialogue can be no more than one part of a
complex theatrical event. The startling, playful speech of Pegeen and
Mike in *The Playboy of the Western World* is the medium through which
we apprehend a complex and brutal reality. It serves to awaken our
imaginative response and ensures our complicity in the way in which
the hero comes to resolve his own problems and those that his arrival
has created among the villagers.The characters in *The Eve of Saint John*
speak a peculiar literary dialect, carefully imitated from the Irish
dramatist, which is designed to suggest in English the richness and
complexity of rhythm and idiom he claimed to have heard in Cardi-
ganshire inn-kitchens. Self-consciously "rich, expressive, powerful",[21]
this language introduces us to a colourful, active and even dangerous
world, where people may court each other seriously or flirt outrageous-
ly, spite each other, get drunk and fight and pay the price of compromise in daily labour. However, this world is only reflected indirectly
in the speech of his characters. The world actually presented on stage,
is not where action commitment would be possible, even inevitable,
Saunders Lewis denies his characters the opportunity to commit
themselves. Because of this discrepancy he failed to achieve more than
a quaint poeticised dialect and trivial humour, certainly nothing like

the "central uneccentric irony" which the speech of Synge's characters introduces to his play.

The Eve of Saint John consists of two short scenes, the first of which introduces and develops the situation of a spirited and attractive young girl who is unwilling to accept the lukewarm and unromantic though wealthy lover her mother intrigues to obtain for her. Megan, Sara and Harri represent different attitudes towards a central question: how far does wisdom or necessity require that we compromise our dreams for the sake of material comfort? The unwilling lover, Harri Richard, confines his dreams to the lonely hours of night-time and earns Megan's scorn. Her mother, Sara, has married a weak and patient man and accepts authority and security as the beginning and end of life. Megan would prefer almost anyone to the spineless Harri and particularly a strong man, "without fear in him of stuff or spirit, and can give a right clout with his hand". Sara arranges a scene where Harri, pressured into an unwilling proposal by her discovery of his theft of Megan's Sunday ribbon, discovers them both folding the thick woollen blankets which suggest the substance of the daughter's dowry. Then she slips out, leaving them to go on with the job and come to an understanding. In the conversation that follows Megan reveals her disgust at Harri's feeble self-concsciousness and fear of ridicule and describes the kind of lover she would have:

> Don't I see him plain before me the moment I shut my eyes? A strong man with a beard would blunt the edge of a new scythe, and great muscles to his chest, and it rough and hairy the time he'd be swinging a sickle in the heat of August and his shirt open for the breeze. Not a sorrowful thin shadow the way you are, but a man would make the church pew of a squire creak when he sat down. A brave, easy, comfortable man.

Megan fears that married to Harri she might yet meet such a man and have to send him on his way, leaving herself fastened "to a bleating calf is afraid of a woman's mocking". To escape from this fate she determines to observe the old custom of preparing a meal for the Devil at midnight on St. John's Eve, who will come in the likeness of the man she will marry. Undeterred by this, Sara sends Harri off to learn a prayer and borrow the corspe bell to protect him from the Evil One so that he can return at midnight and present himself in his own likeness and be betrothed to Megan.

At this point the first scene ends. The second beginshalf an hour before midnight, when Megan is preparing the Devil's meal, including a quart drink and a pipe of tobacco. Harri and Sara are forestalled by a drunken tramp, whom Megan accepts as the image of her lover to be. Her self-deception survives all the ambiguities that arise during a long conversation with the innocent tramp, whom Harri and Sara discover when they enter sleeping with his head on her breast. Their fearful deception is shorter lived than Megan's, for they recognise him soon enough for "the tipsy tinker from Carmarthen". Disillusioned, Megan is is angry, but Harri sees a chance to escape from the women's clutches by urging Megan to accept the tramp as "the very image of her fancy". Repentant, Megan is willing to accept him for a moment when she takes a close look at the sleeping tinker, but Harri bucks at the bargain and has to be brought to heel again by the remorseless Sara. By the time Megan's spirit is up again and all Harri gets when he tries to come terms with her is a slap in the face. She turns from him to the tinker, determined to offer herself and accept whatever she gets in return rather than compromise again:

...do you be seeking another wife indeed, for its brave ways you have with woman, so that they'll be eager for your flatteries and proud of your strong arm. But I'll be marrying myself to my coffin rather than to you, and I'll suffer an eternity of torment before a month of your honeymooning. It's with this tinker I'll be going now, Mam, and taking the gift the devil has sent me, for it's a merry companion he'll be on the roads and we'll have a great laugh together at this night's doings.

She turns to trump to shake him awake. He rises slowly to his feet and delivers the plays last surprise:

Aye, aye, my dear, I'll be moving now, and a deal of thanks to you. For it's my wife will be waiting me these many hours, and she sleeping the night in the loft is above the Vicar's stable.

It would have been interesting to see a third scene showing us the various characters reacting to the turn in the situation introduced by the Tramp's closing words. What is left for Megan in particularto say or do in this last scene? Would she decline to the lesser status of Harri's wife, grateful to her mother for preserving that much for her? Or would she, like the heroine of Saunders Lewis's next play, hold out for her ideal, even at the cost of her comfort? The end of the play as we have leaves Megan, still defiant and demanding, but fooled at all points. She is deprived even of her last gesture, a personal compromise designed to preserve her integrity at the cost of romance.

Saunders Lewis was so deeply under the influence of Synge at this time that *The Eve of Saint John* is almost an imitation of the latter's first play, *The Shadow of the Glen* (1903). Here Synge presents a woman not unlike Saunders Lewis's Megan as she might have been after a few years of marriage to an older Harri. In this case the play begins with the suspicious husband shamming death to catch his wife with her younger lover and ends with her disgusted exit, not with the timid lover, but to wnader the roads with a chance-met tinker who offers the romance and the adventure she craves. The last scene, which presents the husband and the lover settling down to drown their sorrows together, complacently accepting the comforts of the cramped social world, leaves us free to wonder at the woman's bold escape to the wilder world dominated by the elements, a world of poverty, discomfort, perhaps even of madness, but the only escape from the prison house of frustration and respectability.

The very different way in which Saunders Lewis ended *The Eve of Saint John*, without permitting his heroine to make any decision, demonstrates his unwillingness to accept the distinction between the physical world and the social world on which the resolution of Synge's plays depends. This is all the more striking because the play's balanced structure promised just such a resolution. Having no means to resolve it in these terms, clearly he would need to put the problem in a different way.

3. *Gwaed yr Uchelwyr*

Unlike Megan, the heroine of Saunders Lewis's second play is allowed to preserve her integrity, even though at a crippling cost. Faced with the prospect of the endless series of compromises which erode character, she is saved by the idea of tradition, which gives her a framework in which she can define herself in opposition to the social world. Tradition, Saunders Lewis maintained, following Barrès, is a civilising influence in human life, which would otherwise be given up to a struggle between individuals motivated by various low instincts, such as pride and greed. In an ideal situation higher instincts will come into play, such as romantic love, and these will soften and refine human nature and society. However, in some situations even love, which is essentially unselfish, may be corrupted by lower instincts, or may seem to be. In these circumstances only the individual whose character has been formed in terms of a tradition which incorporates values which cannot be corrupted, can preserve the idea of civilisation. He or she will withdraw from social life so as to affirm these values absolutely.

The initial inspiration of *Gwaed yr Uchelwyr* also came from Barrès, but not this time from *Le Culte du Moi*. It was an attempt to rework the theme of Barrès' novel, *Colette Baudoche* (1909), which told the story of a young French girl, who lived through the German annexation of Lorraine after the Franco-Prussian war of 1870. Its central theme is renunciation. Barrès' heroine falls in love with the German schoolmaster who comes to lodge in her home, but renounces that love because she feels that it will necessarily compromise her fine awareness of her own Frenchness. Many years later, after the Second World War, Saunders Lewis was fascinated with a similar story by Jean Bruller, *Le Silence de la Mer* (1942). [22] Although in this later story the emphasis lay on the experience of the man rather than the woman, it ends similarly, with the sad renunciation of love as the only means of preserving the sensibility in which it grows.

Both these stories are set in circumstances of international conflict, in which individuals are compelled to see themselves as representative of their nation, in contradistinction to that of another person. When Saunders Lewis went about the business of adapting the theme he chose a different kind of setting. Welsh history, and even contemporary Welsh life, provide ample material of a similar kind, but instead of taking up some such story he set his play against the background of the conflict between landlord and tenant which dominated the political mythology of Nineteenth Century Wales. Consequently what his heroine was obliged to renounce was other forms of Welshness and particularly the compromises which had led to the present reality of Welsh life. The choice she made was not simply one between tradition and innovation, but was also one between the past and the future, implicitly a negation of the world in which Saunders Lewis himself lived and wrote.

The action is set in the farmhouse of Isallt around the year 1827 and concerns the fortunes of Luned Gruffydd. Though now the daughter of a tenant farmer, Luned inherits, through her father Rolant, the blood of the former landowners, aristocrats who held fast to the traditions of the past and lost their land as a result in the turmoil of the Civil War. Since they returned to the area and took up the tenancy of Isallt, the Gruffydd family have lived in full consciousness of their aristocratic inheritance and have kept alive the ancient cultural traditions. Luned, visiting relations in London, has met the son of the present landowner and discussed with him their mutual dream of renewing the old way of life in the future. The union of these two young people, representing the older, responsible aristocracy and the newer merchant class which has taken its place, would offer positive hope for the future. However, the play opens when the social classes they represent are at the very point of a conflict which will dominate Welsh life for the next half century. From the very first moment the situation demands exactly the kind of delicate dramatic balance which it took all Ibsen's mature mastery to sustain in plays like *Ghosts*.

As the play begins Luned has been out walking with her dog, Gelert; she returns with a hare which he has killed on their land. Unfortunately the incident has been witnessed by an English keeper, who has rushed with the news to Robert Puw, the steward. Puw, jealous of the status enjoyed by the Gruffydd family, takes the opportunity of humbling them by insisting that the dog be shot. His employer, under pressure from other landlords to make a stand against his tenants on behalf of the class he represents, lends his authority to the steward. The penalty for a refusal to comply is ejection from the tenancy. Although he has no recourse but emigration, Rolant refuses to shoot the dog and faces the consequences. Arthur Gwynne, the squire's son, fruitlessly intervenes. His last hopes of effecting a reconciliation are shattered when the farm hands fire the steward's ricks in revenge for the expulsion of the family. In despair, he offers to accompany Luned to America as her husband. Though she loves him, Luned refuses, partly because she is unwilling that he should make such a sacrifice for her, mainly because to consent to any form of compromise would be to abandon the aristocratic standards she has inherited.

To some extent Luned is motivated by an unselfish desire to maintain the standards of her class as an ideal on which the values of other classes are ultimately dependent.In the final analysis, however, her decision is a means of preserving the only identity she has. Having inherited the past, she is unable to compromise with the present. If the contemporary world offers no means of being herself, then she will reject it. "Life will never dominate me," she tells Arthur:

> Mi wnaf fy mywyd yn allor i atgofion fy ngenedl. Mi fyddaf yn lleian i'm gwlad. Ac fe fydd fy nheulu farw gyda mi, ond yn marw heb fradychu eu delfrydau na'u traddodiad.

> I will make my life an altar to the memory of my people. I will be a nun for the sake of my country. And my family will die with me, but die without betraying their ideals and their tradition.

Arthur has no choice but to accept her decision. Her father endorses it, comforting her suffering with the words which echoe the title of the play: "You have noble blood in you, my girl..."

Luned understands that love is not absolute in itself but rather the flowering of human nature in favourable circumstances. Arthur may love again in conditions which permit him to fulfil his social duties. Going to America with her would impoverish his emotional nature because it would amount to abandoning the social responsibilities which sustain it. Her heroism consists in acting on her understanding of the full reality of her situation. Her choice is not between love and duty. Love cannot develop in conflict with duty; so, to go to America as Arthur's wife, even regardless of what this would mean for him, would destroy her. Her identity, formed in consciousness of the past, could not survive an act which would deny the claims of the past on the future.

The decision to adapt this story for the theatre presented Saunders Lewis with one major problem, which in the event he failed to solve. In order for Luned's choice to have any general validity the audience need to have consented imaginatively to the inner logic which leads to it. In his novel Barrès had mediated Colette's renunciation largely by manipulating point of view. The central scene in which she makes her half conscious decision as she contemplates the cathedral of her native town is typical of the novelist's method, moving in and out of the girl's consciousness, weaving together direct sensuous impressions, shared emotions and values which the reader assimilates unconsciously in the flow of the narrative. However, these novelistic techniques were not available to the dramatist. He must find other means to bring his audience to the point of sympathy — in this case to the point at which they are willing to accept the negation of the historical process which has produced their own consciousness and the world to which they owe profound allegiance.

In Ibsen's work, of course, a model lay ready to hand. His *Ghosts*, (1881) for example, showed how a theme could be developed and resolved through action centred on the internal development of a self determining central character. Ibsen's method, however, was essentially problematic. He wanted to show the reciprocal relationship between circumstances and consciousness. He could do this neither by confining himself to the point of view of one character, nor by truly preserving the unity of time. Instead he dramatised the consequences for one central character in the present of a series of events in which he or she had been an actor. These events could not be simultaneously represented but only recalled in discussion, narrated, presented to the minds of characters by symbolic objects or to the audience by indirect references. The balance was a fragile one and often involved restraints and evasions which threatened a decline into melodrama.

No better example of this can be found than the end of *Ghosts*, where Ibsen has to draw the curtain before Mrs Alving can actually decide to accept her responsibility for the situation in which she finds herself and kill her son. The play purports to show us how we pay the penalty for a failure to exercise moral reponsibility through direct action. Were Mrs Alving's experience truly the subject of the drama we would have no interest in Oscar's syphilis except as it occasioned her action. As it is, however, the syphilis is important in its own right, as a symbol of the corruption of a whole generation and a whole society and Mrs Alving's dilemma is likewise important not because it is resolved in action but because it is part of a symbolic display.

On the surface of things the situation Saunders Lewis chose to dramatise in *Gwaed yr Uchelwyr* presents fewer difficulties than *Ghosts* because it is firmly limited in terms of time and focused clearly on the experience of one central character. In fact, however, Saunders Lewis was quite unable at this stage to internalize the action of his play in the way that Ibsen's example suggested. If we turn to another Ibsen play, *Hedda Gabler* (1890), which is closer to *Gwaed yr Uchelwyr* than *Ghosts* in terms of structure, we notice at once that the function of character in Saunders Lewis's play is much more confined. Hedda's actions and reactions dominate Ibsen's play, controlling its whole movement and development. By contrast, the action of *Gwaed yr Uchelwyr* is external. The play develops an idea, which the dramatist is chiefly concerned to project towards the audience rather than develop in terms of Luned's experience.

Both plays begin with the heroine off stage. However, the opening scenes, which prepare us for their appearance, work quite differently. *Hedda Gabler* begins with a scene which establishes the social context and the emotional atmosphere with which Hedda must learn to relate. Even the setting, with the dominant portrait of her father, prepares us for an action in which external stimulus and internal response are to be intricately related a true character study. By contrast *Gwaed yr Uchelwyr* opens with a rather wooden conversation between Luned's parents which sets the ideological context. "Listen again Lowri" are Rolant's opening words, with which he calls his wife's attention to a quotation from the Eighteenth Century Welsh dramatist, Twm o'r Nant, a tenant's complaint about the behaviour of the steward.[23] Within two pages of dialogue, which set the scene and describe the family circumstances, Luned herself comes in. She brings the news of Gelert's misdemeanour, which introduces another dialogue, between father and daughter, in which she questions him regarding the history of their family. When this comes to an end with the entrance of the gamekeeper, Gwilym Rhys, who comes against his will to announce the decision of the steward regarding Gelert, we have been prepared for the action which follows.

This dialogue is essential to our understanding of Rolant's behaviour and provides a context for Luned's eventual renunciation of love and Arthur Gwynne. However, it does nothing more than prepare the audience; it is not in itself a part of the central event of renunciation. It is not because of this conversation that Luned acts as she does. After Rolant has brought his daughter up to date with the family history and the fate of the old nobility, she remarks: "I would love to prove myself one of them." If we ask at this point or, indeed, any other point in the play, why she feels like that, we receive no answer. Hedda Gabler, too, was motivated by a similar striving towards aristocratic aloofness, but it was an essential part of Ibsen's play that the audience should understand this in its social context. Saunders Lewis is quite uninterested in why Luned should feel this. Her mother Lowri responds to the crisis very differently, clinging on to the house and the farm as the only realities in her life. We may assume that Luned has inherited the aristocratic tendency from her father rather than her mother, but this does not go very far towards an explanation of her character.

Gwaed yr Uchelwyr simply takes for granted that Luned is such a person and demonstrates the consequences of her personality, given the situation in which she finds herself. To her wish that she should find an opportunity of showing loyalty to the nobility of her ancestors, her father prophetically replies: "Yes my girl. Perhaps your chance will come next." This remark might be read as arising from Rolant's awareness of the situation and his foreknowledge of how his daughter may be required to act, but it is more obviously a piece of dramatic. irony, a remark addressed by the dramatist to the audience, to sharpen their awareness of the situation.

That irony is deepened by Lowri's entrance with the hare in a basket, together with a bottle of wine and a pound of butter, which Rolant is to take to the steward as a peace offering. No sooner has this been proposed and given its proper value by Rolant's bitter response — "You see, Luned, buying peace at any price is your mother's idea" — than the keeper's arrival announces that the situation has already moved beyond the characters' control. Rolant's decision to seek conciliation regardless and visit the steward opens the way for Lowri to question her daughter regarding her relationship with the squire's son. "Like the devil in the old play" he comes in as soon as this matter is cleared up, to invite Luned to hunt with him on the following day. The conversation which follows allows them both an opportunity to develop as characters; her stubborn pride and his rather unrealistic optimism become very clear. Rolant returns to throw cold water on Arthur's hopes for an easy resolution of the problem. The keeper confirms that his father is well aware of the situation and determined to support his steward. Then in spite of his wife's attempts to delay the crisis, Rolant makes his stand: "I won't take the dog to be shot tonight or tomorrow, or ever!" This opens the way for Luned to close the scene with a significant gesture. Crossing to stand by her father, she turns to Arthur and withdraws her previous agreement to join him in the hunt: "Mr. Gwynne, thank you for your invitation, but I won't be with you tomorrow in the hunt."

Effectively, this is the end of the action. Her deliberate formality should make it clear to Arthur and to the audience where she stands. The Act which follows moves in a quite different direction, though it closes with the repetition of the rejection. It is set one month later, at the time of the auction of the land and the farmhouse, outside the tavern where it takes place. It opens with a dramatic commentary on human nature. A group of farmers are drinking themselves to the point of irresponsibility on the steward's ale. Having reached it, they exit to the auction as Rolant and Lowri enter, accompanied by one of the farm servants. After a few words which fill us in on their intentions they are joined by Luned, who stays to keep her mother company while her father joins the others off stage. Twm, the servant, remains in the doorway to provide Luned, Lowri and the audience with a melodramatic commentary on the auction as it proceeds:

Lowri: Beth sy 'rwan, Twm?
Twm: Robin Llwyd wedi ennill cae'r mynydd.
Lowri: A wyr o, tybed, fod pob cynnyg yn mynd fel nodwydd drwy 'mronnau? A hwythau yn diota ac yn ysbeilio fy nhy...Clywch, dyna waedd arall!
Twm: Maes yr afon sy dan y morthwyl.
Lowri: Mae 'nghalon innau dan y morthwyl.

Lowri: What's happening now, Twm?
Twm: Robin Llwyd's won the mountain field.
Lowri: I wonder does he know that every bid pierces my breast like a needle? As they drink and ravage my home...Listen, there's another roar!
Twm: The river meadow is under the hammer.
Lowri: My heart's under the hammer.

The purpose of this crude device is to ensure that the audience read the auction in terms of its emotional and moral value and so become better able to appreciate the neccessity of Luned's final refusal to compromise. Their awareness of what is happening is further de-

veloped by the scene which follows, in which the steward reveals the
full effect of the arbitrary power with which the situation invests him.
Arthur intervenes once more, but the physical humiliation of the
steward which he achieves, far from relieving the audience, is immediately revealed as an empty gesture when his attempt to conciliate
once more fails. At the end of the Act he fails even to keep Luned on
the stage for a moment longer than her father:

> Luned: Gedwch i mi fynd. Ni allaf wrando ar ddim heddyw. (*Hithau'n
> dianc.*)
> Arthur: Luned, Luned —
>   Llen

> Luned: Let me go. I can't listen to anything today. (She escapes.)
> Arthur: Luned, Luned —
>   Curtain.

The third Act is set at Isallt, two days later, in the evening. The
opening dialogue brings up the possibility that the relationship between Luned and Arthur may yet be a means of saving something from
the wreck, revealing the different attitudes of the father and the
mother. Once this has been proposed, Sion Edward is ushered in, one
of the farmers whose drunken greed had given Lowri such pain in the
previous Act. By now Sion has learnt the extent of his own foolishness
in putting himself in the hands of the steward and faces the prospect
of giving up his own land as well as the part of Isallt he had over-
stretched himself to obtain. His visit serves two ends; it extends our
understanding of the full extent of the social evil which Rolant and
Luned are attempting to withstand in the only way now left open to
them, and it provides evidence of the civilising effect of tradition,
embodied in the Isallt family. This is exemplified further when the
squire's keeper calls on Rolant to save the steward's ricks from
destruction by his own enraged farmhands. His hurried exit gives
Lowri valuable moments in which to tighten the screw on her
daughter's conscience, urging a sympathetic reception of the proposal
which she hopes that Arthur Gwynne will now make.

This scene greatly develops our sympathy with Luned, under her
mother's pressure, as we gradually understand the full extent of her
own suffering and the depth of her feelings. However, before she is
finally put to the test towards which everything has been leading, the
dramatist intervenes with another short scene which he employs,

typically, to double effect. One of the farm hands sneaks back to Isallt from the fire to ask Lowri to take care of his family while he is on his way to Liverpool. Lowri, hopeful of the outcome of Arthur's proposal, says that the family may yet be able to stay at Isallt and Gito's reponse has a direct effect on the audience and on Luned. It tells us quite how important the Isallt tradition is, even to those who contribute to it only indirectly. Gito can only interpret the possibility of relief as betrayal: "Are you telling the truth?...Has Rolant Gruffydd sold us out?..." His distress when he thinks that this has happened shows that the Isallt tradition is of fundamental personal importance to him, even though it affects him only peripherally: "What will become of me, what will become of me?" As for Luned, witnessing this, she is strengthened against her mother's persuasions to refuse Arthur: "Gito, you're right", she says to him, "Heaven sent you here."

After this nothing remains but the last debate between Arthur and Luned, which is finally resolved when she points out to him the essential difference between them. Arthur has no choice but to accept her decision and her father endorses it, comforting her with words which echo the title of the play: "You have noble blood in you, my girl..." The very last words of the play confirm her decision : "Father, you must write to Gito."

This final affirmation emphasises the extent to which the ideology of *Gwaed yr Uchelwyr* is projected through Luned's experience. In this respect she is in exactly the situation of Ibsen's Hedda, whose decisive suicide brings to an end the internal process to which the beginning of the play introduced us and also closes the ideological debate which the action sustains. However, whereas Ibsen succeeds in generalising Hedda's experience, in spite of her wilfulness and childish egoism, Saunders Lewis fails to convice us that Luned's heroic unselfishness is anything other than eccentricity. Ironically, he failed here in the very respect in which later, in plays like *Gymerwch chi Sigaret* and *Brad*, he was to succeed most strikingly.

Part II

1. The Still Turning Word

Gwaed yr Uchelwyr left Saunders Lewis with two related problems, one intellectual, the other technical: how to develop the link between tradition and individual experience on the one hand and the social world on the other; and how to embody this vision in a coherent and integral dramatic action. He was eventually to find the solution to both problems in developing his understanding of human relatedness in *Blodeuwedd* and *Siwan*. But many years were to pass before he did so. *Blodeuwedd*, begun in 1923, remained unfinished until 1948. The intervening years saw Saunders Lewis turn away from the theatre to literary criticism and fiction and immerse himself in practical life and politics. When he did begin to write plays again he faced another period of awkward experiment and adjustment

In 1925, together with others, Saunders Lewis established the political party now known as Plaid Cymru. As its first President and an active politician and journalist, he spent the following decade developing and promulgating his political philosophy. At the same time he had established himself as an important critic and scholar, particularly with his study of the work of William Williams, Pantycelyn (1927), two separate books on the poet, Ceiriog and the novelist Daniel Owen (1929 and 1936) and a novel based on contemporary Welsh experience, *Monica* (1930). Theatre seems to have been far from his thoughts.

It was an invitation from the Welsh Department of the BBC to write a radio play to be broadcast on St David's day, 1937 that brought him round again to drama. The commission was quite explicit in terms of subject and the scope of its treatment. It was to be set in the Age of the Saints and should take some seventy-five minutes to broadcast. His response was his third play, *Buchedd Garmon*, composed while he was awaiting his second trial for setting fire to building materials on the site of the proposed bombing school at Penyberth in the Lleyn peninsular. [1] This was a gesture which might have been expected from a character like Megan Gruffydd of *Gwaed yr Uchelwyr*. The dramatist's speech to the court at Caernarfon during his first trial was an eloquent expression of a political creed based on the philosophy he first articulated in that play.

In the meantime, however, he had undergone his second conversion, the consequences of which for his view of Theatre were to be worked out directly in *Buchedd Garmon* and the play which followed it, *Amlyn ac Amig* (1940). Since 1932 he had formerly abandoned the Calvinist Methodist Church and become a member of the Church of Rome.[2] The instinctive act of reaching out to grasp the reality of the Spiritual community necessarily took him beyond the confines of his father's Church. By 1930 political and theological liberalism had long undermined the Calvinist basis of Methodism until little was left that could have been recognized by William Williams and the early Reformers who had set the course of conflict with the Anglican Church two centuries before. Saunders Lewis's own brilliant, eccentric book on Williams shows how closely he connected the unified social and artistic vision of Medieval Welsh poetry with the radical, individualistic Calvinism embodied in the hymns and religious practices of the early Welsh Methodists. His assessment of the achievement of William Williams was that he stimulated and helped to organize a process by which the integrated vision of the Medieval *cywyddwyr* could be reconciled with the new individualism and self-consciousness of the Eighteenth Century. From the strictly historical viewpoint it would not be difficult to argue that this was nonsense. On the other hand, in view of the fact that the essential drive of late Eighteenth and early Nineteenth Century European literature was towards precisely that integrated vision that Saunders Lewis detected in the work of the *cywyddwyr* and labelled the 'Welsh aesthetic', the argument in his study of Pantycelyn looks far more authoritative.

The fact is that Saunders Lewis was moving forward in the mainstream of contemporary European thinking. His brilliant criticism of Medieval Welsh poetry was part of a wider reassessment of the Middle Ages which was in course of changing the way people looked at contemporary literature and art. In large measure this was a specifically Catholic movement, initiated and developed by several groups of Catholic authors, particularly in France. One aspect of it was the revival of interest in the theological and philosophical system of St. Thomas Aquinas (1225-74), which took place in a series of studies by

writers like Etienne Gilson. This renewed Thomism profoundly influenced social and moral criticism, especially in the work of one of
the French author's whose influence Saunders Lewis openly avowed,
Jacques Maritain (1882-1973). It also had profound effects on the
Theatre, particular among a group of French practitioners and theore-
ticians of whose work Saunders Lewis had been aware from the
beginning. These include Jacques Copeau, whose work at Les Vieux
Colombiers initiated a movement of which Firmin Gémier was an
active participant. This was made a specifically Catholic movement
mainly by the producer and critic, Gaston Baty (1885-1952), whose
study of the Theatre, *Le Masque et L'Enscensoir* (1926), introduced the
idea of 'Total Theatre', a Theatre of movement, deriving directly from
the Catholic Theatre of the Middle Ages, in reaction from the dialogue and text oriented Theatre of the Seventeenth Century.

Looking at Saunders Lewis in this context, however, brings us once
again face to face with an apparent paradox, implied by the structure
and style of his plays. For whereas the Catholic Baty launched a
swingeing attack on the dominance of what he called 'Sire Le Mot'
and the damage done by the logical structure inherited by the Naturalist Theatre from Racine, the Catholic Saunders Lewis was to
demonstrate his willingness to work within the confines of that
Theatre.

The explanation of this is that what Saunders Lewis found in
Catholicism was a revivified Calvinism. This should not seem too
paradoxical. He was very much the direct heir of his own Calvinist
predecessors. His vision of the world derived directly from that of the
early founders of the Welsh Calvinist Movement. Calvin's own authority, however, was the Catholic St. Augustine (354-430) and although he was so violently opposed to the Roman Church in matters
of Church government and ritual, there is little in Calvin's theology
which is inimical to Catholicism as such. Saunders Lewis left the
Church in which he had grown up and to which his forefathers had
contributed so much because it had lost its grasp of the essential truths
which Calvin had inherited from Augustine and particularly its sense
of the substantiality of Christ's sacrifice and the sharp awareness of
sin. He became a Catholic in order to recover the sacramental view of
the world which had been freely given up by his own Church, but in
doing this he renewed his Calvinism rather than revoking it. The world
remained for him a dark and shadowy place from which only occa-

sionally and in torturing glimpses could man achieve the vision of the eternal City of God.

The Theatre of Saunders Lewis embodies, not the Thomism of Baty and Claudel, for whom the created Universe and sin itself are nothing but a means of discovering the Creator, but the Augustinian view. Without denying the essential goodness of the Creation, St Augustine, and after him his Calvinist interpreters, regarded human nature and the human world as corrupt. They emphasised that salvation cannot be earned in the world but can only follow on the free working of Divine Grace in the human soul. Once visited by Grace, however, and consequently possessed of an understanding of how God willed that the world should be, they saw it as the responsibility of the Christian to act in the world as if it were capable of salvation by means of his actions, even though it is not.

The logic of Augustinian theology, so strongly confirmed in the literature and religious practices of the Calvinist Methodist Church, provided Saunders Lewis with a model which permitted the resolution of the paradox which had developed at the centre of his thought. Since his first encounter with Barrès he had been convinced that the individual could achieve himself only in relation to his community; and yet he had never lost the poignant sense of isolation which had first drawn him to the Frenchman's writings. It was the practical manifestation of Augustinianism embodied in the history of the Calvinist Methodist movement in Wales which took him a step farther in his thinking. In particular it was the study of Pantycelyn, whose hymns express a profoundly personal and passionate sense that relatedness to Christ involves estrangement from the world and whose prose works and practical endeavours in establishing the system of *seiadau* reflect his acceptance of the social dimension to the Christian's experience.

Buchedd Garmon records an early phase of this process. Here Saunders Lewis came closer to the Thomistic theatre of Claudel than at any other time in his career as a dramatist and might seem in retrospect momentarily to have faltered in the logic of his own development. *Gwaed yr Uchelwyr* had been based on a convention which demands that every imaginative proposition which the dramatist presents to the audience will be made in terms of character and justified in terms of situation. The audience's rôle in plays of this kind is basically passive: in accepting the situation they will also accept the dramatist's argument. In *Buchedd Garmon*, however, the dramatist taps other sources of theatrical energy; this is a theatre of ritual and gesture, where the audience are drawn in to celebrate the events which the actors enact. In his freer use of the playing space in this play Saunders Lewis is nearer than he had been before or was to be again to the kind of Theatre Baty was advocating and contemporary producers were achieving on the basis of the poetic texts of Paul Claudel.[3]

Even in *Buchedd Garmon*, however, Saunders Lewis would go only so far in this direction. Claudel's stage represents the whole universe. It is defined alternately in terms of soliloquy and prayer and violent action, in which individuality may be swept away and quite extinguished. In Claudel's theatre we may witness the extasy of battle or the wonder of a Divine miracle; the action of his plays defines itself in the breathtaking movement from one to the other. Even in *Buchedd Garmon* Saunders Lewis holds back from exercising this kind of structural freedom. The purpose of this play for him was to develop his awareness of the way in which the ideal of unity and meaning embodied in St Augustine's vision of the City of God might be realised in a concrete social and political environment. What is uncharacteristic in *Buchedd Garmon* is the failure to project the imaginative vision through an action based on personal relatedness. On the other hand it was quite typical of Saunders Lewis that in the absence of such an action he should restrain himself from going further along the path which led to the Claudelian theatre of movement, even though this refusal should incur the consequence of awkwardness and stilted structure.

In *Amlyn ac Amig* Saunders Lewis retraced his steps in some measure, without loosening his hold on what was new to his art in *Buchedd Garmon*. This new play marks a return to the tighter oranization and narrower focus of *Gwaed yr Uchelwyr*. Here the dramatist was attempting to assimilate the new spiritual vision within an action based on the development of a central character. Once again, quite inevitably, he failed, because he could not yet substantiate the relationship between individual experience and the social and spiritual worlds in terms of an internal action. On the other hand, *Amlyn ac Amig* was also a success, on one level at least. Like *Buchedd Garmon*, it showed a mastery of a new poetic dialogue which in itself marked a new level of achievement.

2. *Buchedd Garmon*

It says a great deal about Saunders Lewis that he should have written *Buchedd Garmon* under the circumstances in which he found himself in 1937, dimissed from his post as a lecturer in University College Swansea and leader of a national movement which had failed to make the very slightest impression on the ideology of the British State. Saunders Lewis seized on the opportunity offered by the radio commission to create a dramatic effect different from anything he had attempted before. In *Buchedd Garmon* he exploited the greater freedom of the radio drama so as to appeal directly to the audience's imagination and suggest the spiritual dimension completely lacking in his earlier plays.

For his subject Saunders Lewis took several incidents from the ;ife of St. Germanus, bishop of Auxerre (378-448) and arranged them as a striking commentary on the events in which he himself was engaged. Buchedd Garmon may be read as an expression of everything that Saunders Lewis said in the court at Caernarfon. It is set in the period between 429 and 430, some years after Roman withdrawal from Britain, when Romano-British civilisation was under threat from barbarian invaders. The play assumes that the unity of the Christian Church, which had replaced the unity of the Roman Empire, was essential to the preservation of civilisation. It begins with an appeal to Saint Germanus from the Christian inhabitants of Britain, where the unity of the Church is threatened by barbarian attack from without and the spread of the Pelagian heresy within.[4] The saint answers the appeal and the drama ends with a celebration of his famous victory against the barbarians on Easter Sunday 430. So in the lands which were to become modern Wales the vision of the City of God is realised, even at the moment of its apparent defeat. Garmon's last address to the Britons has very clear reference to the Wales in which Saunders Lewis himself lived and wrote, awaiting his second trial in London after the jury at Caernarfon had failed to agree to find him guilty. "May Wales rejoice;/ Dawn broke on her darkness,/ And she came forth from the prison of fear".

Significantly, the separate scenes of the play are called 'parts', there being no consistent development from one to the other. Through two of them are constructed as dramatic scenes, they relate to each other rather as tableaux. In the first, set in Auxerre, the consecration of the bishop Lupus by Garmon is central. The two travellers, Paulinus and Illtud, are drawn to wonder what is happening in Auxerre; then the situation is explained to them by the doorkeeper, who welcomes them and invites them to take part in the feast. This invitation is the means by which their message is presented and their plea to Garmon granted because they cannot eat until their vows are fulfilled. The dramatist's main purpose here is to present the family of faith, the living reality on which the play is based. The Christian's belief that he is a citizen in the City of God and a member of the Holy family, informs all his actions and relationships. So the arrival of the two monks who have vowed to eat nothing but one daily meal of bread and water until they have delivered their pleas to Garmon must stop the feast. Lupus can only interpret their arrival as a result of the guidance of God:

> Fy nhirion dad,
> Diogel yw gennyf i mai Ceidwad y Teulu Santaidd
> A ddug y cenhadon hyn tros gors ac afon a diffaith
> A thrwy enbydrwydd fforestydd a'r di-feudwy fôr,
> A'u glanio yma'n brydlon yng nghanol preladiaid Gâl
> Er mwyn eu gollwng hwy heddiw mewn hedd o'u duwiol ddiofryd
> A pheri gogniant i'w anwylyd, Alban sant.

> My tender father,
> I am sure that the Keeper of the Holy Family
> Brought these messengers through fens, rivers and desert lands
> And through the impassable forests and the hermitless-sea
> Landing them here today in peace from their pious vow
> To release them today in peace from their pious vow
> And glorify his loved one, Saint Alban.

The remainder of the scene is given over to Paulinus' account of their mission, which presents the dramatist with an opportunity to communicate directly with the audience. They must listen in company with Garmon, Lupus and the gathered bishops, to hear his description of

the state of Britain and the dreadful effects of heresy, undermining the
unity of faith and the walls of the City of God.

A child of four, Paulinus tells them, he witnessed the march of
Macsen Wledig's armies "on the stones of Sarn Helen, out of the city's
hearing" and heard his father lament the passing of the world they had
known: "The end of a long summer, the end of stability, the end of
quarrying stone for houses, the endless end of the centuries of Roman
peace". But his mother's reply had the ring of truth in the child's ear:

> Pan ddarffro heddwch Rhufain fe saif tangnefedd ein Harglwydd;
> Offrwm beunyddiol offeiriaid Crist yw meini saerniaeth ein dinas,
> A chreo ddisyflyd yr Eglwys balamanta undod gwareiddiad.
> Gwir fu ei gair

> When Rome's peace ends, our Lord's peace will remain;
> The stones of our city are the daily sacrifice of Christ's priests,
> And the Church's unshakeable creed paves the unity of our civilisation.
> She spoke the truth.

Paulinus's story sharpens our awareness of the meaning of faith as it
has already been directly demonstrated to us. While they face only the
barbarians the Britons stand firm, confident in their defence of Christ's
Empire. But under the internal attack of heresy they see Christ's vine,
the Church, drooping and declining, "the branch rotting on the stock".

His appeal to garmon is highly rhetorical:

> ...Ond Rhufain newydd, ysbrydol, Dinas ein Duw,
> Etifedd ei thegwch a'i dysg,
> A welais yn llamu o'i llwch;
> Ac iddi gwrogodd fy ngwlad,
> Yn undod un ffydd, un bedydd, un offrwm, un Arglwydd.
> A welaf i yn fy mhenwynni ein deol o hon?

> ...The new Rome, Rome of the spirit, our God's City.
> The inherior of her beauty and learning,
> Which I saw spring from the dust;
> In which my country found strength,
> In the unity of one faith, one baptism, one sacrifice, one Lord.
> Shall I, in old age, see us exiled from it?

In reply Garmon does no more than confirm what we already know.
"The lands of the faith make one country,/ A city, interconnected in
itself" and because of that he will naturally help his brothers in Christ.

Even so there is no sense of anticlimax. The scene is brought to a close by Saint Patrick, whose decision to return through Britain with Paulinus and Garmon thence to undertake the conversion of Ireland, is a final reminder of the reality and practical consequences of the unity of Faith.

In this opening scene Saunders Lewis makes effective use of the chorus of monks gathered to celebrate the consecration. Their intoned interjections greatly strengthen the important gestures of appeal and consent. Paulinus's plea to Garmon, for example, draws from the whole company the forceful interjection: "May God not permit it". Again, at the end of the scene, when Paulinus and Illtud echo Patrick's words: "Let Garmon come to Britain", their words are strengthened and given force by an invocation by the Chorus in the closing words: "Garmon to Britain,/ And Wales to Christ".

Part II of *Buchedd Garmon* is an interlude rather than a part of a continuing action, but it strongly develops the play's central theme. It is based on an incident when Garmon imitates Christ's action in calming the elements during a storm at sea. Above the roaring of wind and waves we hear the voices of the demons who activate the powres of nature to impede the progress of the saint. These alternate with the voices of the monks and sailors, who call on Mary to protect them against the storm. Urged on by the devils, the storm increases until the captain calls on Garmon as the disciples called on Jesus. As he rises and begins to intone the psalm, *De Profundis,* the storm begins to quieten. The scene ends with the sound of the ship being rowed on a quiet sea and the voices of the sailors growing faint in the distance as they chant the invocation to Mary.

In the third part Saunders Lewis returns to a more dramatic manner, but again, it is drama of gesture rather than action. The saint's return to Britain and his victory over the Pelagians must have suggested possibilities for dramatic action, but Saunders Lewis ignored them, choosing to centre on the appearance of the saint to the people the day after the great dispute. The sceene begins with a comic dispute between a blind beggar child and a bad tempered, one legged soldier who has prior claim to beg in the door of the church. This is resolved by the saint, in favour of the soldier, to whom he asks the child to return the alms he has received. Obeying Garmon's instruction, the child then goes into the church and looks up to the Host at the moment

of its elevation before the people. Then the saint explains to the people
the reason for his opposition to Pelagius.

Pa gyfanedd a wnawn,
Pa gyfanedd mewn cariad a pha gwdwylio
Onid ydym yn un yn Adda, yn un yng Nghrist?
A hyn yw drwg y Pelagiaid,
Chwalu undod ein natur, a'n hundod newydd drwy ras,
Fel na bo gwr llen yn un genedl â gwr tlawd,
Eithr ennill, ohono ei hun, ei nefoedd ei hun,
Mewn hunan foddhad diysgog
Yn nydd goresgyniad y Goth.

How should we live together,
How should we build together in love and keep vigil
But that we are one in Adam and in Christ?
And that is the evil of Pelagianism,
That it destroys the unity of our nature, our new unity in Grace,
So that the learned and the por no longer form one nation
But each earns his own salvation
In unshaken self-satisfaction
Under the domination of the Goths.

This powerful indirect attack on modern individualism is the cnetral
statement which the play is designed to sustain. It is followed immediately by the sound of the bell which celebrates the elevation of the
Host, and Garmon's injunction to the people to celebrate the sacrament of the mass which binds the Church and the civilised world in
unity: "Christ's sacrifice is a marriage,/ And therein, in the marriage
which is sacrifice, lies in the unity of the family of Faith". Immediately
after this the crowd discover the miracle of the restoration of the child's
sight, which reveals in practical terms the meaning of the sacrifice. At
the moment of elevation the sacrifice is renewed. Looking up obedient-
ly, in all the fulness of his mischievous nature, the child receives his
sight. So mankind has received the light of salvation, sharing Adam's
sin but made one in Christ.

At this point, introducing Emrys, heir to the imperial tradition of
Rome, Saunders Lewis reminds us again of the political dimension to
his subject, as he did at the end of the first part. Garmon's return to
Britain, a symbolic gesture celebrating the unity of Faith, was shown
there to have led to the conversion of Ireland. Here it is linked to the
development of Wales. The eloquence of the monk, Paulinus, is
matched by that of the young king, Emrys, who pleads with Germanus

to take command of his armies in battle against the English and Pictish heathens. Borrowing Biblical imagery, he depicts Wales as a vineyard, passed down from generation to generation, which must now be defended against the swine which threaten to destroy it:

> Garmon,   Garmon,
> Gwinllin a rhoddwyd i'm gofal yw Cymru fy ngwlad,
> I'w thraddodi i'm plant
> Ac i blant fy mhlant
> Yn dreftadaeth dragwyddol;
> Ac wele'r moch yn rhuthro arni i'w maeddu.
> Minnau yn awr, galwaf ar fy nghyfellion,
> Cyffredin ac ysgolhaig,
> Deuwch ataf i'r adwy,
> Sefwch gyda mi yn y bwlch,
> Fel y cadwer i'r oesoedd a ddêl y glendid a fu.

> Garmon,   Garmon,
> My country Wales is a vineyard entrusted to my care.
> To pass down to my children
> And to my children's children
> An inheritance for ever;
> And behold the swine rushing to despoil it.
> Now I call on my friends,
> Scholars and laymen,
> Come and stand with me in the breach,
> To preserve the beauty that is past in the ages that are to come.

Emrys appeals to Garmon for military help against the barbarians. Again his acceptance is quiet and undramatic, "In the name of the Lord of Hosts,/ I will come, O King". But the scene ends with an invocation which echoes and develops the words which close the earlier scene: "Garmon for Britain,/ And Wales for Christ".

Part IV celebrates Garmon's acceptance of responsibility for the secular condition of the British people. Between the two parts martial music is heard, gradually increasing in sound and continuing to make itself heard above the opening litany. This gives way to an exchange between the watch and Lupus on the one hand, and a messenger sent from the army on the other. This dialogue provides an opportunity to suggest the tiem and the place in which the scene occurs and to provide the background to the victory which suddenly announces itself when Garmon's hidden army is heard declaring itself and advancing upon the enemy with repeated Halleluias. The litany is resumed as the sounds of the victorious army grow distant. The messenger breaks in again with a formulaic description of the battle scene and Garmon is announced to the sound of trumpets. His formal statement of victory is followed by the Lation prayer which brings the play to a close:

Glory to the Father and to the Son and to the Holy Ghost,
As it was in the beginning, is now and always will be,
World without end, Amen.

3. *Amlyn ac Amig*

Like *Buchedd Garmon, Amlyn ac Amig* resulted from an invitation to write a play for radio, to be broadcast on the occasion of Christmas 1940. Saunders Lewis responded by adapting a Medieval tale which derived from an eleventh century French *chanson de geste.*[5] The Medieval narrative is a serenely unquestioning description of the relationship between Mankind and its Creator, whose power and glory interpenetrate every aspect of his Creation. In dramatising this story Saunders Lewis introduced two major innovations. In setting it at Christmas time he took great care to draw out the theological implications of Christ's birth, emphasising the way in which it impinges on the ordinary reality of mankind. Then he changed the focus of the tale, shifting the emphasis from Amig, the leper who is miraculously saved when his friend obeys the Divine injunction to kill his own children and bathe him with their blood. Amlyn, not Amig, is the central character of the play, His bitter, unwilling obedience to the letter of the command is followed by conversion to holiness and sincere wonder at the mercy of God, manifest in the feast of Christmas as in the no greater miracle of his children's survival.

In the story of Amlyn and Amig the Medieval author saw an opportunity to demonstrate the fact that mankind lies in the hand of the Almighty and that human affairs are inseparably a part of the Divine vision. The modern author's eye, however, saw no farther than the stress and tension of the human passion absent from the poem. For him Amlyn is the true focus of attention because his dilemma is typical of that of every Christian. The author of the Medieval Welsh version saw clearly the pity of Amlyn's suffering, obliged to murder his own children to reciprocate friendship, but his portrayal of Amlyn is calm and elegaic. He is aware of the deep pathos inherent in the situation, emphasising it by describing the children waking to greet their father with laughter, but with Amlyn's last words to them he ensures that we remember that their fate is no more than that we all share by virtue of our humanity and as the punishment for sin:

> Lords, my sons, your laughter will be turned to weeping and your happiness to sadness, because your cruel father is ready to show you that Death is your nearest neighbour.[6]

In the Medieval author's Amlyn, in fact, we sense no cruelty, in spite of his unquestioning obedience to the consecrated oath. In the central character of Saunders Lewis's play, on the other hand, in spite of his unwillingness, we see cruelty and harshness, the stubborn blindness of the English Mystery character, Cain, a man struggling to be sufficient to himself, in spite of the evident mercifulness of his Creator.

To compare Amlyn with Cain as we see him, for example, in the work of the Wakefield Master in the Towneley cycle of mystery plays, obliges us to notice that Saunders Lewis is very much less confident in the fundamental technique of dramatic enactment than his Medieval predecessor.[7] The Wakefield Master's Cain blinds and blaggards his way across the stage, confronting and defying God directly, disastrously confident in the solidity of the ground beneath his feet which he will be cursed to water with his sweat. The Medieval dramatist wastes no time in preparing the audience for what he has to say. His ironies are simple and direct, resolved before the audience in the remorse of his characters. By contrast Saunders Lewis creates a complex, sophisticated web of irony, which is never fully resolved on the stage. In spite of his choice to focus the drama on the situation of Amlyn, whose conversion offered a frame for the whole play, he eventually withdraws from action, taking refuge, as it were, in irony. As a result, though the first two scenes of the play are constructed masterfully, the climax they introduce and inform never occurs. In the final scene the play's dramatic energy is dissipated. The theme is completed, but is not achieved in terms of dramatic action.

The central theme of *Amlyn ac Amig* is introduced in Amlyn's opening enquiry "Porter, has the gate been closed?" These words, innocent seeming in the first instance, demonstrate the mastery of the dramatist who brings his character forward at the very beginning developed to a point which we can only gradually understand. For as the play continues we come to see this opening enquiry as quite typical of Amlyn, a man who will defend the sources of order and stability in his life even against God himself. When the play opens, on Christmas

Eve, Amlyn claims faith, but his claim is false. In contrast to his wife, Belisent, he seeks to close his world against God. He advances the moral justification of the Christmas fast – "It is not fitting to go feasting to greet the baby Christ"– but she presents the practical acts of charity in a way that tells us that the story of Jesus has a present reality to her:

> Cadwaf, er hynny, fy Amlyn, arlwy o fwyd a gwin,
> Rhag dyfod rhyw ddieithiwr hwyr
> A churo fel Joseff a Mair ar ddrysau Bethlem.

> In spite of that, my Amlyn, I will keep a supply of food and drink,
> In case some late stranger may come
> And knock like Mary and Joseph on the doors of Bethlehem.

In this spirit Belisent claims the children's right to fulfil the custom of placing a lighted candle in the window, "Because, who knows whether he may not come, as once to Bethlehem Judea/ A baby seeking shelter, or in the guise of a beggar..."

With these lines the central dramatic irony begins to develop, for it is this childish custom which brings Amig to the door and opens their world to the horror of the night's events. Saunders Lewis steadily develops this fundamental irony, resolving it only in the last movement of the play, with the recovery of the children and the manifestation of God's loving kindness to man. As the children set the candle, the choir sing a hymn to Mary, celebrating the obedient humility which made her the door and the source of Light to men. As it comes to a close Amlyn, blind to that Light, refers to the light which the children have set and the blessing it may bring to them and their parents. His blessing to the children, recalling the words of the Hail Mary,[8] forces us to look forward to later events and acknowledge the dreadful weakness and fragility of mankind:

> Y nos hon ac yn awr angau,
> Cadwed chwychwi, fy mhlant, y Tad goruchaf

> This night and in the hour of death,
> Heavenly Father, may my children be kept safe.

Amlyn's blessing brings the first movement of the play to an end. The next begins with his reference to Amig and the friendship between them. Five years ago to the night Amig had fought to protect Belisent

from a false accusation and win her hand for his friend, in fulfilment
of the vow of friendship they had taken. Remembering the occasion,
Amlyn utters words which he will repeat again with very different
feelings: "I will never forget the vow". At this point these words
introduce a flashback to the scene when the oath was taken by the two
friends. This might have signalled the introduction of a new dimension
of action. After all, if Amlyn's conversion is to be the subject of the
play, it would be natural to expect the dramatist to make use of the
freedom of place and time which the modern stage allows to dramatise
his internal development. However, this flashback scene is in fact no
more than a mechanical device, allowing the dramatist to fill in the
audience's knowledge of the situation. The oath is important not
because it is consecrated, like the vow of the characters in the original
tale, but because Amlyn has anchored his life on it, making it an
irreducible element which survives even his love for his children. As
such, however, it is not more than another kind of selfishness, though
buried deeper in the recesses of his being.

After this interruption the action of the play proceeds with an ironic
anticipation of Amig's entrance. Belisent wishes that Amig might be
there to share Christmas with them. The dramatist makes use of this
to draw our attention to the friends' twin baptismal cups, presented
to them by the Pope, preparing us for the later identification of the
leper by this means. Then the scene takes a new direction, as the bard
praises his lord and lady, ironically increasing our awareness of the
fragility of the human happiness which is so soon and so rudely to be
shattered. We have now reached the dramatic climax of the scene, with
the knocking at the castle door, heralding the approach of the leper,
attracted in the dark of the night by the children's candle. His entrance
is delayed for a few moments, while the dramatist further intensifies
the audience's sense of irony with Belisent's pious response to her
husband's concern: "Christ will never bring anyone to sadness on this
night/ If you believe in his name". The Fool's response to her sharpens
the irony still further, as he warns that Christ rarely brings mankind
the kind of peace they anticipate themselves: "Neither did He come
to bring men peace,/ He sometimes played strange tricks with a
sword". Until this point the irony has mainly related to our immediate
expectation of Amig's entry. This remark of the Fool's forces us to
look farther forward, and specifically to anticipate the children's death,
which takes place between the second scene and the third. Belisent's

reply confirms this tendency – "May there be no mention of swords tonight."

The final movement of this first scene concerns the recognition of Amig, itself a joyful occasion, in spite of the sadness Amlyn and Belisent feel in welcoming their friend as a homeless, hopeless leper. In dramatic terms the enacted welcome is itself a culmination, which aptly brings the scene to an end, especially as it allows them to play a Christ-like role. Even here, however, the sense of irony is dominant. "You have children?" Amig asks; "God be praised for that": and it would be difficult to find another single line which has more different ironical reverberations. Beneath the childless man's rejoicing for his friend we are aware that the children will be the occasion of the horror to come; and yet at the same time we anticipate the final realisation that joy of another kind will ensue. Amlyn's last line, however, another repetition of the terms of his vow, prevents us from anticipating too much and returns us to an earlier phase of awareness. "And between us," Amig says, reminding his friend of their oath, "may there never be untruth". Amig replies, as we would expect; "I will never forget the vow." Far from a virtue, this loyalty is the substitute for a more humble faithfulness which should transcend the selfishness of Amlyn's self-regarding friendship.

The play's second scene enacts the visit of the Angel and the conversation which follows between the two friends. It is certainly the best piece of dramatic writing that Saunders Lewis had produced up to that time. Without going far beyond the frame presented in the original story, he develops quite new dimensions to the action. In response to the Angel's injunction Amig and Amlyn develop clearly differentiated characters. We come to see Amig as the type of the true Christian, whose selfish emotions have been subsumed by humility. Amlyn, on the other hand, reveals himself to be lost in self concern, bitter because he cannot protect himself from God, to whom he should be turning humbly for protection. Both men find the situation they are in cruel almost beyond the point of sufferance. Under pressure, Amig confesses his dishonesty and evasiveness, but he has the strength to resist the subtle temptation that Amlyn offers him, to dismiss the voice of the Angel as the invention of the Devil. Amlyn fails to undermine the clarity of mind which rests on simple faith in God's goodness. "Will you swear to me that it was an angel?" he asks. Amig replies:

Na thyngaf, am na wn. Ond d'wedaf imi gredu

Mai Raffael oedd, a rhoi fy mhwys ar Dduw
Na'm gedy Ef fi'n anrhaith i Ddiawl...
Ni ofyn Duw i tithau ond barnu'n ôl dy olau,
Ac os rhag ofn cythreuliaid neu falais fy nghalon i
Y berni'n wag fy neges, yna bydd dawel dy ysbryd,
A gosod hunllef heno o'th gof.

I won't swear because I don't know. But I will say that I believed
That it was Raffael and that I relied on God
Not to leave me prey to the Devil...
God only asks of you that you judge according to your own lights,
And if, in fear of devils or the malice of my heart
You judge my message to be false, then quieten your spirit,
And put tonight's nightmare from your mind.

In fact, however, Amlyn cannot dismiss what Amig has told him because he lacks his friend's faith in God's goodness. Amig listened in faith to Raffael's message and never doubts it. Even so, in pity of his friend, he urges him to ignore the message:

Mi daerais i â'r angel yn unig er osgoi
Byr gur y siarad hwn. A thybiais yn fy angerdd
Mai drosot ti yr ymbiliwn: felly mewn gweddi ar Dduw
Mae calon dyn yn ei dwyllo.
Tithau, gwnaethost a ellaist. Ffordd Dduw, nis deall dyn.
Dos, gyfaill, i'th wely'n awr.

I struggled with the angel only to avoid
The brief pain of this talk. And in my agony
I thought I was pleading for you; so even in prayer to God
Man's heart deceives him.
You have done what you could. Man does not understand God's way.
Friend, go back now to your bed.

Amlyn cannot take this alternative because he insists on judging God according to his own nature. If Amig is telling the truth, he argues, then God is malicious; if he lies, then friendship – the foundation of his own certainty – is destroyed. Amlyn's dilemma actually arises from the fact that God is not real for him. In the place of God he puts the solidity of his vow, re-enacting the oath to assure himself that his friend is telling the truth in order to justify his condemnation of God:

Tynghedaf di er y llw,
Ac fel y cadwer d'enaid,

Ai gwir i'r hwn ddaeth atad
Ddweud fel y d'wedi di?

I charge you on the oath,
And as your soul may be saved,
To declare whether it is true that he who came to you
Did speak as you have reported.

Amig's simple and sad reply – "True, my lord, too true" – leaves Amlyn with only one recourse, which is to justify his own bitter hatred of God in what he will experience as cruel, destructive, self-murder. His last words promise this, though the audience may not know him well enough to understand them: "I will never forget my vow."

In concluding this second scene Saunders Lewis must have been aware that several possible courses lay open to him as a dramatist. He could have decided to stay with Amlyn and approach the task of dramatising the remaining action from his point of view. This might well have seemed the most natural way of proceeding, in view of the fact that Amlyn's experience is central to the play.

A scene like Othello's murder of Desdemona might have provided a model for a scene enacting his murder of the children. However, he decided not to provide such a scene, nor to enact the miracle of the healing as it was originally conceived. Instead he decided to change the pattern of events so as to separate the healing from the murder of the children, sending Amig to the church as a leper alone, there to be healed by immediate and apparently unconditional Divine intervention. This enabled him to increase Amlyn's isolation, to create a more dramatic contrast between Amlyn on the one hand and Belisent and Amig on the other and to concentrate dramatic attention on the moment when he reveals to them what he has done. However, the decision also brought with it several problems which he was unable to solve satisfactorily. As a result, the play founders in this last scene, just as it should be increasing in power and effectiveness.

The action with which the scene begins does not arise from the situation of any of the main characters. Nor does it reflect on the central themes of the play. In dramatic terms it is scaffolding, designed to sustain a dramatic situation which cannot stand independently. The conversation between the porter and the maidservants clumsily serves several functions. It permits us to locate the central characters and allows us to balance them in our minds as two separate groups, the isolation of which promises a dramatic confrontation — Belisent and

Amig are returning from the church, confused and joyful witnesses of the mercy of God; Amlyn sulks in the corner. It also provides a frame upon which the dramatist can stretch the audience's awareness of the irony which emerges here again as the dominant note. So the girls repeatedly ask Amlyn for permission to awake the children, thereby keeping their fate before the attention of the audience.

The climax of the scene is to be the moment when Amlyn draws Belisent and Amig into his own pit of bitterness, telling them the price of Amig's cure. In order to postpone this moment and properly to prepare the audience for it, Saunders Lewis entrusts the narrative of what has happened at the church to the subordinate characters of the Fool and the Bard. The rather crude comedy which results serves to heighten further the audience's sense of irony, increasing their sympathy with Amlyn and the shock with which they greet his outburst of violence "Woman may the Devil choke you!" This in turn introduces the explanation which takes place between the three central characters, heavily marked by irony, which can be appreciated fully only by the audience.

There are several stages to this process of revelation. Firstly Belisent and Amig attempt to explain Amlyn's violent and confused behaviour, which they are unable to understand because they are to varying degrees ignorant of the circumstances of the miracle they are celebrating. Belisent knows nothing of the angel's visit and Amig, who slept through what happened afterwards, is unaware that his friend has acted on the angel's injunction. There is consequently a double focus to the scene. We note and learn from their response to Amlyn's climactic narrative. Belisent's response is particularly important, illustrating a simple, profound acceptance. At the same time we note the change which takes place in Amlyn as he is forced to contemplate what he has done and why he has done it. Re-enacting the bitter defiance of God, he softens to acceptance of what has happened in despite of himself.

With Belisent's simple response, the central action of the play is over. While she goes to seek the children, the bard sings a hymn which combines references to the Massacre of the Innocents and the Book of Revelations with the *Kyrie eleison, Christe eleison* of the Mass.[9] The dialogue which remains records for the benefit of the audience the final miracle and the change it brings about in Amlyn, prepared by his own suffering to understand and accept for the first time the relationship between Man and God which is symbolised in the Christmas story.

The play ends as the choir sings the Latin carol 'Adeste, fideles', while, according to the stage directions, the characters "go towards the crib". Were *Amlyn ac Amig* to be performed as a stage play this would present problems which would not arise in the case of a radio production, for which, of course, it was composed. The choir makes a considerable contribution to the play. Each scene is brought to a close with a carol or a hymn. At the end of the first and second parts the choir sing Christmas carols; in the first scene there is a hymn to Mary sung alternately by men and women. Were the play to be performed in a theatre, in the presence of an audience, the producer would have to decide whether to let the choir share the playing area with the actors, or, indeed, whether to make them double as members of the court. The problem does not arise so obviously in a radio play, because we never see them, and yet it still exists. To the extent to which members of the radio audience do conceptualise the action of the play, they must be aware that the choir exists as an entity other than the characters. In Ancient Greek tragedy the choir is also quite clearly understood to be apart from the actors, although they may also take part in the action, but this presented no problem for contemporary audiences. They saw the actors and the choir, like themselves, as part of a larger cultural and conceptual entity, the City, which the theatre reflected. Lacking a similar concept, modern audiences react differently to the way in which stage space is disposed. They must understand the choir as in some way placed between themselves and the characters, who are confined to the space and time suggested by the situation they enact.

In *Amlyn ac Amig* this has a two-fold effect. It allows the dramatist to retain a greater degree of control over the audience's response than would otherwise have been possible. It also increases the celebratory element of the Christmas drama at the cost of reducing the dramatic element. In fact Saunders Lewis has taken great care throughout the play to enclose the action he derived from the medieval tale within the audience's awareness of the theological meaning of the feast of Christmas. Several devices work to this end, in addition to the element of song. Subordinate characters like the Fool and the Bard, who are not involved in the central action, are employed to manipulate the audience's awareness of the situation. The dramatist's main instrument, however, is the irony which he weaves throughout the play's fabric.

Irony is a device which necessarily encourages the audience's self-awareness because it can only arise when they interpret something which is happening on stage in a way which is not possible for the characters concerned to do. However, as we see in the work of some of the dramatists who develop it most finely, it may be presented as an integral part of the dramatic event, so increasing its authority and power. When we watch Oedipus quarrelling with Creon or questioning the Shepherd, the dreadful irony which arises from our awareness that he himself is the man he seeks to punish increases our interest in the process of gradual discovery by which we will find release.

In *Amlyn ac Amig* the situation is quite different. On one level the irony which Saunders Lewis borrows from the original narrative does reinforce the dramatic interest of the situation. So when we hear the maidservants or Belisent herself urging Amlyn to let the children be awakened, we share his painful awareness of the real situation. However, we also know that they are alive and this knowledge separates us from him, distancing us from his painful consciousness. This level of awareness is sustained and developed throughout the play by other ironical references which remind us that the outcome of the action will be a strengthening of faith and a justification of God's way with man.

Particularly important are the many references to Mary, the perfect example of the faithful soul who willingly grants unquestioning, selfless obedience and thereby becomes the instrument of God's mercy. Mary and Jesus bring together the two themes of obedience and suffering which are necessarily bound together as the means by which the will of God and the salvation of man are effected. Consequently we can never feel implicated in Amlyn's situation. We are always aware that we are part of the Church, possessed of the knowledge of God's mercifulness.

It is not the purpose of the play to enable us to win through to this knowledge with the central character. Saunders Lewis rejects the opportunity to implicate us in Amlyn's guilt by enacting the murder in our presence. He also rejects the challenge of dramatising Amlyn's conversion. He gives us a speech which relates his past actions and his present grief, followed by one which records his subsequent change of heart. However, there is no action which mediates between these two statements. One has only to compare Shakespeare's treatment of Leontes's conversion in the last scene of *A Winter's Tale* to see what is lacking here. Shakespeare, of course, has his own problems with Leontes, which are notoriously evident in the early parts of the play.

However, he solved the difficulty he faced in the later scene, the difficulty of enacting a process of inner change, by showing us Leontes's reaction to the statue of Hermione.

To understand the way in which Saunders Lewis chose to treat his subject in *Amlyn ac Amig* we need to draw back a little from the text to a point from which we can analyse the world which the play in general portrays. There are three types of character in *Amlyn ac Amig*. At the centre, Amlyn himself, who is without true faith but who may win through to it through suffering: Amig and Belisent, who already have it and to whom, consequently, in the terms proposed by the play, nothing can happen: and the remaining characters, the Porter, the Fool, the Bard and the other members of the household. This latter group is also beyond the reach of the action, for a different reason; although they lack deep faith, they are never tested. There is a striking contrast here between Saunders Lewis's play and T.S. Eliot's *Murder in the Cathedral*. Eliot's chorus, unlike Saunders Lewis's choir and his subordinate characters, are involved in the action, which does represent a spiritual test for them. Though they do not share the Archbishop's ability to live in the light of his faith, they rejoice in his spiritual victory, in which they share by virtue of their own spiritual suffering.

The immediate explanation of the difference between the two dramatists is theological. Eliot sees the world as penetrated by the Spirit. Though he shares Eliot's Catholic vision of the Church, Saunders Lewis is unable to believe that it actually exists in the world to the degree that *Murder in the Cathedral* implies. His *Amlyn ac Amig* embodies a compromise vision. The human world of drama, in which Amlyn lives and suffers, is untouched by his suffering. Nor is it illuminated by his victory. Indeed, the central assertion of the meaning of Christmas is made indirectly rather than directly, nor is it fully enacted. It is as if the dramatist could not bring himself to trust his medium. He is unwilling to obliterate himself, but clings to the power he can exercise directly on the audience. We can only conclude that his unwillingness results from a degree of uncertainty regarding the relationship between the world of man and the world of the Spirit. Some such explanation is necessary, for in *Amlyn ac Amig* he set out to dramatise the victory of the Spirit, came close to success and then, almost as if deliberately, drew back.

Part III

1. Myth and History.

"You might imagine that it had been written especially for the recitation competition at the National Eisteddfod", Saunders Lewis commented ruefully in 1957 on the "rhetorical poetry" of *Buchedd Garmon'*. By the time, he came to revise and extend the first two Acts of *Blodeuwedd*, as he put it himself, he had "quietened down quite a bit".[1] "Dramatic poetry," he tells us in the Preface to *Blodeuwedd* (1948), "is the poetry of conversation." The central characters in *Blodeuwedd* and *Siwan* (1956) are poets in their own right, endowed with the ability to express feelings and sensations which lie far beyond the reach of consciousness and yet without losing the ring of natural speech. In contrast to the language of earlier plays, the unrhymed verse of *Blodeuwedd* and *Siwan* achieves the poet's expressed aim of conveying the speech rhythms of people who thought and felt as intensely as they spoke. By this time the comparison with T.S.Eliot had turned in Saunders Lewis's favour, for in the plays which succeeded *Murder in the Cathedral* Eliot had failed to create a dramatic medium in which the different levels of discourse blended naturally.

Though clearly evident in dramatic dialogue, this was by no means simply a matter of language. The underlying factor which sharpens our awareness of the awkwardness of the language of plays like *The Cocktail Party* (1949) and *The Elder Statesman* (1958) was Eliot's failure to work out an appropriate dramatic action arising from the relationships between his characters. In *Blodeuwedd*, on the other hand, Saunders Lewis did find a way of developing his subject by means of an action which was, recalling Szondi's term, 'interpersonal'. In practical terms this meant that psychological analysis arose from contact between the characters locked together in the action; and that action itself could only develop through dramatic interchange and discourse as the characters reflected on their mutual situation and the way the behaviour of others impacted on them.

Reading *Monica,* the novel he published in 1930, is perhaps the best possible preparation for understanding the way in which Saunders Lewis developed during the years when, as he put it himself, he had abandoned the theatre for the cause of nationalism.[2] His starting point in *Monica* is the rejection of contemporary reality implied in *Gwaed yr Uchelwyr.* The novel is a study of the isolation and consequent break-down of the individual in a suburban world where no real community or relatedness is possible. It reveals a mistrust of the immediate human world which goes far to explain the relative failure of the dramatist in *Buchedd Garmon* and *Amlyn ac Amig.* Saunders Lewis had adopted Barrés' idea of community as an antidote to subjectivity and as the way of true freedom, but where could community exist if not in the world? In *Blodeuwedd* Saunders Lewis was able to answer this question for the first time. By 1948 he had acquired new confidence in the ability of human beings to inform their relations with meaning. This made his return to the theatre, in a very real sense, a 'happy return'.[3]

The basis of this new confidence was an acceptance of the interdependence of the individual consciousness and the social world. *Gwaed yr Uchelwyr* had shown how the individual could define himself in opposition to the world in which he lived, on the basis of ideas derived from the past. *Blodeuwedd* is based on the understanding that tradition can be mediated through the present. Recognising that his consciousness is actually an aspect of the world on which he reflects, the hero of Saunders Lewis's mature drama is free of the self-disgust which destroyed the characters of *Monica.* A conscious acceptance of the forces and the structures which have moulded consciousness and identity frees the individual from isolation and impotence. His exercise of will becomes an objective expression of the forces which have come together to form him. Having been freed from the romantic illusion of self-sufficiency, he is also free of the guilt which follows from the romantic hero's inevitable failure to experience coherence and harmony in his relationship with the world. So this new hero and, more frequently, heroine – need not, like the characters of Ibsen's later drama, compound unhappiness with guilt. He will experience freedom in choosing how his consciousness will be disposed in the world; but he will not be responsible for a failure which follows from the conditions of the world.

This view of human character was ultimately responsible for Saunders Lewis's renewed choice of the theatre as a medium of expression and for the shape and structure of his mature drama. His characters come to him fully formed, a part of the world they live in; the action of his plays represents moments of crisis in which they experience the freedom of determining the way in which they relate to it. Unlike Ibsen, he is not concerned to relate their present actions to their past experience. His method is clearly reflected in his description of the way in which Racine developed the action of his Bérénice:

> Gwelodd Racine frawddeg fer mewn pennod o lyfr hanes gan Suetonius: 'Anfonodd Titus, ymherodr y Frenhines Bernig, y dywedid ei bod wedi ei diweddio iddo, ymaith o'r ddinas, o'i anfodd ef ac o'i hanfodd hithau.' Y mae'r Lladin gwreiddiol yn fyrrach dipyn na'm cyfieithiad i. Ond dyna'r cwbl. O'r frawddeg fer honno fe gyfansoddodd Racine drasiedi Bérénice, un o'i weithiau mawr ef, sy'n dal ei swyn a'i nerth ar lwyfan Ffrainc hyd heddiw; ac nid oes fawr ddim yn stori'r ddrama honno nad ydyw eisoes yn y frawddeg fer Ladin uchod; a drama o bum act yw Bérénice. Sut y llwyddodd ef? Trwy dynnu allan o'r sefyllfa ei holl ystyr, ei holl resymeg, a thrwy ddatblygu'r cymeriadau i'w cyflawnder eithaf.

> Racine saw a short sentence in a chapter in Suetonius's history: 'The Emperor Titus sent Queen Bernice, to whom he was said to be engaged, away from the city, against his will and hers.' The original Latin is a good deal shorter than my version. But that's all there is. From that short sentence Racine composed the tragedy, Bérénice, one of his great works, which maintains its charm and strength in the French theatre even today; and there is scarcely anything in the story of that play that is not already in the short Latin sentence above; and Bérénice is a play in five Acts. How did he do this? Through drawing out the whole meaning of the situation, its whole logic, and through developing the characters to their fullest potential. [4]

Like Titus and Bérénice, Blodeuwedd and Siwan came to the dramatist through the medium of narrative, rooted in a specific, though distant, reality. He is not concerned to ask how they came to be as they are, but rather to create a space in which they can develop the logic of their being. The sharp reality of their speech and action in the dramatic world in which move together confirms at once their independence and their relatedness to the larger world. The responsibility which makes them interesting and gives them strength and dignity, follows from this duality, which enables them to grow under the hands of the dramatist to become, like the characters of the greatest drama – the drama, Saunders Lewis said, of Aeschylus and Sophocles – "Symbols of life and the fate of humanity and the forces which work in them and through them."

It is in respect of the way in which his characters relate to the world that Saunders Lewis differs from Jean Paul Sartre, whose plays otherwise reflect a strikingly similiar awareness of the way in which theatre may focus attention on the dramatic moment when the individual defines himself in relation to the past and determines his future. This awareness underlies the basic similarity between the two dramatists in the way they define the stage in terms of the relationship between inner experience and the outer world of other people. In Sartre's case, however, there was a fundamental ambiguity in his view of the relationship between the individual and the world which introduced an element of weakness into his drama. In *Huis-Clos* (1944), which is structured around a series of relations worked out directly in the presence of the audience, we see how well he had applied lessons learnt from Ibsen. His three characters come together after their separate deaths to work out the consequences of their past lives in the world by tormenting each other in the eternal present of Hell. The reason why they are in Hell is that they have all refused to accept the reality of their own freedom and they remain there because they continue to do so. This point is made dramatically at the end of the play, as the door of the room swings open, leaving them each with the freedom of choice which they refuse to exercise. In theatrical terms, however, there is an element of ambiguity in this ending. Throughout the play, both in the past action which the characters report, in giving accounts of themselves to the others and in the present action, human behaviour is presented as essentially social. It is only in relation to other people that the individual may achieve or avoid the act of self definition in which freedom consists. However, the open door at the end of the play seems to posit another dimension, which is neither the social world of real life, nor the equally social world of the after life.

The strength of Sartre's implicit argument in *Huis Clos* derives from the fact that the audience has had access to both these worlds, indirectly, through narration, and directly through action, and so recognizes their similarity to each other and to the one they themselves inhabit. This is all the stronger because in the end we remain together with the three characters, facing a door through which we have no reason to believe that we may pass. This ending, in fact, reduces to a negative the freedom which is posited throughout the play as the proper condition of the human being. It must be imagined by the audience as a state of non-relatedness, even as non-being, essentially different from that which they share with the dead characters.

The difference between Sartre and Saunders Lewis in this matter appears very clearly in the comparison between *Blodeuwedd* and *Les Mains Sales* (1948). The two plays are similar in that they end with dramatic acts of self-definition, which are also voluntary acts of self-extinction. Sartre's hero, Hugo, walks from the stage to meet the Party executioners; Gronw goes patiently to meet his death off-stage and Blodeuwedd exits on a note of bitter defiance, rejecting Llew's forgiveness and the whole human world. In both plays the stage is defined similarly as a space in which the individual consciousness may be seen reacting to external stimulus in relation to others. A stage defined in terms of the consciousness of an individual is emptied of meaning when he leaves it and the audience's awareness of this must greatly strengthen their reaction to the debate which is concluded in this way.

However, the ending of *Les Mains Sales* is relatively weak compared to that of *Blodeuwedd* because Hugo's withdrawal from the stage alters the way in which it is defined – it is now occupied by another character whose loneliness symbolises the failure of relatedness in a world where personal integrity is impossible – and this sudden change in point of view is not assimilated into the action itself. *Blodeuwedd,* on the other hand, ends strongly. The heroine's exit, following from her refusal to accept the limits of merely human experience, completes the thematic statement of the play. In theatrical terms this is a strong ending because it is reinforced by the audience's awareness of the stage as the point of contact between the existential and the social self. When Blodeuwedd leaves the stage the audience are left with the cynical Gwydion and the sadder, wiser, Llew, in the social world which forms their consciousness and in which alone human life may be lived.

This is not to say that the author of *Blodeuwedd* had achieved a completely consistent view of the relationship between the individual and the world. In this respect, in fact, the comparison with Racine is a little misleading. In plays like *Andromaque* (1667) and *Britannicus* (1669), if the audience are permitted to hope for a moment that the human world may prove anything other than irredeemable it is only in order to deepen the bitter sense of irony which they are eventually to be left with. While he was writing *Blodeuwedd* and *Siwan*, there remained an element of ambiguity in the way he thought about the relationship between the individual and the community which led to an occasional awkwardness in the way he handled the audience's awareness of the playing space.

Rather than Racine, this puts us in mind of his contemporary and rival, Pierre Corneille, whose work was very much in Saunders Lewis's mind at this time. In his *Polyeucte* (1641), to which Saunders Lewis devoted two appreciative articles in December, January 1949-50,[5] the balance of Corneille's theatre is also often in doubt because of a similar ambiguity regarding his attitude to the world. Occasionally this led to problems which he could not solve within the terms he had set himself in a particular drama. So, for example, he was uneasy about the definition of the stage in *Le Cid* in the scenes where he brought Rodrigue and Chimène together in her appartment.[6] In *Polyeucte* he achieves consistency, but only by enclosing the on-stage action, which reflects internal crisis and processes of change, within a framework of off-stage action presented through narrative. The threatened arrival of an envoy from the Roman Emperor initiates the action of the play and from then on the emotional and moral crises which we witness on stage develop in relation to a connected series of off-stage events which are reported to us and which, though not themselves the focus of attention, are ultimately of greater importance than what happens on stage.

Saunders Lewis's dramatic method in *Blodeuwedd* and *Siwan* involves a similar attempt to balance on-stage and off-stage action. In *Blodeuwedd* we are constantly aware of the immediate, off-stage world of the court and of the larger world of Gwynedd and the whole territory of Math and of Dyfed, where Blodeuwedd and Gronw might have fled to escape the anger of Llew and Gwydion. The balance between this off-stage world and the immediate world of inner action and reaction, however, is not always consistently held. There are times in *Blodeuwedd* when Saunders Lewis creates an uneasy sense that his stage represents at one and the same time a free, inner space, and an enclosing, outer space. Likewise, in *Siwan*, he finds it difficult to control our awareness of the stage as representing the private space of relatedness and as a more public world, in which inter-personal action can take place and even as representing a more open space where the characters can acquire the value of objects to the external social world. In this respect, though they embody an attitude to the social world with which audiences are more likely to be content than with the more consistent, harsher vision of the later plays, these two plays mark no more than a transitional phase in the consistent development of his theatre.

2. *Blodeuwedd*

The characters and much of the action on which *Blodeuwedd* is based are drawn directly from the early Twelfth Century redaction of the story of *Math, Fab Mathonwy*, the fourth 'cainc' of the Mabinogi. Saunders Lewis kept faith with this original to a surprising degree, in spite of the difficulties involved in adapting the story for the stage. However, his version incorporated a far-reaching re-interpretation which is so natural and compelling that it seems always to have lain there, awaiting discovery.

Blodeuwedd retells the story of Llew Llaw Gyffes, a nephew of Gwynedd's king, Math, whose illegitimate birth shames the king's sister, Arianrhod, causing her to refuse him recognition or baptism. The child's uncle, the magician, Gwydion, pitying him, employs his magic to avoid the consequences of the various curses Arianrhod imposes on him: that he will never have a name or arms unless he receives them from her and that he will never find a wife from among the sons of men. To avoid this latter curse Gwydion makes a maiden from flowers who becomes Llew's wife, but she, revolting against the confinements of marriage and court life and resenting her husband's tameness and self-centredness, plots with a lover, Gronw ap Pebr, to bring about his death, in spite of Gwydion's protection. They seem to succeed, killing Llew and ruling in his place, but Gwydion recovers him, so that at the end of a year he returns with three hundred men and they face the alternatives of flight or destruction. Gronw chooses to remain and accept his punishment at the hand of Llew because a year with Blodeuwedd has taught him that the freedom she offers is no more than a form of madness. He seeks, as he puts it, to return to the confines of humanity through death, the only gate remaining open to him. Blodeuwedd, defiant to the end, claims that she has done no more than fulfil the nature with which Gwydion himself invested her. Llew accepts her arguments; but Gwydion, with the magician's cunning, turns them against her, returning her to the wild in the form of an owl who, hated and shunned by other birds, will never know the experience of community.

The most important change that Saunders Lewis introduced into his version of the tale concerned the role of Gronw ap Pebr. In the original version Gronw is obliged to receive a blow from Llew as the only appropriate restitution for the wrong he has done him. The author of *Math, Fab Mathonwy* takes it for granted that Gronw has no means of refusing restitution, given that Llew is alive to ask for it, but he shows Gronw trying to avoid its consequences. Firstly he seeks a substitute from amongst his followers, who, in refusing, earn the title of the unfaithful 'teulu': secondly he asks for the right to hold up a stone between himself and Llew as protection. Here the story-teller is confronting traditional material which he feels obliged to rationalize in some way. When Saunders Lewis came to adapt this material for the stage, he shifted the emphasis entirely, making Gronw accept his punishment willingly.

It would certainly be difficult to over emphasize the importance of this innovation, either in thematic terms or in terms of dramatic technique. Until the dramatic change of direction in Act IV, Gronw plays a minor role, quite predictably the younger lover, something of a pawn in the battle between Llew and Blodeuwedd. His betrayal of Blodeuwedd in Act IV changes the whole course of the play, releasing great dramatic energy. This is appropriate because it carries the main burden of the play's philosophical statement. If we look back to *Gwaed yr Uchelwyr* we see Luned renouncing personal fulfilment through marriage and motherhood for the sake of personal integrity. In *Blodeuwedd* Saunders Lewis has separated out the constituent elements of love and identified them as the sources of different kind of self fulfilment. Llew yearns for a kind of love which would authenticate or reinforce his sense of self, but he is not prepared to pay the high price required in the absolute commitment to his lover. Llew can offer only a conditional commitment, because he has only a conditional sense of self. In relation to his mother, to Gwydion, to his role as ruler, he has come to consciousness of himself, though that consciousness brings with it a sense of yearning which he looks to Blodeuwedd to satisfy. For Llew love means children, fatherhood, a return of affection and loyalty as the basis of marriage as a social institution. Saunders Lewis refers to this form of 'tame' love as *cariad,* distinct from the wilder, more passionate, unconditional *serch,* which Blodeuwedd offers and Gronw accepts. This irreducible element of wildness in human nature is the basis for a different concept of self, unconditional and unconfined.

Taken as a whole the story of Llew records the process by which a man abandons desire. At the beginning of the play Llew is sulky and disappointed because he cannot achieve his dream of love. Deceived by Blodeuwedd to believe for a while that he may grasp what once seemed unattainable, he learns through suffering and sympathy with his wife, that desire may destroy everything on which human life is based. Gronw's story is the dramatic enactment of disappointment, more poignant than anything experienced by Llew. This is the disappointment that follows surfeit rather than failure. *Blodeuwedd* represents the fate of those who cannot transcend their own, irreducible yearning, which later, in *Siwan,* survives even the re-establishment of love and understanding between husband and wife.

When Gronw goes back on his love bargain and chooses to align himself with Llew rather than Blodeuwedd he is rejecting the idea that the self can exist in isolation. He sees it as choosing sanity, even at the price of death. Yet essentially this is the same choice that Luned makes. By now Saunders Lewis has come to think that it is possible to possess the world through the sense of community, but his vision remains pessimistic. Blodeuwedd, banished to the darkness of the woods, Gronw savagely slaughtered and Llew alone, sadder and wiser, accepting exile and isolation as the lot of humankind even in the midst of their fellows.

As the title suggests, the play centres on Blodeuwedd's experience and much of its dramatic energy derives from the tension in her situation. In Blodeuwedd Saunders Lewis saw a parallel to Euripides' Medea, an outsider who suffers rejection and who in turn rejects human society and human kind.[7] Both women, though they are inhumanly savage and destructive, direct a powerful criticism against the human world, in which civilisation is won at the price of betrayal. Blodeuwedd is snatched by Gwydion's selfish, cynical magic into a world which is empty of all the things which make it real and comforting to Llew. She has no family, no history, no responsibilities and although her husband offers to fill her world, he does so only conditionally on her fulfilling a bargain which she herself has never made. The play begins at the point when she makes her first, clear demand on Llew, and in doing so becomes fully conscious of herself for the first time. Filled with a vague sense of foreboding, she asks first Llew, then Gwydion, to stay with her, rather than going at once to visit Math and leaving her alone for the first time since her creation. When they refuse and leave she is saddened and afraid because in forcing her to confront her loneliness they oblige her to recognise and accept her freedom, the freedom of a creature who has been created without the ties of habit which hold human morality together.

However, the dramatic focus of the play is not determined by the shape or quality of Blodeuwedd's experience. Nor is she central to the play in the way that Euripides' heroine is. In fact Saunders Lewis tended to distinguish between the 'epic' quality of Ancient Greek drama in contradistinction to the "psychological sword crossing" which characterised modern drama and gave its characters their peculiar kind of vividness.[8] The complex 'dramatic' rather than 'epic' action of his play arises from the fact that it is the situation of Llew which dominates it. Blodeuwedd's challenge to him through Gronw initiates a direct dramatic movement centring on her, but Gronw's betrayal changes the play's direction, reinforcing the viewpoint from which the audience had originally entered the play. Once Gronw has left the stage Blodeuwedd too must follow him, leaving the world, as it were, to Llew and Gwydion.

To appreciate Gwydion's rôle in *Blodeuwedd* we need to be aware of the whole legend. Gwydion's magic and his friendship for his brother involve him in the rape of a maiden in Math's court. The king punishes them by turning them into three different wild animals, alternately male and female, for a year at a time, during which they mate together and have offspring, whom he turns into human beings at the end of the three years, when he restores the brothers to their original shape. So Gwydion has an experience of the wild which puts him outside the human pale in a sense. His punishment has reduced him to a point when he has acquired a quite non-human wisdom, understanding the emptiness of craving and desire, even the wild yearning of Blodeuwedd.

Gwydion offers us a critical perspective which, though we cannot share it, lacking his experience, helps to distance us from the situation which Llew introduces at the beginning of the play. When it begins Llew and Gwydion are together on the stage, but no indication is given of what they are doing. When Llew speaks it is to summon someone from beyond the stage and order him to ask Blodeuwedd to come to say goodbye to them. Saunders Lewis manages to off-load a good deal of necessary information during this first exchange — a quite respectable dramatic convention, which allows the audience to locate the action as part of a given chain of circumstances and in a given place and time. Shakespeare does this quite barefacedly in the second scene of *The Tempest,* which audiences accept quite willingly as the calm after the dreadful opening storm. Here, however, it has a different effect, because it makes us more aware of the imagined space beyond the stage than of the stage itself. What is happening before us on the stage is no more than a means of referring the imagination to the space occupied by Blodeuwedd, who is not here, and that which will be occupied by Gwydion and Llew, who reminds us: "We will travel three hours yet today, while it is light,/ Gwydion and I, and the soldiers".

The conversation which takes place between the two men while they await the entry of Blodeuwedd gives us a good deal more information about the background to the action and the situation of Llew, who laments Blodeuwedd's coldness, her wildness and distance from him. It is important that we should understand Llew, of course, but in preparing us in this way Saunders Lewis is giving us no more than an attenuated form of drama. What is happening on stage constantly refers to something else and somewhere else, firstly the events leading up to Blodeuwedd's creation, then her behaviour during the year of their marriage. Gwydion's demonstration of cynicism helps the dramatist over his difficulty. Gwydion in effect is laying down one of the base lines of the drama, our awareness of which will affect our response to the behaviour of the other characters. In dramatic terms, however, his rôle here is strange. His conversation with Llew is not really a conversation. He stands between Llew, who is telling a long story about past events, and the audience, commenting on the story as it goes. He can do no more than soften our awareness that the play has yet actually to begin. When Llew concludes his poetic report on his relationship with his wife and Gwydion sees her coming, it is something of a relief, though the line in which he anounces it has a touch of bathos: "Here's Blodeuwedd".

With the entry of Blodeuwedd the stage space is full for the first time and the drama comes to life. The scene that follows, her request and its refusal, initiates and in dramatic terms justifies, her betrayal of her husband and the subsequent action. When Llew goes from the stage, leaving her with the empty platitudes of husbandly concern, we must be prepared for her revolt.

In the next movement the maid servant Rhagnell is important. Her lack of understanding of Blodeuwedd draws us closer to the heroine while her unquestioning acceptance of her mistress also influences us at a moment when we might otherwise tend to distance ourselves from her. The introduction of Rhagnell as a character no doubt owes much to the example of Corneille and Racine, especially to the latter's example in plays like *Phèdre* (1677), where the Queen's companion, Oenone, plays a similar rôle. The *Penteulu*[9] is a similar character. Like Rhagnell, he mediates between the three central characters and the world, enabling the author to strengthen his control over the audience's response at important times. He is also brought into the action to an extent which is very unusual in Seventeenth Century French drama, though to a far less extent than Rhagnell herself. Though she is never more than a secondary character, her behaviour and her fate deepen the audience's capacity to respond to the strange and savage history of her mistress.

Explaining herself to Rhagnell, Blodeuwedd is also communicating indirectly with us on behalf of her creator. We have already seen how Saunders Lewis gives the passionless Llew the restrainedly passionate description of Blodeuwedd at the moment of her first creation, rather as Shakespeare gives a speech of brilliant poetic praise of Cleopatra to the pedestrian soldier, Enobarbus.[10] Addressing Rhagnell, Blodeuwedd goes far beyond the bounds of dialogue and presents a hauntingly poignant impression of a human life lived beyond the pale of humanity:

> O, ni deelli fyth,
> Fyth, fyth, fy ngofid i, na thi na neb.
> 'Wyddost ti ddim beth yw bod yn unig.
> Mae'r byd iti yn llawn, mae gennyt dref,
> Ceraint a theulu, tad a mam a brodyr,
> Fel nad wyt ti yn ddieithr yn y byd.
> Mae'r man y troediodd dynion yn gyfanedd,
> A Gwynedd oll, lle bu dy dadau gynt,
> Yn aelwyd iti, yn gronglwyd adeiladwyd
> Gan genedlaethau dy hynafiaid di;
> 'Rwyt ti'n gartrefol yn dy wlad dy hun
> Megis mewn gwely a daenwyd er dy fwyn
> Gan ddwylo cariad a fu'n hir yn d'aros;
> Minnau, nid oes i mi ddim un cynefin
> Yn holl ffyrdd dynion; chwilia Wynedd draw
> A Phrydain drwyddi, nid oes dim un bedd
> A berthyn imi, ac mae'r byd yn oer,
> Yn estron imi, heb na chwylwm câr
> Na chadwyn cenedl. Dyna sut yr ofnaf –
> Ofni fy rhyddid, megis llong heb lyw

Ar fôr dynoliaeth.

O, you will never understand,
What pains me – never, never – nor you nor anyone.
You don't know what it is to be alone.
For you the world is full; you have a home,
Relations and family, father, mother, brother,
So you are not a stranger in the world.
Wherever men have trodden is familiar to you
And all Gwynedd, where formerly your fathers dwelt
Is home to you, a shelter built
By generations of your ancestors.
You are at home in your own land
As in a bed prepared for you
With loving hands by one who long awaited you;
For me there is no familiar way
Among all the ways of men; search through Gwynedd
And through Britain – nowhere is there a single grave
Belonging to me, and the world is cold,
A foreign place to me; without the ties of love
Or chains of nationality. That is how I fear –
Fearing my freedom, like a rudderless ship
On the sea of humanity.

This intensity of poetic expression is not merely the means by which Saunders Lewis develops the symbolic dimension of the action. In practical, theatrical terms it is a rock on which to anchor the attention of the audience at the point when he is confronting a difficult technical problem which arose in adapting the narrative description of the arrival of Gronw Pebr. The author of the tale managed this matter very skilfully. He describes Blodeuwedd responding to the sound of Gronw's hunting horn, seeing the hunt go by and sending a servant to enquire who they were; in his narrative we read of the hunt continuing on its way, of how they kill the hind and find themselves benighted as they flay the carcass and feed the hounds. So they return to the court and Blodeuwedd, fearing to break the laws of hospitality, welcomes them.

In the play Saunders Lewis takes up the hint provided by the Mabinogi author's use of the horn and uses it as an external measure of Blodeuwedd's internal state. So we hear the horn sounded four times – once at the end of the speech quoted above, introducing a further speech in which Blodeuwedd issues a threat to her absent husband: "Without him,/ Without lineage, my life is anchorless/ And in my blood Nature's challenge, Nature's danger." The second time we hear it is after Rhagnell's question, which must surely also be ours: "Tell me. What wild storm races through your flesh?" There is a danger here, of which Saunders Lewis must have been aware. The sound of the horn means little to us in itself, unlike, for example, the sound of the train in Gwenlyn Parry's *Y Twr,* which the dramatist has time to define for us, so that we can share the characters' response to it. There is no reason why we should respond to it in the same way as Blodeuwedd, so the dramatist has to find some other way of making her excitement seem real to us. There is another problem here, too. Coming from outside the stage space, which has been very narrowly defined by Blodeuwedd's recent speeches, (almost soliloquies, because they are not really addressed to Rhagnell), the sounds weaken our sense of immediacy. Sensing this, Saunders Lewis uses Rhagnell to strengthen the on-stage action. Blodeuwedd draws Rhagnell to her, puts her hand on her heart and marvels to find it beating quietly – "...as tranquil as the heart of an oak tree in a wet winter." This strong natural image provides a good example of the way in which poetry can reinforce a dramatic movement. Here the dramatist is over-defining Rhagnell's stolidity so as to shift his audience a little nearer to Blodeuwedd and increase their sympathy with her wild, instinctive response to the call of the hunting horn. As it sounds a third time it is very close:

> Clyw, ferch. Corn hela. Hela rhwng y coed,
> A'r carw'n chwipio'r tir yn chwyrn o'i ôl
> Fel rhwyfau'n taro'n don...O, mae natur
> Mewn hoen afradus acw yng ngloddest byw,
> A'r heliwr yntau'n un ag egni'r fridd –
> Mi allwn garu heliwr...

> Listen girl. A hunting horn. Hunting among the trees,
> With the stag scattering earth behind him with his heels
> Like oars beating water...Oh, Nature is
> Yonder in prodigal joy in the glory of life,
> And the hunter himself sharing earth's vigour –
> I could love a hunter...

This speech is a natural climax to the dramatic movement which began with Llew's exit. In the few moments of actual time that have passed since then we have traversed a good deal of dramatic territory. Those closing words, "I could love a hunter", conclude the process of Blodeuwedd's self discovery and contain, of course, the promise of action which is soon to be fulfilled. As she speaks we hear the horn for the last time, this time more faintly, dying away as the hunt passes by, giving Blodeuwedd the impetus finally to ask the question which must have been there in the back of our minds since we first heard it: "Go, go, girl,/ And ask who is hunting."

What follows reminds us how fragile is Saunders Lewis's control of theatrical convention at times. Rhagnell goes out for a moment before returning to say that the hunt is over and the huntsman approaching the court. For a moment here the poet and the dramatist part company. "What is he like?" Blodewedd asks, and Rhagnell replies: "Young, and on horseback like a hawk riding the air." This vivid answer is an important poetic link, between her mistress's previous speech "I could love a hunter" and her next command: "Fetch me/ Golden cups, and the wine I tasted/ On the morning of my creation, and fetch me fruits,/ Cherries, red apples and pears..." This highly charged poetic enactment helps us over a difficult transition between promise and fulfilment. In poetic terms it transforms the unseen hunter into the proper and natural object of Blodeuwedd's passion. In practical terms, however, the transition is far less satisfactory. Once again Saunders Lewis has momentarily emptied his stage space. While Rhagnell is off stage Blodeuwedd has nothing to do. Of course an enterprising director will find something to occupy her and the resulting stage business may well be effective and productive in its own right. However, this will not conceal the fact that the dramatic focus has shifted awkwardly. Presenting us with an object of attention which is off-stage, Rhagnell makes us uncomfortably aware of the fragility of the conventions which govern the way in which we interpret the stage space. She has seen too much, too quickly and has given us too much work to do in adjusting and readjusting our ideas about the relation between the flexible space represented by the stage itself and the inflexible world to which it relates.

For the remainder of this middle section of the Act the dramatist maintains a delicate balance between what we may call the 'real' time of the action and the actual playing time. Blodeuwedd orders Rhagnell to receive Gronw and prepare him for the feast. Only one speech intervenes between Rhagnell going out to execute this order and her returning to announce that the feast and the guest await her mistress. The weight of this speech, however, compensates for the shortness of the interval. It is a soliloquy in which Blodeuwedd claims the authority of natural law as justifcation for her action: "Freedom and excitement are my elements;/ My law is desire, the lust, that drives the seed/ To break through the earth and face the sun." Then – it might seem, strangely – both Blodeuwedd and Rhagnell leave the stage and the dramatist's direction suggests a lowering of the lighting to convey the idea of the passage of time before Blodeuwedd and Gronw enter the stage together.

Several alternative courses might seem more natural at this point. Might we not have expected to witness the meeting between Gronw and Blodeuwedd and the gradual strengthening of their mutual attraction? There are many precedents for such a scene. *The Tempest* comes to mind again, where we find the famous first encounter between Ferdinand and Miranda; and in a different vein the first meeting between Olivia and Sebastian in *Twelfth Night* or the scene in which Benedict woos Beatrice in *Much Ado About Nothing*.[11] Practical considerations might have affected the dramatist's decision not to present such a scene. Saunders Lewis was always conscious of the limitations of the amateur or semi-professional companies his plays were likely to be produced by. He might, however, simply have ended the scene at this point, committing the feast to the interval of time that elapses between scenes rather than pointedly excluding it from the action.

It is clear, in fact, that Saunders Lewis saw the whole of this Act as a continuous development, culminating in the ritual celebration of natural love transcending the laws and customs of civilised life. Two factors seem to have influenced him in planning its structure. He needed particularly to control the distance between the audience and the lovers and the degree of our sympathy for them. He also wanted an opportunity to formalize and dignify what might well have come across as a natural and consequently rather casual process of attraction and involvement. In emptying his stage at this point he is effectively redefining it as a more private interior place, neither hall nor bedchamber, where the lovers are free to explore and articulate their relationship. He is also ensuring that the action is kept within the original frame provided by the opening conversation between Llew and Gwydion.

In the remainder of the scene Gronw Pebr has an opportunity to confront the full reality of what he is doing. There is nothing casual about his seduction; it must fully involve his conscious will. So when he eventually pledges love to Blodeuwedd he formally renounces honour, tradition, the customs of his family, the integrity of his caste. Time, and even life itself Gronw renounces as he drinks from the cup: "Tonight/ I would choose to die in your arms,/ Rather than wake in some tomorrow without you." Blodeuwedd has won a victory over humanity itself, which she celebrates in her closing speech. For her this victory was essential, enabling her for the first time to escape into her own body from the prison of a relationship imposed on her. Purposefully she celebrates her own birth with the wine she tasted when she was first born into imprisonment. Everything she does at this point is done with the design of obliterating the first year of her creation, the year of false life, and we cannot but sympathize with her as she does it. So her words to Rhagnell, as she orders her to prepare the bed she slept in that first night with Llew strike us as a dignified and formal commitment to life rather than preparations for a sordid act of adultery. Yet even in her final, joyous and assertive speech there is an element of irony:

> Ymysg teuluoedd ni bydda' i'n unig mwy;
> Dy wenau di yw f'achau i a'm hawl
> Ar y ddynoliaeth. Un ewyllys sydd
> Mewn dail a dynion; ni all defod frau
> Na moes na barn gaethiwo'r galon a glyw
> Belydrau serch yn taro. Tyrd, f'anwylyd,
> Nyni piau byw, a charu yw bod yn rhydd.

> I will no longer be alone amidst families;
> Your smiles are my lineage and my claim
> On humanity. One desire makes us one
> With the leaves; no fragile rite
> Or custom or opinion can enslave the heart which feels
> The beam of love. Come, my dear,
> Life belongs to us, and love is freedom.

Only at the end of play can Blodeuwedd find true freedom, the same freedom which Llew endures and accepts. Even as she speaks these words at the end of Act I, we recall the story of her creator, Gwydion, whose three years of punishment in the wild remind us how far below the level at which mankind finds it possible to endure life that equality of human and vegetable nature exists. Blodeuwedd's tragedy is that she can exist at this level, but only by means of someone else, who cannot.

The second Act opens at a point three days later than the first, as Gronw is preparing to leave, and ends after the return of Llew. It is again interesting to see how Saunders Lewis has treated his source. The author of *Math, Fab Mathonwy* arranges this part of his narrative around two traditional devices. The first is the guest's ritual request for permission to depart, which is repeated three times. On the second day Gronw suggests that Blodeuwedd extract from Llew the secret of how he may be killed. Then on the third day, fearing Llew's return, they part. The author of the tale then utilises another traditional story-telling device to explain how Blodeuwedd deceives her husband. After a day spent in pleasure-making they retire to bed and she refuses to speak. Asking the reason, Llew gives Blodeuwedd the excuse she needs to explain her worry lest he be killed and so get possession of the secret.

Saunders Lewis disposes of this structure. His second Act is based on the apposition of the same two ideas, but they are arranged quite differently. Shifting the emphasis wholly onto Blodeuwedd, he makes her responsible for the suggestion that Llew must be killed and introduces a protracted farewell between the lovers in which she gradually leads Gronw to the conclusion that Llew must die. This is balanced against a second powerful scene in which she extracts the secret from Llew. In dramatic terms this involved overcoming a problem which, as usual in his theatre arose from difficulty concerning the relationship between stage space and the off-stage world from which characters enter. Gronw's exit and Llew's entrance must not come too close together. As in the case of the feast, Saunders Lewis could have solved this probem simply by separating the two scenes completely, but as we have seen, it was important to him to maintain continuity. At this point he wanted to keep the dramatic focus firmly on Blodeuwedd and to maintain control over the way in which the audience respond to her. This latter point is particularly important in Act II because what Blodeuwedd is actually doing is likely to undermine any sympathy we might have had with her. She reveals herself here as savage, treacherous, scheming and bloodthirsty.

He found the answer to these problems in Rhagnell, whom he used so as to maintain control of our responses to Blodeuwedd. The Act begins with a conversation between Rhagnell and the Penteulu, whose sour, critical response, doubtless suggested by the memory of Gronw's *mintai*[12] in the Mabinogi, provides us with a kind of moralistic base line for the Act. It is difficult not to agree with Blodeuwedd's sharp reproof of the Penteulu: "Goodness help him if he has no more faithful followers than you." Ironically, we will eventually come to accept the Penteulu's reponse: "What's it got to do with faithfulness? He sells his birthright as the price of his lust, and his only virtue is that he's too

hotheaded to know fear." Gronw, too, will bitterly accept this view of
what he has done, but at this stage, so soon after witnessing the ritual
consummation of their mutual love, and still under the charm of
Blodeuwedd's awakening to life, we find it easy to accept Rhagnell's
more patient, passive attitude.

In this opening exchange between the Penteulu and Rhagnell there
is something of a sexual clash between the male and the female
viewpoint, which indeed, is implicit in the whole play. Blodeuwedd's
complaint against Llew and Gwydion is the ageless complaint of the
female thoughtlessly exploited by the male, the savagery of her protest
against them much softened by our awareness of their power and the
certainty of their ultimate victory. Rhagnell greatly reinforces this
aspect of the play. Her patient kindness and loyalty to Blodeuwedd
has great influence on us as the response of a creature of the same
world, closer to her by virtue of her sex than any of the other characters
can be. Her rôle is that much more important because it is towards
her that Blodeuwedd's conscienceless malignity is most fully exercised. The scene in which, suspicious of her loyalty, Blodeuwedd
attempts to strangle her with her hair, was brilliantly conceived as the
means of separating Gronw's departure from Llew's arrival. Following
the lover's farewell, in which Blodeuwedd deliberately seduces Gronw
to step with her beyond the pale which marks the end of all human
restraints, this scene makes it possible for us to enlarge our own vision
and see her in a different light. The creature revealed here is beyond
the reach of the Penteulu's reductive morality. Blodeuwedd will kill,
and not for a humane, romanticised love, but for the freedom of
physical lust. Gronw's faithfulness means nothing to her; only his lust
will guarantee his steadfastness:

> A gedwi di dy chwant? Mae chwant yn gryf
> I ddal ewyllys megis saeth i'w nod
>   Pan rwydo bwa ffyddlondeb. Edrych arnaf.
>   Llanw dy enau â blas y cusan hwn
>   A'th ffroen â sawr fy mynwes...Dos yn awr.

> Will you keep your lust? Lust is strong
> To hold the will as an arrow keeps to its aim
> When the bow of faith is broken. Look at me.
> Fill your mouth with the taste of this kiss,
> And your nostrils with the perfume of my breasts...Now go.

The scene with Rhagnell intensifies our awareness of Blodeuwedd's
inhuman wilfulness and gives us a glimpse of its dreadful fragility. Even
at the price of savagery Blodeuwedd lacks power over humankind. She
may kill Rhagnell, but has no control over the pathetic mixture of
female sympathy and pity which makes her faithful to her. When
Rhagnell quietly leaves the stage to drown herself in the fourth Act she
shows a degree of passive strength which Blodeuwedd can neither
share nor overcome. Through Rhagnell we become aware of Blodeuwedd's weakness, which is what attracts her human loyalty, not her
apparent, primitive strength. It makes us patient with Blodeuwedd and
enables us to see the tragic dimension to her character. Like Medea,
and like Macbeth, her destructiveness is childlike, a protest against the
experience and consuming fear of weakness.

At the end of the Act there is a second scene between Rhagnell and
her mistress, which includes Blodeuwedd's apology to her and closes
with the bitter message she sends to Gronw: "Tell him how happy my
husband is, and that today the court is full of song and dance as if it
were a holiday." Again this scene palliates our awareness of Blodeuwedd's cold-blooded treachery by strengthening our understanding of
the weakness which lies beneath the surface of her passion. Her
question to Rhagnell: "Do you love me?" is a pathetic attempt to
understand her and attracts Rhagnell's honest explanation: "You are
simple Lady, like a child,/ And destructive as a child. Who, knowing
you, would not pity you?" After the scene between Llew and Blodeuwedd we need this reminder of what we had previously glimpsed of
Blodeuwedd's weakness, and having given it the dramatist is free again
to prepare us for the savagery of the third Act, leaving us with
Blodeuwedd's cruel message as the closing words.

The message points us towards the savagery of the third Act and the
murder of Llew very straightforwardly, which in dramatic terms is
necessary after the complexity of the earlier, climactic encounter
between Llew and Blodeuwedd. The irony is striking from Llew's first
greeting to his wife: "My stainless wife", but it is Rhagnell who sets
the tone of the encounter, with her ironic truth-telling: "...since you
left her I found her weeping her heart out on that couch, her body
shaking with pain and fear..." This gives Blodeuwedd the cue to tell
her husband the truth, at any rate about herself, and in doing so in
some measure to justify herself in our eyes, because we cannot but
notice his persistent failure to see any explanation of what she is saying
but that he wishes to see. Llew never stops to reflect on the misery of

unloving love which Blodeuwedd hints at, so he misses the clue to the
bitterness of his wife's grief and swallows the lie willingly. All through
this scene he is developing a massive selfishness, which is all the more
striking because it preserves an element of cautious awareness of the
world around him. Bearing this scene in mind we will be more than
ready to sympathize with something of Blodeuwedd's bitterness in Act
III, as she urges her husband forward to receive what she hopes will
be his death blow. Yet at the same time, there is something which saves
Llew. In his selfishness is he not drawing very close to the loneliness
to which Blodeuwedd herself has confessed and with which we have
learnt to sympathize? As Llew glories in his dreadful delusion we must
sympathize with him in a strange way, not as the lover betrayed where
he had a right to expect love, but rather as the essential human being,
weak and lonely and looking for comfort and fulfilment in the only
place he can look and yet never find it – another human being.

> Llawer tro, Flodeuwedd,
> Y bum yn dymuno f'angau. Ond yn awr
> Mae blas ar fyw fel blas afal ar ddant,
> A'th gariad di yw'r gadair yng Nghaer Siddi
> Nas plawdd na haint na henaint a fo ynddi,
> A minnau yno'n frenin,
> Heb neb na dim a'm diorsedda mwy,
> Nac ofn na hiraeth na chwaith angau'i hun,
> Cans digyfnewid yw brenhiniaeth cariad.

> Many times, Blodeuwedd,
> I wished for death. But now
> Life has a taste like the juice of an apple against the teeth,
> And your love is the throne in Caer Siddi
> Where plague and disease and old age can never come,
> And I am a king there
> From whence no one may ever dethrone me,
> Neither fear, nor longing, nor death itself,
> Because love is changeless.

The powerful irony of this speech does not flow over into the question
which Blodeuwedd then asks him: "Is anything changeless among
men?" Later events will bring an answer to this question and unite
both husband and wife together at least in bitterness.

In adapting the phase of his source material included in Act II
Saunders Lewis faced considerable difficulties. In the first instance he

had to simplify the Mabinogi version of the circumstances in which Llew could be killed. The original has Llew standing on the banks of a river with one foot on a water trough and the other on a billy goat! Having dispensed with the goat, the dramatist had to find a way of bringing Llew to the scene and getting him into the position in which to receive Gronw's blow. The way he did this not only solved the immediate problem but gave him an opportunity to increase the dramatic weight of the event and deepen its significance.

The irony introduced in the earlier scene in Act II between Llew and Blodeuwedd is greatly increased here by the device which Saunders Lewis makes her use to bring her husband to the river bank one year after his return to her. During that year Llew has been lulled into trusting happiness, while Gronw damns himself, preparing the poisoned spear which is to kill Llew every Sunday during the sacrifice of mass.[13] Now Blodeuwedd has hinted that she is pregnant and the promise that she will present her husband with an heir gives a new, bitter twist to the irony of his confident contentment. This irony, however, cuts in more than one direction. In the first instance it greatly increases our sense of Blodeuwedd's cruelty; at the same time it also develops our awareness of his selfishness and his blindness to Blodeuwedd's real feelings. There is a moment when Blodeuwedd almost seems as if she is willing to draw back from what she is about to do, when she says: "Oh Llew that you could never once/ Look at me and say: You, you are enough for me. If you said that..." At this point her husband's blind self-preoccupation seems wilful: "I will say that when I see you with your son in your arms."

The irony here works so as to involve Llew in responsibilty for what happens to him. That is, the audience, knowing the real identity of Llew's 'son', and knowing that Llew should be seeing something of what they see, can scarcely avoid feeling that he is wilfully moving towards the predestined conclusion of the scene. Something of this is implicit in the story on which the play is based, for everything depends on Llew's willingly creating the circumstances in which he can be killed. Dramatic enactment would necessarily increase this element, for the audience, seeing Llew's collaboration, must in some degree wonder at it. Saunders Lewis greatly developed this awareness by the device which he employed to get Llew onto the trough, ready for the blow. Indeed, in noting the way in which the different elements of this scene reinforce each other, it is difficult not to wonder at the degree of dramatic craftsmanship involved. When Llew first comes to meet his wife he observes the fact that she is barefoot. The way in which this arises itself reminds us of the constant element of tension in their relationship, which should have made it impossible for Llew to be lulled into such a degree of blind contentment. Explaining her early rising, Blodeuwedd compares herself to a rabbit – "The shimmering of the dawn drew me like a rabbit to bathe in the grass." Llew's reply "And like a rabbit, too, you came barefoot?" attracts a retort which has just the slightest edge of sharpness: "Only a husband would notice a thing like that". Such small points as these gather in our minds and add weight to remarks that Llew himself should notice, as when Blodeuwedd later asks him: "My Llew, do you still fear all wild things?" At each of these points, however, Blodeuwedd carefully picks herself up. So she follows this remark with a question which takes Llew's attention in a quite different direction: "Will you make me shoes as you did for your mother?" As Llew follows the course marked out for him Blodeuwedd has the opportunity to draw him in to retell the story of how, disguised with Gwydion as a cobbler to make Arianrhod shoes, Llew killed a wren with a blow from his needle and received his name from his mother: 'Llaw gyffes', 'Skilful Hand'. Even here Blodeuwedd betrays herself, as she asks: "Is that when you killed the wren with the spear?" This should prepare us and indeed, it might well warn the complacent Llew of how she is to lure him on to the trough, persuading him to act out the killing of the wren in the trough as if in the boat on the banks of the Menai beneath Arianrhod's court.

At the very last moment Blodeuwedd gives her husband another chance to escape his fate, knowing by now that nothing will suffice to warn him. "And at that moment," Llew says, lost in contemplation of the victory over his mother's hatred, "With the needle between my fingers–" and Blodeuwedd tauntingly interjects: "A needle, not a spear". Undeterred, Llew continues: "I aimed at it" and Gronw finishes his sentence with his own words and the blow: "Like this".

There is another dimension to the action up to this point which we have not yet observed. Retelling the story of Llew's victory over his mother means that there is a dual focus to the scene. The audience are aware that the characters are approaching the murder step by step together, but they are also in some measure distracted from the immediate present of the scene on the river bank by the narration of that other long past story which takes up the central part of the Mabinogi tale. This creates a complex overlay effect. At one level they are watching a scene of betrayal; at another they are aware that in some measure the victim is collaborating in his own destruction; and then they are also reminded of the whole sad story of his struggle to escape from his mother's curse. Reminding us of this history and showing us a man who is unable to escape from his own past, Saunders Lewis deepens our sympathy for Blodeuwedd and at the same time builds up our awareness that all three characters, husband, wife and lover, or if you wish, father, mother and son, are alike subject to the same sad and inevitably frustrated longing which all men share.

This complex, central scene is set between two shorter scenes which prepare us for it and reinforce its effect. The first, which begins the Act, presents the meeting between Blodeuwedd and Gronw when they set the scene for Llew's murder and the usurpation of Ardudwy. Here Blodeuwedd is in control and Gronw relatively uncertain, sure of his love and confident of his aim, but seeming somehow in need of a little of Blodeuwedd's single-minded determination as she tells him: "Bind your will to mine/ to raise him up to the trough..." The second follows the murder, when the rôles are reversed and Blodeuwedd is suddenly shaken by the absoluteness of death. Here the play's pervasive irony has a new function, strengthening our awareness of the fragility of their victory. "Uttering a screech and going," Blodeuwedd reflects, significantly, "Is that how it will be with me when my time comes?" Again a little later she says to Gronw: "He fell like a flower. Is that how/ You will die?" And her gloomy hesitancy draws from her lover the ironic reproof which stamps the meaning of action on our consciousness: "Come, girl/ You're like an owl, not your lively self." After this little remains of the scene. The stage empties again for a moment before Gwydion enters to find the body and take it away. The Act closes with his gentle care, as he urges the soldiers: "Now carefully...gently...quietly..."

The central event of the final Act of *Blodeuwedd* is Gronw's desertion of Blodeuwedd, which occurs just before the arrival of Llew and Gwydion. Everything that happens before this prepares for this sudden, dramatic change of direction, yet without seeming to. The Act begins with a long scene between Rhagnell and the Penteulu which develops what was only suggested in the similar, shorter scene in Act I. The immediate effect of this scene is to delay the development of the principal action, which must begin when Gronw and Blodeuwedd hear that Llew is alive and on his way to Ardudwy with Gwydion and three hundred men. The purpose of this scene is to develop our awareness of the strain and tension which has underlain Blodeuwedd's

year-long 'hour' of fulfilment and freedom. When Blodeuwedd even
ually enters we discover that she has known, or at least suspecte
Gwydion's rescue of Llew ever since the night of the murder itsel
when she saw the Penteulu return from his fruitless mission to bur
Llew's body. The Penteulu's sardonic mixture of loyalty and scorn
also an important point of reference for us, for it helps to re-establis
something like a norm of human conduct. Rhagnell's response to
prefigures Gronw's, for she betrays no fear or surprise, even thoug
she has gone through the motions of defending herself against it unt
it is absolutely certain and incontrovertible. Then she adopts some
thing of the Penteulu's bitter playfulness in presenting the news to he
mistress; and after she has completed this message she says no mo
and exits silently when Gronw tells her to prepare Blodeuwedd'
journey, to drown herself in the river.

The short dialogue between Blodeuwedd and the Penteulu whic
precedes the entrance of Gronw reminds us how little Blodeuwed
for all her inner, instinctive knowledge, understands, or even wants t
understand, the world of men. Her petulant spitefulness leaves th
Penteulu unaffected. Accused of disobedience, his answer is unhesi
tating: "Is that worse than being slave to a woman?" When Gronw
enters we see the real understanding between them, which has survive
the two years of Gronw's enchantment and the Penteulu's bitte
sulkiness. So their relationship is immediately recovered and reaf
firmed in the few lines of enquiry and response which follows Gronw'
entry. This concludes with the sudden, formal transfer of lordshi
which is the first substantial sign of what has happened to Gronw. A
this stage we can only suspect its motivation and there is a further dela
in explaining it. Answering Blodeuwedd's uncertain questioning
Gronw begins his explanation: "I won't come./ I've been mad for
long time;/ I am mad no longer." We cannot understand this fully unti
we hear Gronw's long and bitter speech to Blodeuwedd just befor
Llew's soldiers burst onto the stage. At this point it seems a strange
almost discordant note, in Gronw's quiet, determined converse wit
the Penteulu:

> Teg yw dy gerydd, wrda, teg dy gynnig,
> A theg i minnau wrthod. Mae arna'i ddyled
> I Lew Ardudwy, ac fe'i talaf heddiw
> Yma, fy hun, heb ofyn meichiau neb.
>
> Your chiding is just, and your offer,

And my refusal too is only fair. I am in debt
To Llew Ardudwy and I'll pay it today,
Here, myself, asking no-one to stand bail for me.

We notice here quite how much Saunders Lewis has changed the character he found in the Mabinogi, for in that account Gronw did all he could to avoid the consequences of the punishment which he welcomes in the play. In the rest of the scene he strengthens him at Blodeuwedd's expense. Gradually we notice that it is developing as a reverse image of the earlier scene between the two lovers on the morning of their separation. There are echoes of other scenes, too. So when Blodeuwedd goes towards Gronw, still uncertain, as he is insisting that the Penteulu leave, he turns her away with words rather similar to those she used at the beginning of Act III, when she was intent on keeping his mind firmly on the projected murder.

At this point the scene begins to break up. As Blodeuwedd refuses to leave without Gronw and a soldier enters to warn of Llew's imminent approach, everything becomes uncertain. Rhagnell's absence is noticed, without being explained, and even Blodeuwedd's steadfastness is open to doubt as Gronw calls to mind the example of Helen of Troy, who in some versions of the story is described as compounding her betrayal of her husband by treachery towards her lover.

When the Penteulu and the soldier leave there is a moment's pause, but the explanation we expect does not follow immediately. In the short series of exchanges between Gronw and Blodeuwedd uncertainty increases until the climactic, ironic misunderstanding between them. Urging escape, Blodeuwedd repeats the phrase Gronw had used to her in that earlier scene of farewell: "Horses still wait in the gate/ Freedom in the stirrup. Why don't we go?" Gronw's reply is deliberately, bitterly ironic: "Freedom is here, with you". Inevitably Blodeuwedd misunderstands him, not once, but twice, in spite of Gronw's repeated explanations: "My freedom is not in your arms...my death is coming. I choose that,/ And that choice is my whole freedom". His final speech enlightens Blodeuwedd and us alike, telling us how far he has travelled quite alone in the year of his "freedom" with Blodeuwedd, towards the ground occupied by Llew and the idea of love which Blodeuwedd earlier, cruelly mocked:

I beth y bydda'i byw? I brofi am oes

A brofais eisoes, y syrffed sy yn y cnawd
A'r gwae a'r gwarth o ganwaith ofer syrffedu?
Bedd heb yfory yw dy serch; ni chwardd
Baban ar dy fynwes; nid oes grud yn dy gaer;
Ond yn y nos bu swn adyn o'i go'
Yn udo ar fronnau cryfion yn y tywyll,
Brathu budreddi a chrechwen gwdihw.
Collais i lwybrau dynol i ddilyn ffagl
A phibau hud y gors, a suddais ynddi,
Cofleidio seren, ystlum ar fy min;
Heddiw daeth bollt i'm taro a deffrois;
Mi welaf Benllyn, gwelaf fy mebyd yno,
A'm gweld i'n awr, och ffiaidd, a'th dremio dithau —
Gwell gennyf i na'th gusan gleddyf dy wr.

Why should I live longer? To experience for a lifetime
What I have already experienced, the pointless surfeit of the flesh
And the misery and shame of repeating it a hundred times?
Your love is a grave; no baby smiles
On your breast; there's no cradle in your court;
But in the night there's been the screech of a madman
Howling in the darkness over unyielding beasts,
Mouthing filth and the grimace of owls.
I left the ways of mankind to follow a will o the wisp
And the magic pipes of the bog, and I sank in it.
I embraced a star and found a bat sucking my lip.
Today a bolt struck me and I awoke;
Now I see Penllyn, I see my childhood there,
And see myself now, loathsome, and your gazing —
I'd rather your husband's sword than your kisses.

Throughout *Blodeuwedd,* in one way or another, we have been trying to resolve the three-cornered relationship between Llew, Blodeuwedd and Gronw. Several times it has seemed to resolve itself, either ironically or in real terms. Now Gwydion's magic has opened a new perspective and enabled the characters to enact what would otherwise remain unresolved, perhaps even undeveloped. In recovering Llew, Gwydion gives us a chance to discover the brotherhood which underlies rivalry, spite, the selfishness of lust. So when Gronw goes out with the soldiers to await his death, Blodeuwedd is left alone, as previously Llew had been. Unlike Gronw, Blodeuwedd has learned nothing and regrets nothing. She is still childishly suspicious and spiteful once she is obliged to confront the human reality of what she has done, but now, faced with Gwydion's frightening power, at least she can honestly accept her own weakness and convert it to strength. Llew is unable to resist her arguments, because he is forced to acknowledge that his own selfish craving made him blind to her weakness and her need. The difference between them now, what keeps them apart, and ultimately justifies Gwydion's final use of his magical power, is that Llew is willing to accept his helplessness, whereas Blodeuwedd must still strike out. Her loneliness by now, no matter what caused it, is no greater than his. She justifies her viciousness by harping on Gwydion's responsibility for her fate. She will accept neither forgiveness nor even the sadness of the scene soon to take place at the riverside, for which she is responsible more than Gwydion or Llew. In the end she calls down her own punishment on herself. It is one which Gwydion alone could impose and which he alone, who has lived with his brother as a beast of the forest, could understand.

3. *Siwan*

Written six years after the completion of *Blodeuwedd* and reflecting a continuing preoccupation with the relationship between *serch* and *cariad*, *Siwan* might be thought represent a correction of the earlier play. Whereas *Blodeuwedd* presented *cariad* as the basis of ordered social life, opposed to the insanity of serch, *Siwan* presents a more measured view, recognizing the persistence of unsatisfied desire even within a stable, secure relationship, which sustained precisely that extensive edifice of social and cultural achievement of which Llew Llaw Gyffes selfishly dreamed.

However, it would be a mistake to think of *Siwan* in this way. Even in *Blodeuwedd* Saunders Lewis was aware that the relationship between desire and restraint can never be anything but problematic. In the final analysis his sympathy went with Blodeuwedd rather than Llew. "*Blodeuwedd* is not outside human nature," he told a correspondent, "but the woman, the eternal Eve...And it is she who wins the debate in the last Act, isn't it?"[14] In fact the story of *Siwan* must have been in his mind during the time when he was still working on the final version of *Blodeuwedd*. He refers to it in an article on the women of the royal house of Gwynedd which was occasioned by the marriage of Princess Elizabeth in November 1947. The story of Siwan's love affair with the Norman Lord of Brecon, the father of her son's wife, as it was told in the Medieval chronicle, *Brut y Tywysogion*, he found "the strangest of all the Queens of Gwynedd":

> Gynnil yw'r hen fyneich yn adrodd yr hanes. Efallai fod Siwan ei hun yn teimlo'n ddolurus am y tro. Efallai fod tendio a glwyfau'r iarll ifanc brathedig, y Norman chwerthinog anturus, wedi deffro'i nwyd. Rhyddhawyd ef ymhen y rhawg, ond ar wyl fawr y Pasg dychwelodd i brif ddinas Gwynedd, y llys yn Aber ger Bangor. Rhywfodd fe ddaeth awgrym o'r hyn a oedd ar gerdded i glustiau Llywelyn. Dywed rhai mai Hubert de Burgh ei hunan, prif weinidog Lloegr ar y pryd, a fradychodd y cariadon. Ganol y nos torrodd Llywelyn i mewn i ystafell ei frenhines

a dal y ddau ynghyd. Taflodd ei wraig i garchar. Codwyd crocbren, medd traddodiad, ar y gwastad gerbron neuadd y brenin, ac ebr y Brut:

Y flwyddyn honno y croged Gwilym Brewys ieuanc gan Lywelyn ab Iorwerth wedi ei ddala yn ystafell y tywysog gyda merch Ieuan Frenin, gwraig y tywysog.

Aeth ias o ddychryn drwy Loegr oll a Ffrainc; canys yng ngolau dydd ac o flaen torf fawr y crogwyd blodau marchogion y Norman. Ni feiddiodd Brenin Lloegr ymyrraeth. Blwyddyn wedyn maddeuodd Llywelyn i'w wraig ac wele hi'n ôl yn ei gyngor cyfrin ac yn ei fynwes, ac yn llysgennad drosto yn llys ei brawd. Rhaid bod edrych craff ac eiddgar ar ei hwyneb enigmatig yno. Pum mlynedd yn ddiweddarach bu Siwan farw.

The old monks told the story sparingly. Perhaps Siwan herself was feeling mournful at the time. Perhaps tending the wounds of the injured young lord, the lighthearted, adventurous Norman, had awakened her senses. After a while he was released, but at the great Easter feast he returned to Gwynedd's capital, the court at Aber, near Bangor. Somehow a hint of what was afoot came to the ears of Llywelyn. Some say that it was Hubert de Burgh himself, Prime Minister of England at the time, who betrayed the lovers. In the middle of the night Llywelyn broke in to his queen's room and found the two together. He threw his wife into prison. According to tradition a gallows was raised on the green near the king's hall and, in the words of the Brut:

That year young Gwilym Brewys was hanged by Llywelyn ap Iorwerth having been caught in the prince's room with his wife, the daughter of King John...

A thrill of horror went right through England and France; for the flower of Norman knighthood was hanged in broad daylight and in the presence of a great crowd. The King of England dared not interfere. A year later Llywelyn forgave his wife and received her back into his privy council and his bed and as an ambassador on his behalf at her brother's court. There must have been a sagacious look on her enigmatic face there. Five years later she was dead.[15]

Siwan's story, so sparingly told in the *Brut,* raised a question more intriguing than *Blodeuwedd.* For Siwan was at once the faithful Queen and the faithless wife and she was both these things not in the far away world of magic and myth, but the concrete world of Thirteenth Century Gwynedd. Blodeuwedd was a creature of flowers who came to live amongst men, but in a world of myth and magic. Siwan was born the illegitmate daughter of King John of England and came at fifteen to live in Medieval Wales, as the wife of Llywelyn ap Iorwerth, one of Gwynedd's most successful, expansionist princes, in a turbulent age. "Among the chieftains who battled against the Anglo-Norman power", according to the historian, Sir Edward Lloyd, Llywelyn's place, "will always be high, if not indeed the highest of all..." and his patriotic statesmanship, "will always entitle him to wear the proud style of Llywelyn the Great".[16] When he died, in 1240, he left "a strong and prosperous principality" to be handed over to his son Dafydd, in whose interest he had set aside Welsh laws of succession so as to exclude his older, illegitimate son and ensure the stability of the state he had established. In doing this it is assumed that he was influenced by his wife, who collaborated in everything he did, acting on several, critical occasions as ambassador between her husband and her father and brother in the interests of her son's inheritance. As Saunders Lewis put it, no other woman of Gwynedd's princely house was ever so able a politician as Joan. "In effect and in practical terms," he wrote, "she was the Foreign Secretary for Wales during the reign of Llywelyn ap Iorwerth...Without doubt she was the most wonderful and the most interesting of all the Queens of Wales".[17]

Together Llywelyn and Siwan achieve in the real world what Llew dreamt of creating in legendary Ardudwy:

> Fe godwn inni deulu yn Ardudwy
> A fydd fel llwyn o'n cwmpas. Yno tyf
> Y gwiail ifainc gyda'r henwydd praff,
> A byddwn megis perllan glyd, gysgogol,
> A chariad yn fagwyrydd rhyngom ni
> A chwaon oer unigedd.

> We will raise up a family in Ardudwy
> Which will be like a grove round about us. There will grow
> Together the young saplings and stout timber,
> And we will be as if in a snug, sheltered orchard,
> Our love a hedge, protecting us
> From the cold winds of loneliness.

Llew's dream becomes a bitter nightmare, because Blodeuwedd is unable to accept the conditional love he offers. The historical lovers succeed because they share the willingness to compromise, requiring nothing but that which is possible. In their success, however, they discover disappointment and dissatisfaction. Their marriage, though based on mutual trust and firm friendship, cannot protect them from the winds of loneliness and unsatisfied longing.

At thirty-five, married to the fifty-seven year old Llywelyn for twenty years and the mother of four children, Siwan accepts the love of the

youthful Gwilym de Brewys, lord of Brecon. As yet unable to return
his love, Siwan nevertheless is strongly attracted by his passionate
wilfulness, which is very like that element of wildness in Blodeuwedd
which Llew suspected and mistrusted. Siwan is well aware of the
danger implicit in *serch*. She tells Gwilym: "There is no place for the
disorder of love in the government of the family and land." On the
other hand she has come to feel that in the cautious, measured,
expenditure of energy for the achievement of political ends she risks
losing something of herself which is precious.

Siwan and Llewelyn have built their relationship on the assumption
that business and pleasure are necessarily opposed and that there is
danger in trying to bring them together. In Gwilym she finds someone
who habitually throws caution to the winds because it is inimical to
the freshness of experience which alone makes life worth living.
Gwilym's foolhardiness, his willingness to gamble everything for the
sake of the insubstantial moment, makes her afraid for him, but also
draws her close to him. She feels nothing of that wildness herself. The
passionate energy which she is sensible of inheriting from her father
never overcomes the cautious wilfulness which has become a stronger,
second nature. She gives herself to Gwilym almost sadly, not thinking
too much of the value of the gift, rather formally, to mark her regret
for the things which have passed her by. Gwilym never loses his awe
of her, even in the moment of surrender, nor ever understands her
answer to his question: "And why, Siwan? Why, my generous giver?"

> Am dy fod di'n cofio blas pethau
> A bod blas yn darfod mor fuan:
> Am iti chwerthin ar berigl
> A bod bywyd ar antur mor frau:
> Am fod dy orfoledd di yn fy ngallu
> A bod rhoi iti d'orfoledd yn bêr.
> Am ei bod hi'n awr yn galan Mai.

> Because you remember how things taste
> And that they fade so quickly;
> Because you laugh at danger
> And because life at hazard is so fragile;
> Because to satisfy your passion is within my power
> And because to satisfy it is good.
> Because tomorrow is the first of May.

surrender'
Act a) Peryneth

This is nothing like Blodeuwedd's impulsive and demanding *serch*. Siwan wants to associate herself with something she feels she has lost. She delays the moment of surrender as long as she can, to enjoy the sensuous awareness of what she is doing. Ironically, when she eventually goes to bed with Gwilym it is too late. Llywelyn's men are about to break down the door. By then it is an act of defiance, an open, public acknowledgement of something which is no longer even true. For one moment Siwan declares herself beyond compromise, even though she must know that she can never escape it.

It is ironical, too, that all through the years when Siwan thought she was merely a partner in a politic, trusting, relationship, she was in fact the object of her husband's passionate love. The play's first Act ends with the discovery of the lovers and Llywelyn's determination that Brewys will pay for what he has done not merely with his life but by enduring the humiliating death of a criminal. The confrontation between Siwan and her husband in this scene evokes from him a passionate outburst of hatred which Gwilyn immediately understands and threatens to reveal as the reaction of the disappointed lover. Blinded by her own assumptions about her husband, Siwan fails to see this, and her failure brings about the tragic, wasteful hanging. Her appeal to Llywelyn for Gwilym's life is made on what she assumes is the basis of their relationship, the cautious, responsible behaviour of a politician. Llywelyn interprets this as contempt, arising from her belief that he is incapable of feeling in the same way as her lover. To disprove this to himself and to spite her, to pay her back for her failure to intuit and appreciate the truth, he hangs Gwilym and imprisons her.

In the third and final Act of the play, which takes place exactly a year later, husband and wife face the consequences of their actions. In the intervening year everything that Siwan had prophesied has come true. Llywelyn's enemies, and especially Hubert, Duke of Gloucester, enriched by the reapportionment of Gwilym de Brewys's Breconshire inheritance, have grown in power to the point when they threaten the security of Gwynedd. Llywelyn has little choice but to declare war, even though the circumstances are unfavourable to him. Now he asks for Siwan's counsel and support, on the basis of their mutual interest in the security of their son's inheritance and the twenty year alliance between them. Now Llywelyn explains to his wife the love which he has always felt for her, but concealed, conscious of the discrepancy in their ages and satisfied with creating a princely heritage for her son as a secret sign of homage. The love which he confesses is very like that which Gwilym had decribed in the earlier scene. When Gwilym first saw Siwan, years before, he fell in love with her at once, stealing a rose from beneath her feet to treasure secretly. Later, a wounded prisoner in Llywelyn's castle, he swooned when Siwan kissed him. He compares his love for her with Tristran's love for Iseult. If there is, as he says, flame in her kiss, it is not the destructive flame of Blodeuwedd's love, but rather a sign of warm acceptance of his idealised adoration. Siwan acknowledges that the source of his emotion is similar to that which motivates the saint. Love and sanctity, she says, "are as madly prodigal as each other, both despising the world". "My flame" is how the fifty-seven year old Llywelyn refers to Siwan, when at last they explain their feelings to each other. "[W]hen you came a maiden to Snowdonia, like a silver birch sapling," he tells her, "My heart leapt suddenly as if I had seen the Grail." Llywelyn attributes all his achievements to the inspiration of his love for her. When she returned from her first embassy to her father, confident and happy, and turned to embrace him, Llywelyn says, "I had no language/ To express my rapture; I controlled the trembling of my body;/ But after that night I was terrible to my enemies..."

"Llywelyn, I didn't know," Siwan replies, "I didn't know." And now, of course, after the execution of Gwilym, the knowledge comes too late. They come together again on the basis of mutual acceptance and forgiveness, but without expecting ever to displace the sadness and guilt for what has happened. Llywelyn has changed least, though now he is more open and honest. He has learned something during the year of loneliness, reflecting on the storm of hatred and malice which destroyed Gwilym and undermined his own life's work and Siwan's will to live. Her suffering has marked her more deeply. When she agrees to return to live as Llywelyn's wife she asks for one favour, which is that she may be buried alone, in the Franciscan abbey across the Menai straits, which she could see from the window of the tower where she has been imprisoned. She accepts Llywelyn's claims on her only up to the grave. After that she claims the freedom of loneliness. The association with St Francis reminds us of Gwilym, of course, and of what he had earlier said: "I'll turn to Francis's prayers when I lose Fortune and you." We remember from *Amlyn ac Amig* that the saint has gone beyond the selfishness of love, gambling all on God's love, without asking return.

Siwan no longer has the strength to do this. She lacks the complacency required to live quite happily within the bounds of *cariad,* content with the achievements of a love which conforms to the restrictions of social life. Indeed, that is why Saunders Lewis was interested in her at all. She and Llywelyn both have come to understand that human beings are essentially lonely and that their attempts to escape from that loneliness may be terrifyingly destructive. What they have won is the experience of choice in their marriage, that is the conscious engagement of the whole personality. This is what all Saunders Lewis's characters seek; but having found it, these two acknowledge that it can never be complete. There are elements of human nature which can never be brought within the sphere of choice; an element of danger, of hazard, must always remain and the only proper object of the gamble is God Himself.

Siwan has lost the chance ever to make that gamble of total commitment to God. Her year's imprisonment has given her ample opportunity to reflect on what she has done. When Gwilym made his mad leap into the dark at the end of the rope, with Siwan's name on his lips, he achieved his own kind of saintliness. The image of his lifeless body hangs in Siwan's mind, sapping her strength. While she was in prison she could in some measure shield herself by attributing the tragedy to Llywelyn's hatred of her. When she hears from him what his motive was her disillusionment must deepen. She has the wit and honesty to force him to confront the element of egoism in his love, refusing to be overwhelmed by his share of the responsibility for what has happened:

> Gwrandewais arnat a dysgu: fi a halogodd dy wely,
> Fi hefyd a grogodd fy nghariad, fi roes y Deuau i Hubert,
> Fi a beryglodd deyrnas Dafydd drwy'r rhyfel hwn,
> Fi a ddrylliodd y ddelw 'roedd dy fywyd di'n lamp o'i blaen
> Di ferthyr y serch priodasol.
> Ac yn awr cyn ymadael i'r frwydr fe'm derbynni'n ôl i'th wely
> A'm llorio â gras dy faddeuant i wylo mewn llwch a lludw...

> I listened to you and I learnt: it was I who stained your bed;
> I, too, hanged my lover; it was I who gave Hubert South Wales,
> Who endangered Dafydd's principality through this war,
> I who smashed the image which your life, lamplike, illuminated,
> You, the martyr to married love.
> And now before leaving for the battle you will take me back to your bed,
> Flooring me with gracious forgiveness to weep in sackcloth and ashes...

She tells him, too, that his situation is worse than her own. She has the memory of a glorious moment of commitment when Gwilym died, whereas Llywelyn has nothing but the ashes of his own love:

> Fe grogwyd Gwilym,
> Neidiodd i'w dranc gan ddiasbedain f'enw
> A chafodd ein serch awr anterth gogoniant poen.
> Felly y cofia'i o mwy: achubwyd rhagom
> Awr y dadrithio, y cogio cusanu, yr hen alaru a'r syrffed.
> Ond rhaid i ti, os maddau, fyw gyda lludw dy ddelw
> A chofio'r hunlle di-gwsg y nos y diffoddwyd fflam serch;
> Bydd gorwedd gyda mi yn dy wely fel cysgu'n fyw yn dy fedd.

> Gwilym was hanged,
> He leapt to his death, my name ringing out on his lips
> And our love had its moment of sublime agony.
> That's how I'll remember him: we were saved
> The moment of disillusionment, the pretending to kiss, the surfeit and the fatigue of it.
> But if you forgive me you'll have to live with the ashes of your image
> And remember the sleepless nightmare of the night when your love's flame was extinguished.
> Lying with me will be like being buried alive.

Yet Llywelyn has energy and commitment left which she doesn't have. He acknowledges Siwan's sad philosophy, but without her listlessness. "What is life but a gamble?" he asks her. "This war of yours is choice, not chance," she answers, but the fact is that it is merely the consequence of his earlier, mad, angry gesture of defiance. His reconciliation with her has transformed it from a gesture of hatred to one of love. The image he had of her may have been smashed, but his love remains and can still motivate him to vigorous, triumphant action. "Will you take me like that," Siwan asks, "with nothing but good will?" "Good will *is* love," Llewelyn replies. Of course, the word he uses is *cariad* rather than *serch,* but its effect on him could hardly be more striking if it were otherwise: "Siwan, my wife,/ I will go rejoicing from my room to the battle; / I'll look forward to your war as to a race, and I'll run it like a giant."

It is at this moment that Siwan asks her favour of her husband, which he understands quite clearly as a refusal to commit herself beyond the point at which their relationship formerly stood, the measured, politic commitment of a state marriage. Llywelyn accepts this for what it is, but he shows no dissatisfaction. The play ends with a trumpet peal which anticipates the victory which is to come, with Llywelyn triumphant over his old enemies and the throne of Gwynedd secure for the foreseeable future. Llywelyn's last act before this is to turn to Alis, Siwan's maid, and promise her as a husband the bravest youth amongst his following "So long as he pleases you..." Alis had been married before. We remember her telling Llywelyn about her brief marriage to one of his troop and their parting one morning as he rode off to battle, leaving her, "With a milky kiss, among the laughter of the soldiers." "A fortnight," Alis says, "and it was all over. We were beginning to know each other." Llywelyn's response is a sad reflection on his own marriage: "Every husband and wife are beginning to know each other/ Whether married for a fortnight or twenty years." However, this cynicism does not prevent him from remarking on her bravery in bearing her grief: "You too are brave...You didn't stop living." Typically Alis disclaims the praise, but her words have a special significance in terms of the debate between impulse and control on which the play is based: "Did I have a choice?" Llywelyn tells her, and tells us, that the choice exists for everyone. Life, he says, is an "awful gift for everyone." We are bound to remember this conversation at the end of the play, when Llywelyn calls Alis in and promises her a new marriage. The promise and its acceptance remind us of the courage which is essential if life is to continue. Nor will this be merely a compromise existence. Alis lacks the self-consciousness necessary for full awareness of choice but exercises it nevertheless.

Alis's example helps us to keep Siwan's case in perspective and to see the tension between impulse and control in her experience differently. Siwan is exceptional in that her dilemma arises from an experience of freedom greater than that possessed by the average person, of whom Alis is a good example. It is also accompanied by a degree of alienation and detachment greater than normal. There are many things which Siwan has never done, such as attending a hanging, or keeping Maytime with the youths of the village. On the other hand she has exercised power freely, ordering many men to prison, without understanding what it was.

It was Saunders Lewis's response to this problem of perspective which dictated the shape and structure of the play. The need to generalize Siwan's experience could partly be satisfied through the medium of language, as he was well aware. However, difficulties arose from the way in which he had seen his subject in the first instance. The enigma of Siwan's behaviour dictated the two contrasting scenes, with

Gwilym as faithless wife and with Llywelyn, recognized once again for her loyal and indispensible service. Something else was required in order to ensure the audience's sympathy and understanding and to extend the reference of her story to the outside world. Part of the answer to this problem was the introduction of the scene where Siwan, from her prison, listens to the preparations for Gwilym's execution and hears his final, defiant cry asserting the supremacy of love over romantic death. To represent Gwilym's execution directly lay outside the scope of his theatre, for it would have taken us quite outside the frame of the relationship which defines his stage, giving it solidity and psychological depth. On the other hand, he needed to present the execution because Gwilym's behaviour was to be an important reference point in the remainder of the play and because Siwan's response to it was an essential part of the experience concerned in the play as a whole. Describing it indirectly enabled him to achieve these aims, but only at the expense of a degree of awkwardness which his poetry can only partly conceal. It is difficult to imagine quite how the second Act could be presented successfully in the theatre. There are two problems. Firstly, Siwan herself is reduced to a state of passivity which is acceptable in dramatic terms only if it is the absolute centre of attention. We may compare her situation with that of Richard II during his famous soliloquy which dramatises the prisoner's painful frustration and indecision.[18] In dramatic terms Richard's weakness has become dramatic strength because it is played out in soliloquy. Conversely Siwan's moral strength tends to undermine her dramatic interest. From the point at which she learns the purpose of the gallows and falls unconscious to the floor she has nothing to do but to await the confirmation of Gwilym's faithfulness to himself and her.

The second problem consists in the use that Saunders Lewis made of Alis in this scene to inform Siwan and the audience of what is going on outside the room. Here we should pause to consider a point that is often made in defence of *Siwan*, which is that as a radio play, it should not be expected to be adaptable to the theatre. Saunders Lewis himself emphasised the difference between the two types of play when writing about Sir Thomas Parry's play about *Llywelyn*. He wrote:

> Hwyrach fy mod yn cam farnu'n llwyr; ond y mae drama radio, yn fy marn i, yn wahanol iawn, yn ei ffurfiad cyntaf ym meddwl yr awdur, i ddrama theatr. Gweld golygfa, ie, ei gweld, ar ei munud anterth y bydd y crefftwr gyntaf wrth lunio drama i'r llwyfan, gweld ystum a chasgl o

bersonau o gwmpas yr ystum neu'n ei lunio. A gyfer drama radio y peth
a gydia'r rhannau ynghyd yw un neu ddau brif ymadrodd a ail ddywedir
ac a glywir dro ar ôl tro drwy gydol y rhannau.

Perhaps I am entirely incorrect, but in my opinion radio drama differs
greatly from theatrical drama in the way it first forms in the mind of the
author. In shaping a play for the stage an artist will first of all be seeing
a scene in its climax, yes, seeing it, seeing a gesture and a group of persons
gathered about it or effecting it. What holds a radio drama together is
one or two principal expressions which are heard again and again
throughout the separate parts.[19]

Certainly *Siwan* displays all the characteristics of a radio play. The
most casual reading will reveal lines and even short scenes which are
designed to convey information which would be presented visually in
a play designed primarily for the theatre. However, there are other
aspects of the play which, though they would be concealed in a
broadcast performance, are not to be explained in this way. There are
several incidents in the play which are problematic with regard to the
time required to perform them. For example, at the point when
Gwilym has realized Llywelyn's secret in Act I, the latter orders that
he be gagged. This must be an extremely awkward moment in performance. The actor playing the soldier who executes the order will have
to have something ready to act as a gag and to have rehearsed the
operation over and over again if he is to do it quickly enough to conceal
the fact that the author has provided Llywelyn with no more than a
verbal device for stopping Gwilym's mouth. In fact he has ample
opportunity to continue his joke at the husband's expense.

The awkwardness of the off-stage sound effects in *Blodeuwedd* is
repeated here in this first Act. While Gwilym and Siwan are talking
they hear various sounds which warn the audience that Llywelyn is in
the offing. These sounds must be loud enough for the audience to hear
them, and yet indistinct enough not to be plain to the lovers – a difficult
effect to manage on any stage, though of course easier on the radio,
where the audience will be better able to respond to the sounds directly
themselves and at the same time to attribute an appropriate response
to the characters.

Perhaps the most serious problem in this scene arises when Siwan
and Gwilym eventually realize that Llywelyn is about to arrive. The
stage direction reads: "The tramp of soldiers, with the sound of shields
and spears is heard nearby." Siwan's response is to say to Gwilym:

"Come to the bed. I give myself to you my darling". Then we have the second stage direction: "The door is burst open and Llywelyn rushes in accompanied by armed soldiers." Again this must be difficult to present convincingly on the stage because there is no time left for the action of loving which Siwan announces and which Llywelyn is to discover. It is going to be difficult to actually get the lovers to bed and time the arrival of the outraged husband in the presence of an audience who will react to events as they see them enacted in a given space.

A radio broadcast will be much easier to manage, but the underlying difficulty will remain, because it arises not from the dramatist's failure to conceive the action visually but from the nature of the action itself. As is so often the case in Saunders Lewis's theatre, Llywelyn's violent entry is no more than a device to arrange the transition between one phase of dialogue and another. It is effective because it enables the dramatist to shift the dramatic focus and to change gear, as it were. The love-making of Siwan and Gwilym is of little interest to him. Indeed, it could be no more than the starting point of the process of reflection which led to the composition of the play. The purpose of the play is not to present this event but its psychological background.

Gwilym and Siwan's love-making is in fact no more than a frame on which the dramatist hangs the debate between them – a debate which could never have taken place on the terms which he presents. There are obvious dangers in this situation. Lovers who talk rather than act, as Siwan persistently does, run the risk of being misunderstood. Saunders Lewis, however, with great dramatic skill, turns to his advantage the audience's awareness that this whole scene is no more than the preparation for something which never happens. At several points during the scene he brings the doubt to the surface and resolves it in the interest of the audience's greater understanding of his characters. So Gwilym voices our first doubt – is Siwan afraid? – and her response to the question adds greatly to our sympathy for her. "You're not afraid of me Siwan?" he asks, and she explains: "No, not at all; but you awaken things in me/ Which do frighten me." Later, with natural impatience, which perhaps by now some of the audience may share, Gwilym reminds his mistress that the bed waits them. Again Siwan delays, inviting him to the window, to breathe the fresh night air because, she says: "I'm giving all my senses freedom tonight." In this way the dramatist strengthens our awareness of the extent to which Siwan is acting consciously, freely and in full control, all the elements of her nature in subordination to her will.

This involves a delicate dramatic balance. It is quite possible that if someone were to tell us what happens in this first Act, rather than telling us the story on which Saunders Lewis has based it, we should get a quite different impression of the heroine. We might well recall John Donne's famous poem, 'The Extasie': "But O alas, so long, so farre/ Our bodies why doe we forbeare?" and begin to suspect that her reluctance requires an explanation other than those which the dramatist himself introduces into the text. Is Siwan capable of a instinctive, loving response at all? Is she not, perhaps, merely playing with Gwilym's feelings in order to discover whether she has any herself?

That we never ask these questions during a performance or a reading of *Siwan* is because we are actually quite aware that they would be mistaken. As a character Siwan does not have the independence of authorial control which would leave us free enough to entertain them. We are in fact quite aware of the dramatic convention on which the play is based, and that the dramatist is claiming the freedom to vary the dramatic focus considerably, even at times to stretch the dialogue to the point at which the framework of a given character is threatened. Such a moment occurs in Act II when Alis is describing the behaviour of the crowds who have gathered to watch the hanging of Gwilym on the castle lawn. There is more than one historical anachronism here, which the dramatist consciously allowed himself because he actually wanted us to be quite aware that Alis's comments apply as much to Twentieth Century Wales as to that of the Thirteenth Century, if not more. He was expanding here a suggestion made in his sources that Llywelyn might not have been able to control the hatred of his followers for Brewys. His point, however, has no bearing on the historical relationship between Welsh peasantry and Anglo-Norman aristocracy, but is rather an explicit attack on the emotional nationalism of the Welsh mob, which never issues in the measured, controlled commitment required in defence of the modern Welsh nation. This was something which had been on his mind quite recently and was an important part of the process of thinking involved in the composition of *Siwan*. In an article in *Y Faner* in March 1949 he returned to the Medieval chronicles to tell the story of Owain Gwynedd's victory over his own feelings in the interests of positive, responsible action. "Feeling too strongly for one's country," Saunders Lewis argued, with a touch of apparent paradox, is a bad thing. Instead he advocated "Intellectual love, steady, unwavering good will, above all, will..." because that conscious will issues "in actions, not in feelings."[20]

When Alis is describing the "herd of devils and damned souls" who scream their hate of Gwilym from the foot of the gallows, she is reflecting the convictions of her creator. Hearing their screams from off-stage, and with the image of Siwan's suffering before us, we are likely to share her revulsion, but we will be quite aware of the political point which is being made, somewhat at the expense of Alis's integrity as a character. This is an extreme example of something which is happening all the time in *Siwan,* and indeed, must be happening in all drama, although it may sometimes be completely concealed. From the first moment of the play the audience must be aware that the dramatist is creating a complex tissue of symbolic meaning which is primarily what makes his characters interesting. The resonance and quality of dramatic action arises from the way it is presented to us, not merely from the fact that it takes place in our presence. It has often been observed, for example, that the first scene of *Siwan* is heavy with symbolism. Siwan's derobing is not a casual act but a semi-conscious preparation for the affair with Gwilym, concerning the meaning of which the audience are entirely conscious. This action is stretched out through the medium of dialogue to enable us to develop awareness of the dramatic situation. This is not merely the situation in which the characters find themselves, as individual human beings to whom we respond as if they really exist in the time and place proposed by the action. It is also the wider, symbolic situation of a princess who is momentarily freeing herself from the responsibilities of office, a wife who is choosing adultery, a woman who grasps at the possibility of self-fulfilment a moment before it will be for ever too late.

The function of dialogue in *Siwan* is to make us aware of all the different aspects of the heroine's situation and at the same time to provide us with a firm framework within which they may be seen in relationship to each other. In Act I this convention is exploited very fully, especially to off-load historical information and to create atmosphere, though rarely to the point when the integrity of character or action is threatened. As we have seen, in Act II Saunders Lewis does reach this point, stretching dramatic conventions to the point when a theatre audience at least would become uncomfortable. In Alis's description of Gwilym's execution we have what is virtually a play within a play. At this point Siwan has been reduced to almost complete immobility. Indeed the artist here has almost exchanged one genre for another, abandoning the directness of drama for the indirectness of narrative. To some extent the messenger's report of Classical Greek and Neo-Classical French tragedy provides a precedent for this, as in the decription given of the death of Hippolytus in Racine's *Phèdre*.[21.] The purpose of this device is to allow the dramatist momentarily to expand the dramatic focus without losing control. With the end of the messenger's speech we return to the place and time represented by the stage, which is largely determined by the thoughts and feelings of the central character or the opposition between two very clearly defined characters.

What is different about this use of the device is that it concerns a present event rather than something immediately past. Saunders Lewis is bringing before the attention of the audience an event designed to affect the way in which they read the current situation on stage. Consequently it represents a significant expansion of the stage space; in effect he is imposing one space on another. This raises the question of why he should not have chosen to have played the whole drama out in this larger space. Another dramatist taking up this story might have chosen to present a wider range of characters, with greater freedom of time and space. In this case the emphasis would have been on movement and event rather than dialogue and the problems which arise in *Siwan* would have been avoided. Saunders Lewis's play represents a compromise between two alternatives which is sometimes rather uneasy. He makes frequent reference to the larger world. The play is full of references which emphasise the particular place and time, ranging from the songs of Marie de France[22] to the bark of the famous hound, Gelert. On the other hand, he never allows the action to overflow the confined space of Siwan's room and her prison, or to draw in characters other than the small group of four, two of whom are clearly subordinate to the two protagonists.

In Act III this compromise is fully justified in the level of dramatic interest the dramatist succeeds in achieving. The Act begins, typically, with the entrance of the maid servant, Alis, to Llywelyn, to announce the imminent arrival of Siwan. It closes with the second entrance of Alis, who comes to prepare for the formal reinvestment of Siwan and the ceremonial exit of Siwan and Llywelyn from the privacy of the stage to the public world of war and politics. Alis acts in both these scenes, though in different ways, as a mediator. Firstly she prepares Llywelyn and the audience for the entrance of Siwan, softening the atmosphere, as it were, which is necessary after the violent ending of the previous Act. Then, later, her simplicity and naturalness help to blur the sharp transition between the intense privacy of the dialogue between husband and wife and the public world they are about to re-enter together. In between, while Siwan and Llywelyn are together, we have a scene of great resonance, where the whole philosophical statement of the play is realised for us in the intimate dialogue between them. What happens here is that what both husband and wife have learned in loneliness and suffering apart during the intervening year is confirmed and modified in relationship one with another. The climax of the scene is Siwan's attack on her husband and his humorous acceptance of defeat. This in turn, as Siwan understands, involves her defeat, for husbands are at their most dangerous at the point when they concede the superiority of their wives. What is most striking here is that amongst the ashes of their relationship they are still able to create and sustain something which is strong enough to support a whole society and a civilisation. This is in a sense their own achievement, looked at as characters; but in another way it is Saunders Lewis's achievement as a dramatist, for he has made it real for us. The awkwardness of Act II and the woodenness it is not difficult to detect at other parts of the play are the conditions of this success. Neither Classical economy alone, nor the free, heroic movement of Romantic drama would permit of this particular achievement. *Siwan,* in fact, represents the triumph of compromise.

Part IV

1. To Cast Out Fear

Only two years separate *Siwan* and *Gymerwch Chi Sigaret?*, but in that short period Saunders Lewis had developed a new preoccupation which determined the shape and substance of his mature theatre. *Siwan* and *Blodeuwedd* had been concerned with the problem of identity; the next group of plays, which begins with *Gymerwych Chi Sigaret?* and includes *Brad* (1958), *Esther* (1960) and *Cymru Fydd* (1967), confronts the problem of evil in the modern world.

In different ways all the plays of this period were felt to be controversial. *Gymerwch Chi Sigaret?*, for example, was attacked variously as a pro-Catholic tract and as anti-Communist propaganda. *Cymru Fydd* offended many by its remorseless psycho-sociological analysis of modern Welshness. Defending himself, Saunders Lewis explained that for him drama was not a mode of persuasion but rather an attempt to explore what he called "the wondrous and awful greatness of human nature." If his plays irritated and unsettled audiences, it was because they were implicitly critical of the way in which we more or less contentedly live in the world. They represent a radical criticism of materialistic humanism from within.

These later plays are a part of the mainstream of Western literature which made its appearance as early as 1902, with Joseph Conrad's *Heart of Darkness* and which developed more strongly as the century wore on, with books like André Malraux's *La Condition Humaine* (1933), the German, Gunter Grass's *The Toy Drum* (1959) or American Kurt Vonnegut's *Slaughterhouse Five* (1969). These writers share a preoccupation with the fragility of the human world and the stable appearances on which emotional security and even sanity depend. This awareness had made itself apparent in Saunders Lewis's writing as early as *Amlyn ac Amig* (1940). As time went by he became increasingly sensitive to the perverse and destructive tendencies which seem implicit in human behaviour, spreading outward from an inner centre of weakness and fear. Publication of the Nazi atrocities after the war and the destruction of Hiroshima and Nagasaki only served to give clearer focus to this anxiety.

In Europe and America in general this awareness was essentially problematic where drama was concerned. Undermining confidence in the solidity of the immediate social world and the stable definition of human character, it also undermined the traditional plot and even the medium of dialogue itself. Western humanism as it had developed from the writings of early Nineteeenth Century Romantics, regarded the individual as the source of value and meaning. Society, an accretion of individuals, was meaningful in so far as it provided opportunities for emotional fulfilment. From the point at which the essential soundness of human emotion was called into question this individualistic Humanism became difficult to sustain. Saunders Lewis, however, preserved his confidence in character and in dialogue because he also maintained his confidence in human freedom and the possibility of self definition. This derived from his view of human emotion. For Saunders Lewis, deriving his view of human nature from the Calvinist tradition, regarded the emotional dimension as neither the source nor the test of value, but rather a response, at varying levels of complexity, to a fundamental experience of weakness. What dictated the shape and direction of an individual's life was the degree of honesty and courage which governed his ability to acknowledge this weakness. Evil itself seemed to consist in a perverse and vain attempt to manipulate weakness in others in order to distract one's attention from its existence within oneself.

The only real guarantee of human strength was religion, but any civilised code or tradition offered an escape from isolation and a means of preserving the freedom of choice on which indviduality itself ultimately depended. In the final analysis, as *Brad* shows us, the finest tradition contains within itself the seeds of corruption, but in spite of this tradition remains an essential condition of individuality. Free recognition of a model outside the self permits a kind of self development in which the emotional weakness deriving from material vulnerability could become a form of strength. The price paid for this in material suffering could be dreadfully high, a price that most human beings would revolt from, even at the cost of sacrificing their personal security. The comparitively few people who are willing to pay it are the central characters of these four plays, which embody an essentially tragic vision.

Writing in the *Radio Times* on the occasion of a broadcast of *Gymerwch Chi Sigaret?* in 1965, Saunders Lewis explained how it fitted into the overall pattern of his theatre. He began by quoting an old Latin poem which celebrated the idea of pure love. His play, he conceded, was a religious play, not by virtue of the fact that the characters are religious or discuss religion, but because of its central concern; for "any play which presents pure love is necessarily a religious play." The main point of his argument here is that human love is essentially selfish, a grasping, possessive tendency, but has within it the seed of unselfishness, which under certain circumstances may grow. It is this implicit and latent contradiction that makes human love essentially dramatic and makes it, as he puts it, "open its arms to tragedy".[1]

What Saunders Lewis refers to as 'pure' love is an emotion which sustains spiritual values instead of subverting them, and in doing so is transfigured. This is not necessarily a Christian concept. The *Antigone* and *Electra* of Sophocles treat the concept of pure love, he says, and are consequently religious. Greek drama, of course, was never far from Saunders Lewis's thoughts, and it is clear that the example of Antigone inspired his interpretation of the story of Iris and Marc. For Antigone recognises a value over and above all other values, including romantic love and even her immediate duty to the state as it is set out in Creon's opportunistic political decrees. She must go through the form of burying her brother, although Creon has forbidden it for reasons of state, because that is the responsibility imposed on her by the gods. The clash between Antigone and her sister Ismene, who pleads for compromise, develops the fundamental source of the play's drama. It is also the ultimate source of Saunders Lewis's own drama. Antigone's love for her brother is not simply an emotion; it is a duty, fulfilment of which is the highest form of self-fulfilment. For the self survives death, and, as she tells her sister: "My time with the dead will be longer than the time I spend with the living. I will lie with them for ever."[2]

In *Gymerwch Chi Sigaret?* Iris has a similar vision. As Marc tells Calista, if his love is like a claw, hers ressembles an open hand, transcending selfish desire. She loves him, "as if eternity existed". In Marc she sees not merely her lover, but an unbaptised soul, from whom she cannot bear to think that she will be separated for eternity. In the dreadful circumstances which annihilate Marc, thrusting him down into a cowardly, self-destructive obedience to the régime, Iris is able to preserve herself intact. They represent an opportunity which fills her with hope and fear. This is not merely or even primarily an opportunity to obtain two passports and escape from danger, though she longs for such a resolution. Far more important to Iris is the chance to win Marc's salvation and consequently to achieve a far different kind of happiness than that which he envisages. Unfortunately Marc himself does not understand this until it is too late. He attains to it only when the illusion of earthly happiness has been torn away from him, through the dreadful knowledge that he is responsible for her destruction.

From time to time there has been a good deal of discussion as to whether such a thing as a Christian tragedy is possible. If Iris and Marc are to be re-united in eternity, can we look on their story in the same way as that of King Oedipus, Antigone or Othello? Saunders Lewis would answer that we do respond in the same way. Art can only concern itself with experience; and the experience of these lovers is harrowingly destructive. Iris in a sense is beyond the reach of tragedy because her faith is so strong that she considers the bargain that she has made to be a fair one. Though she is quite aware of the danger she runs and knows that is is quite unlikely that she will escape torture and death, she can dance happily because she sees a chance to win Marc's love for ever. The opportunity to exchange for a different kind of experience the human happiness to which he clings desperately brings her a measure of joy which outweighs suffering. Yet the choice of suffering and death rather than compromise and corruption is one which she would willingly have avoided. Marc suffers more because he has to live longer and has to do so without her strength of faith and clarity of vision. It may be that in the next life we would look back on the story of their suffering as Chaucer's Troilus looked back on his own that is, with a mixture of wonder and amusement [3] — but until then our spiritual vision can never be anything but cloudy. Trapped in circumstances over which they have no control, they preserve their love and prove it, at the cost of everything else which gives meaning and substance to existence. Something is left to Marc at the end of the play, certainly, but equally certainly it is nothing that human perceptions may measure or appreciate.

It might be objected that Saunders Lewis's modern tragedy ignores the matter of class. Is not Iris's uncompromising clarity of vision the result of her social position? The representative of a defeated and vanishing class, her critical detachment from the world is an unconscious but predictable compensation for the loss of the privileged position into which she had been born. Saunders Lewis would have accepted this, arguing that the elevation of character which is a condition of tragedy is possible only for an individual who has been nurtured within a tradition in which the idea of duty and individual responsibility plays an important part. Marc's vulnerability derives directly from the fact that he has grown up in a world without tradition.

However, although character may be in some degree dependant on class, Saunders Lewis would not draw the Marxist's conclusion that human character is permeable by the material world. In the Preface to *Cymru Fydd* he observes that Communism is similar to Christianity in requiring from its followers an act of conscious engagement. The difference between, them, he argues, is that the Communist's commitment to the material world requires a surrender of the will which is increasingly difficult to justify. Commitment to spirit, he argues, is more realistic and reasonable than faith in a world which may be destroyed at any moment by the nuclear bomb. It also has the advantage of preserving the integrity of the moral will and the reality of human freedom which depends on it.

The human condition is presented in Saunders Lewis's theatre as essentially the same in all times and places, regardless of material differences. At the same time, his drama is also obtrusively concerned with the circumstances of life in modern Europe and particularly in Wales. In the post-war period, though he withdrew from practical politics, Saunders Lewis continued to be actively involved as a commentator on the world about him. Then in 1962 he broadcast the lecture on the future of the Welsh language which eventually led to the establishment of Cymdeithas Yr Iaith Gymraeg and continues to influence the aims and methods of the language movement. *Cymru Fydd*, set in Wales in the early phase of the language campaign, is the only one of the four plays of this period which reflect his involvement directly. Even there his view was characteristically detached. In *Cymru Fydd* the poignant and bitter sense of fragility which preoccupies even the strongest of his characters is at once something specific to the modern Wales and a manifestation of the problem of existance itself.

On the other hand in a play like *Esther*, which reflects a brooding preoccupation with the workings of evil in the world at large, Saunders Lewis constantly finds opportunities to reflect on the circumstances of life in modern Europe and in post-war Wales. The Biblical story permits him to reflect directly on more recent sufferings of the Jews. Fearless of anachronisms, as always, he ensures that his central characters, exiled in Persia at a period some five hundred years before the birth of Christ, remind us directly of the fate of their descendants in Europe under the crueller government of the Nazis. He also insist that Welsh audiences note the reference of Esther's story to their own immediate situation. The insidious fear which masters Hamaan is also the motive of the modern slave; as it can distort the life of the individual, Saunders Lewis reminds us, so it can destroy the life of a nation.

This dual focus gives us the key not only to the philosophy, but also to the shape and substance of Saunders Lewis's mature theatre. It is a theatre in which the audience is far less passive than the Naturalistic style of setting would suggest. Irony and anachronism oblige the audience to be aware of the debate which the play sustains. To some extent, of course, this debate is contained within the action itself. Characters discuss their situation and measure different possible responses and as they do so the audience develops a passive awareness as in Naturalistic theatre in general. However, anachronistic references to material which could not have been a part of the historical consciousness of the characters presented on the stage and the insistent patterns of irony, ensure that the audience develops an awareness of the dramatic presentation as such, that is, as a complex cultural event in which they are taking part.

We may recognize here something of the alienating effect most commonly associated with the theatre of Berthold Brecht. Saunders Lewis never takes it so far as to effect the estrangement of the audience; on the contrary, the Naturalistic style of presentation, the setting and the dialogue, all work to prevent that from happening. His theatre was designed to generate and to articulate a precisely balanced awareness of the general and the particular, of man as potentially free but only in acknowledging weakness and dependence. It is a theatre which accepts the corruption of the social world and yet asserts the potential goodness of human nature. It is a tragic and an heroic theatre in so far as it asserts the capacity of the individual to preserve himself intact in spite of the corruption and destructive power of the world. However it differs from the theatre of Ancient Greece in that the latter enclosed within it the total human world it represented. The relationship between protagonist and Chorus on this stage reflects the inescapable relatedness of individual and group in the Greek City world. In Twentieth Century Wales Saunders Lewis is faced with the task of creating this relationship in the theatre precisely because it does not exist within the immediate social world and of defining its limitations.

To achieve this task Saunders Lewis developed the balance between emotional involvement and ironic detachment which is characteristic of his mature theatre. It also governed the way in which he defined his stage space and shaped the action of the plays he wrote at this time. The stage is more fully defined by the audience's awareness of the nature of the action than ever before. Consequently the occasional awkwardnesses apparent in *Blodeuwedd* and *Siwan* have almost disappeared. In *Gymerwch Chi Sigaret?* the audience have a more informed awareness than any of the characters and even have greater visual access to the playing space. In *Brad* they have information which sharpens their critical awareness of the way in which the main characters are acting. Esther's triumph, in the third play of the period, is not completely shared by the audience; at the end of the play her subjective experience, beyond the reach of the theatre audience, removes her from us a little, reminding us of the integrity of joy as of suffering. Finally, in *Cymru Fydd* , while we share the playing space with all the characters, who have the same freedom of access to it as we do, yet we have an ability to reflect on their relatedness which they lack themselves. The whole play can only be realised in our experience of them, rather than in their experience of each other.

In these four plays, and especially in *Cymru Fydd*, Saunders Lewis achieves mastery of his particular art. They express a fully realized vision of life, not merely in terms of language and action, but in terms of theatre. For the debate which each of these plays sustains as it might be sustained in other forms of literary fiction, is here also articulated in terms of the experience of the audience. That experience, essentially a combination of passivity and active assessment, is shaped in terms of the vision of human life that Saunders Lewis presents. The heroic action asserts the necessity of confronting and coming to terms with human weakness as the only real form of strength and security available to us. The theatrical experience involves a similar pain. Although it is vicarious, it is nevertheless real to us and we seek and find a way of coming to terms with it in the wisdom and understanding which the form of the play offers us and which in itself is a form of strength. Confronted with the fate of characters like Colonel Hofacker in *Brad* or Bet, in *Cymru Fydd*, the words of the Welsh version of the Lord's Prayer might well echo in our minds "May we not be tested..." as they have been; but this itself, for Saunders Lewis, is a substantial point won. The confession of fear is the essential precondition of honest living.

2. *Gymerwch Chi Sigaret?*

Gymerwch Chi Sigaret? (1956) is set during the Cold War in an East
European Communist State where Catholicism is strong — presum -
bly Poland — and in the city of Vienna, still occupied by the Four
Powers. It concerns two married lovers, Iris and Marc, she a committed Catholic, from an upper class family with a tradition of patriot-
sm, he an Agnostic, from a family without traditions, who have met
and fallen in love while working for the Resistance during the recent
war. Now, after the war, Marc is employed as a clerk in the offices of
the Secret Police. The play records the process by which, caught in a
cruel dilemma which offers no release except through physical or
spiritual destruction, they are torn apart from each other.

The play begins when Marc comes home early to announce to Iris
that he has been given the task of executing her god-father, Phugas,
who conducts a pro-Catholic, anti-Government campaign from exile
in Vienna. Marc is chosen for this task by his employers because they
know of the connection between Iris and Phugas and also know
circumstances of her family history which give Phugas particular
reasons for trusting her. These circumstances, of course, will make the
treachery of her arranging the meeting between Phugas and his murderer all the greater, but Iris's alternative is death for Marc and herself
and for the baby she is carrying.

Faced with this dreadful dilemma, Iris sees a way forward, which
may offer a physical escape and will certainly ensure that Marc will
not damn himself by comitting the murder. Firstly she swears she will
never see him again if he does kill Phugas; next she asks him to go
straight to Vienna and throw himself on the mercy of the Americans,
asking them to arrange refuge for her in their Embassy. Unfortunately
Marc lacks faith in her word. Having determined to kill Phugas and
return to her, he wastes valuable time trying to justify the murder to
himself. On the point of doing it, the rosary which Iris has given him

falls out of the cigarette case in which his gun had been concealed and he breaks down. Now, too late, he throws himself on Phugas's mercy. The agents who waited outside for him are already on their way to report his failure and in spite of the efforts of the Americans Iris falls into the hands of the Secret Police. Desperate with anxiety, Marc waits to learn her fate, which is confirmed during a brief, cruel, telephone call from the office where she is being held. Their hope is that Marc's despair will cause him to use the second cigarette case they have given him to kill himself. Saved from this by Phugas's sister, Calista, he decides instead to join Iris in her faith, is converted to Christianity and will serve her cause as Phugas's assistant for the remainer of what life may remain to him in these dangerous circumstances.

Although, however, *Gymerwch Chi Sigaret?* is the tragedy of two lovers, as a play it concentrates much more on Marc than on Iris. Saunders Lewis was aware of this as a problem during the process of composition, and drew our attention in the Preface, to the fact that Iris is necessarily absent from the stage after the First Act as " horrifying difficulty". This meant that he had to get through everything that happens between the husband and wife in one Act and the only way of doing this was to sustain a very long dialogue. He felt that the second Act presented no problem in this respect because the pace and interest of the action would carry the audience through.The third and final Act, however, presented two further difficulties. To complete the working out of Marc's conversion he had to introduce a character who could act as a spokesman for Iris. This is Phugas's sister, Calista, who has no function in her own right and consequently runs the risk of being either uninteresting or too interesting to the audience, distracting attention from other characters.

Then, "for the sake of the formal unity of the whole play" he felt that he had to build the closing Act around the experience of hearing Iris' voice on the telephone and to introduce the vision of her "in cameo" "to intensify the impression". In theatrical terms this is a weak device. Seeing Iris in the hands of the Secret Police certainly intensifies our sense of her suffering and Marc's distress, but it also distracts us to some extent from what is happening on stage, in our presence, in Marc's mind. When Saunders Lewis suddenly extends and alters the nature of the stage, lifting the rear curtain and presenting Iris directly to us, he is shifting the point of balance of the action, as it were, from Marc to the audience. Were the action actually to centre on Marc's experience the direct presentation of the telephone conversation would be irrelevant and distracting — a one-sided conversation, allowing us to focus all our attention on Marc would be sufficient.

The device of the 'phone call is a way of ensuring that the audience do not simply experience Marc's distress but also their own disappointment. By this time, after all, Marc understands his wife thoroughly. The telephone call adds neither to his understanding nor to his suffering, which will be extended through the seeming eternity of his separation from her. However, its impact on us is important. We need this last, dreadful glimpse of the lovers together so that we will fully understand their love for one another.

Given the difficulties involved in dramatising the story one would imagine that Saunders Lewis might have considered presenting it in another way. Either film or novel would allow direct presentation of the all important process of decision which takes place between the end of Act I and the beginning of Act II. The novel would allow us to share Marc's thoughts at this stage and later, when in Phugas's flat. It would permit the author to balance action against reflection in an interesting way. The film, far more restrictive in terms of the amount of interior action it can present, would permit the creation of a strong visual image of Marc, tormented by doubt, against the background of the material and human world by which he was oppressed. Moreover, both novel and film are capable of certain kinds of subtlety which are impossible in the theatre. In the former external action and dialogue gain immeasurably in significance by being presented against the background of internal action. In the latter any given visual or verbal sign provided by the actor is perceived in a fixed relationship with other signs, all under the control of the director.

The choice of film may not have been open to Saunders Lewis because of financial considerations. Indeed, only now is film becoming a possibility in Wales, because of technical developments and changes in systems of funding. He had already tried his hand at the novel, however, with *Monica* (1930) and as his story, *Merch Gwern Hywel* (1964) was to show, the various forms of fiction remained open to him all the time. In fact we must look at the choice of theatre, with all its disadvantages, as a positive choice, directing our attention to what Saunders Lewis saw as central and essential in the material his imagination presented to him, something which he could only present in terms of the larger, cruder gestures of theatre, and within the restrictions of the theatrical stage.

We must bear in mind that the artistic purpose which lay behind *Gymerwch Chi Sigaret?* concerned, "the awful greatness of human nature". What interests Saunders Lewis in Iris and Marc is not the difficulty of the situation in which they find themselves, nor primarily the suffering which they endure, but rather the capacity they have for winning spiritual gain from that suffering. Consequently he has no wish to present the process by which Marc convinced himself that Iris would not hold by the vow she had made, but rather that which led to the triumph of love over fear and hatred. This priority dictates the structure of the play. The first Act belongs to Iris and culminates in the plan she presents to Marc. His response to this is necessarily confused by his own fear and his reluctance to make the leap of faith that Phugas later talks to him about. As a theatre audience we are painfully aware of this fear, but we do not share it. Having a different standpoint, we perceive Iris's behaviour independently, and in a way which is carefully controlled by the dramatist. Marc, absorbed in his own experience, is far more shocked and disconcerted than we can be. For we have had the opportunity to observe the different stages by which Iris comes to her decision.

The opening Act of the play turns around two separate dramatic moments. The first is when Iris asks her husband if he believes his own justification of the projected murder of her god-father, Phugas, and Marc throws her to the floor: "Go to hell you bitch! I've been doing my best to believe it since this morning". Iris's response is the first indication of how far apart they are and how far Marc must travel before he can begin to understand the depth of her love for him. His anger is positive proof that he is not corrupt. This means that his situation is more dreadful than it might have been — had he been able to murder Phugas innocently, as it were, without seeing it as a crime, it would have been open to him to lead a happy and successful life from a worldly point of view. Such a state of mind, however, would foreshadow spiritual death and separation, not merely ultimately, after death, but even in life, because Iris's love is of the kind that necessarily develops a spiritual dimension.

The phase of action introduced by this gesture culminates in the powerful, humanistic argument which Marc puts forward to convince Iris that the murder would be the lesser of two evils. On the one hand, Phugas, a voluntary soldier in the battle line, who will fall only to be replaced by another. On the other, Marc, Iris and their unborn child, all 'innocent' in the sense that they are uncommitted and uninvolved in the battle which is being fought for the world they live in. Iris's reaction, as her husband reveals the full horror of their situation, is very human — "I'm afraid Marc. Because of what I'm carrying in my womb." At this stage she sees no way forward, but although these words seem a confession of weakness, they are actually quite ambiguous. She is afraid because she will not acquiesce in the crime which would remove the threat. She knows that to accept her own fear as a principle of action would deepen it immeasurably and would ultimately enslave them both. Working together as partisans during the German Occupation, they have both known — overcome fear and this common experience makes the difference between them now more striking. Marc's courage cannot help him; seeing no escape from danger, he succumbs to fear.

The argument which he presents to Iris is similar to the one with which Ismene tried to dissuade Antigone from burying their brother. Refusal to murder Phugas will be ineffective — "He chose his path, and if I don't shoot him he'll be killed by someone else." Having no choice, they will bear no responsibility; accepting the world is a neccessary condition of living, a biological imperative: "The only way to live at all in this socialist world is through accepting it and obeying...You can only give birth to your child if you accept this fact".

The techniques which Saunders Lewis employs at this stage give rise to a complex irony which again reminds us of Sophocles. He introduces two Biblical quotations. First Iris adopts the words which Jesus uses when he reproves Simon Peter for trying to turn him from the path to the Cross (Matthew 16,23); "Get behind me Satan! You are an obstacle in my path..." Puzzled, Marc asks her what she means. Her reply seems to amount to a withdrawal from the spiritual commitment implied by the quotation — "Nothing, nothing, I was blaspheming. My head's not clear...I'll be alright in a minute." The confession of very human weakness apparently pulls her back from this spiritual commitment and her next words seem to confirm — "I'm beginning to see my way". Marc accepts her words at face value and continues to hammer home his argument; "There's only one road. We have to take it." But Iris's reply to this again has a Biblical echo, which should warn us that her indecision and confusion are resolved: "It's a pretty narrow road. I doubt if there's room on it for two". (Matthew 7,14; Luke 13,14) Marc, of course, has no reason to think that she is doing anything other than bending to the pressure he is putting on her. However, her words actually show that she is beginning to overcome her fear and gain strength and clarity of vision again. When Marc unwittingly answers her with words that echo Ruth's declaration of loyalty to her mother in law, Naomi (Ruth,1,16), she accepts them as a confirmation of that vision.

At this point the action takes another turn, as Iris explains to her husband the background to the request that she tell Phugas in her letter to him that Marc will carry a message from her dead father. A theatre audience could hardly fail to sense the release of tension in this phase of action, which finds its explanation in her agreement to write the letter. The explanation, however, is not what Marc expects it to be. His relief is an ironical introduction to Iris's apparently paradoxical behaviour in swearing that if he murders Phugas she will never see him again. Instead of explaining at once, Iris teasingly increases Marc's confusion until she finally reveals the path which she has discovered. It leads, she claims, to freedom, a word which he takes up, questioningly, and she repeats "Yes, freedom." Even here there is irony, for the preceding scene has prepared the audience to understand how far the lovers still stand apart. The freedom Iris seeks is not primarily a freedom from torture and death, but a freedom from fear, which may be obtainable only at the price of suffering. Fear still clouds Marc's mind, preventing him from seeing that the path which Iris has discovered is the only one open to them. In making the vow on her rosary Iris is trying to fix in her husband's mind the fact that he cannot compromise without destroying her. There is never any doubt of his love for her or of the fact that he does understand her at the deepest level. That is why he tells her, "If we lose, I'll devote my life to revenge." But Marc lacks the courage which faith gives. This is why before she sits down to write the letter, Iris gives him her rosary, the symbol of her vow, which will remind her husband who she is. When he remembers it will be too late to win the freedom she had hoped for but not too late to win a different kind of salvation for them both.

Before the next Act begins Marc has decided to ignore Iris's oath and to carry out the instruction to kill Phugas. In doing this he is untrue to his love for her. This explains the sudden reversal of feelings which occurs when he opens the cigarette case to kill her godfather and her rosary falls to the floor. His refusal to believe that she means what she has said is a quite deliberate rejection of her. He tells Calista; "The choice was forced on me. She knew that when she took that cruel oath. She knew it when she gave me the rosary to keep. That's why I insisted that it was a lie."

Had the rosary not fallen out of the cigarette case at that moment Marc would have killed Phugas and returned home safely, to find that he and Iris were lost to each other for ever, like Orpheus and Eurydice. The shock of seeing it is so great that he attributes it to deliberate thought transmision on Iris's part. Calista sees it rather as the result of prayer. In literal terms, of course, the American security agent who searched Marc at the door before letting him in to visit Phugas, is responsible. No matter how we choose to interpret this, the underlying factor is Iris's determination to do everything she can to convince Marc that she does mean what she says and so to ensure their safety.

Act II begins with Phugas talking on the telephone. Calista comes in, dressed to go out and asks him about his conversation. His answer introduces us to their situation, which is developed throughout the dialogue which follows until Calista goes out. By this time we have learned a good deal about the perilous business Phugas is engaged in; we know he is ill and even likely to die at any moment; and we have been prepared for the entrance of Marc. Through this dialogue we become aware of the strange, attentuated life the brother and sister lead, isolated and enclosed, quite lacking opportunity to develop their emotional natures, yet strangely content. Calista's complaints lack energy. The difference between her and Phugas in the matter of the coffee is slight, scarcely concealing the underlying spiritual commitment they have in common.

When Calista has gone out, Marc enters and of course it is important that he comes into a room which we already occupy in a sense that could not hold true were the story being told through the medium of novel or film. We welcome Marc into a situation which is familiar to us, which clearly relates to the world to which Iris has already introduced us and which we understand better than he does. In the conversation which follows between Phugas and Marc we are again strangely detached. We know that Marc is giving a false impression to Phugas in an attempt to bolster his own confidence. Phugas's reaction greatly strengthens our feeling that the murder Marc contemplates is indeed an act of barbarism which would undermine his own sense of decency and make it impossible for his marriage to continue. Phugas makes us aware of the inner meaning of Marc's behaviour, the effect of which is to depreciate his wife immeasurably. "Is there some advantage to you," he asks him, "in insisting that your wife could plan falsehood?" And of course, Marc's tormented outburst — "Yes. My life itself depends on a promise being a lie. I'm risking everything on that" — reveals the strain he is under.

As time goes by in this scene tension increases, for we know that time is scarce if Iris's plan has a chance of success. The source of this tension does not arise from our expectation that Marc will actually kill Phugas. Were he to do this and then simply to walk out, the action as it has been defined up to that point would simply fail to develop. Saunders Lewis has designed the whole scene for what it can tell us about human nature. Marc taunts Phugas, attributing his concern at the suggestion that Iris herself is implicated in the plot to disappointment that the old social values have vanished from the world. Phugas's reply is more than a defence against this assertion:

> Mae rhywbeth dyfnach na hynny'n fy mhoeni i, yr ofn fod bradychu a gwerthu cyfeillion wedi mynd yn beth normal a naturiol ymhlith poblifainc fy ngwlad i, ofn fod cywirdeb ac anwyldeb a haelioni a hunan aberth a chadw ffydd wedi darfod...

> Something deeper than that is worrying me, the fear that betrayal and selling friends has become a normal and natural thing among the young people of my country, fear that truthfulness and tenderness and generosity and self-sacrifice and keeping faith have come to an end...

These qualities are not merely the decorations of a given social class, but essential conditions of the love which Marc is desperately trying to protect. Without them, as Othello said, when his own love seemed hopelessly tarnished, "Chaos is come again." [4]

The central point of the Act comes with Marc's words to Phugas as he prepares to shoot him and which provide the title of the play. From this point on, after Marc's collapse, the action concerns the explanation of what we already know to Phugas, to Calista and then to Captain Christopher, the American security officer who protects Phugas. The dramatic interest here turns on Marc, as he begins to live with the consequences of his decision not to trust Iris. With Marc's explanation the responsibility for action is removed from him to Christopher and when this process is complete the Act has reached its natural conclusion. Before that happens the telephone rings and Phugas receives and announces the news that his pilot has been captured and smuggled into the Russian sector of the city. This anticipates the ending of the play — Marc, being a pilot, will take the place of the one who has been kidnapped. So he finds a natural way of defining his own attitude and marking the end of the action which began with his early return home to Iris at the beginning of Act I.

Act III has a deceptively simple structure, leading up to the climactic telephone conversation between Marc and Iris when she is in the hands of the Secret Police and culminating in his final surrender to Iris and commitment to her religion. At first glance it would appear that the action is presented to the audience as if from the viewpoint of Marc himself. Certainly it is true to say that the climactic incident is Marc's capitulation, following his last conversation with Iris. From the end of the second Act to the point when Marc takes the rosary from Calista, falls to his knees and kisses it, the audience are waiting for the conclusion of Iris's plan, which should have followed immediately on Act I had Marc been able to keep faith with her.

From the point of view of dramatic structure it ultimately makes no difference whether Iris will prove to have escaped or to have been captured. Her plan will be fulfilled in one way if not in another. In the first instance, however, we wait for confirmation of our fears and while doing so we follow the movements of the characters, who are also waiting. They engage in a debate which reflects directly on their own response to the situation and indirectly on ours. We are also directly involved in this debate by virtue of our own reponsiveness as audience. As Marc, confronted with suffering, battles with fear, so do we, less immediately involved of course, but painfully aware of some aspects of the situation to which he is relatively insensitive.

Once the climax is over, the two points of view, Marc's and our own, are brought together, but for the greater part of the prolonged scene, they are separate. The relationship between them may be traced through the pattern of irony created by the various references to the idea that Iris may be preserved in safety. When Marc expresses this hope. of course, he is thinking of his wife's material safety, but , aware of the story of the pilot and warned by Calista, we know that the only final security is death itself and what lies beyond it. After the telephone conversation Marc himself becomes aware of the irony of his previous insistence on putting Iris somehow beyond risk, but we, though dimly, perceive that irony much earlier. That is the key to the particularly painful awareness from which we too seek release as the action proceeds, following the debate between Marc and Calista, Christopher and Phugas, with keen attention.

The Act begins with a deliberate release of the tension which was built up at the end of the previous scene, when the fate of the pilot was suddenly announced. The threat introduced there cannot be forgotten, but is certainly suspended for a while during the light-hearted conversation about tea drinking. The dialogue between Marc and Calista which follows recapitulates and confirms much of what we have learnt during the previous Acts about Iris and Marc in relation to each other. We hear Marc confessing and explaining his behaviour as a protest against Iris's love. Then, towards the end of the conversation, he asks Calista whether she thinks the 'phone will ever ring, for him to hear, "her voice, like a star, in safety?" Marc is as yet unready to accept the implication of Calista's reply:

> Mewn diogelwch? 'Rych chi'n gofyn am lawer, Marc. Pa ddiogelwch a welodd neb honom ni yn y rhan yma o Ewrob ers ugain mlynedd? 'Does dim ond un diogelwch.

> In safety? You're asking a lot Marc. What safety have any of seen in this part of Europe during the last twenty years? There's only one kind of safety.

We, however, can hardly avoid recognising and accepting what she implies and of remembering it throughout the discussions which follow.

The dialogue which follows immediately on Phugas's entry strengthens our awareness of the fragility of human security. Introducing the story of the pilot again, it takes us back to the end of Act II, re-establishing the tension and insecurity we felt then. Marc's challenge to Phugas as a result of hearing it extends our awareness of what his own situation implies: "Phugas, how can you believe in God?" Answering Marc, Phugas makes us painfully aware that there is no escape from suffering and indeed, that all committed action must necessariy increase the sum of suffering in the world. The co-existence of opposing forces cannot even be dismissed as the result of random circumstances; enemies, as Phugas puts it, with bitter humour, are locked into an embrace like that of lovers.

Captain Christopher's entry into the room, ostensibly to tell Marc that his request for political assylum has been granted and so to organize the waiting period, as it were, also gives Saunders Lewis another chance to widen the debate which he has initiated. Marc's sudden and 'unamerican' question to Christopher — "Do you believe in God?" — becomes the occasion for us to notice the way in which fundamental issues come to seem peripheral or merely private in societies which have established a degree of apparent material security. Christopher's stiff, Anglo-American response is the more noticeable because we have already been alerted to these cultural characteristics in Calista's earlier remarks about the Englishman's tea-drinking habits. Defining Christopher as a type in this way clearly helps Saunders Lewis to bring us closer to Marc and so to bring a strong dramatic focus to bear on him at this point, not as an exception to the human rule but rather as a type of the ordinary man who takes refuge in indifference and thereby endangers his innermost life. This awareness is strengthened even by the irony which underlies his words: "If only I could hear her voice!" Knowing the issue of events, we may be superior to Marc and yet it remains true for us that hearing Iris's voice will provide the key to resolving the dramatic action.

At this point Phugas gives another turn to the debate, introducing material which Saunders Lewis quite unashamedly borrowed from Pascal's *Pensées*[5] He mentioned this in his Preface to the play, making it clear that he had made little effort to bury the borrowed material in the experience of his characters, any more than he had attempted to disguise anachronisms, such as the fact that Marc is aware of the conversion of Paul Claudel but unaware of the more famous precedent which took place on the road to Damascus. He is content at this point for his audience even to become conscious of the double dramatic focus, following the debate between Marc and Phugas with close attention because it relates to the way they themselves are responding to the dramatic situation. The argument Phugas derives from Pascal is not perhaps a simple one, though it is advanced quite simply and naturally in the course of their conversation. Phugas turns Marc's protest against the proposition that God exists into an argument in favour of faith. The injustice of the world and the sum of suffering argue against the proposition of a just God, Marc would argue. Phugas, in reply, accepts the absurdity of the human situation. Life is indeed governed by accident. So, he says, why not assume that God does exist and that somewhere reason is to be found? Assuming that God does not exist is the same as making no assumption at all and the experience of living obliges us to assume something. Marc has in fact tried to assume that God does not exist, but he failed to act on that assumption, prevented by his love for Iris. What can he do now but the very thing she has plotted to oblige him to do, which is to act as if there is indeed an eternity in which their love may endure?

As Phugas advances the last proposition in his argument Marc screams his protest: "Lies! Lies! Christopher's a witness that I haven't lost everything yet. I haven't lost Iris yet!" Ironically his protest betrays his inner acceptance of Phugas's argument. "I've got Iris to put on the board", he tells Phugas; "I'll bet on Iris." What he hopes to do is bargain with God for Iris's life. If she is saved, then he will believe. But no one could make such a bargain unless he already believed. Calista protests against it. "You can't bet with Iris's life. You haven't got the right!" she tells him, because Iris has already bargained her own life for the very prize which she is about to win — Marc's salvation. "Bargaining can be hard," she warns him, but even up until the last moment, when the telephone rings, Marc is still resisting his own conviction; "If I hear her voice —"

So Marc is dragged towards conviction, in spite of himself. Even after he has heard Iris's voice and understood the whole situation, he is far from safe. Phugas resolves the persistent irony, telling him; "Iris is safe" and Marc shows that he understands what this implies about his previous stubborn blindness: "I heard her voice telling me she was safe!..."

It is possible that Iris's plan would not have ensured her physical safety in any event and she must have known that Colonel Krechlen was unlikely not to have put her under surveillance from the moment Marc left. However, he has no means of knowing anything but that his doubting her has led to a substantial delay and has contributed to the failure of the plan. In his despair he is very vulnerable to the suggestion that lies behind the message Iris is forced to convey to him during the telephone conversation between them. Now, in a state of shock, he is seriously at risk of responding to the 'phone call in the way his employers hoped he would and turning the second cigarette case against himself.

Saunders Lewis makes this final uncertainty into an opportunity of reminding us for the last time that we have been witnessing the working out of a strange and painful love story. He uses Calista to this end and as a means of strengthening the impact of Marc's conversion on the audience. It is important at this point that Saunders Lewis and Iris have an interpreter on stage who is superior in understanding and sensitivity to the other characters, to Marc and to ourselves. Calista shows that superiority when she intuits what Marc is about to do, which we have no means of doing; this gives her the authority to deliver the last, difficult message, after which, the action can come to a close. She reminds Marc and the audience of the inner meaning of the story, with which, like Marc, we have been struggling during the course of the play and she draws a conclusion which we might well have been unwilling to draw for ourselves. Explaining the full extent of Iris's sacrifice, she completes the process of conversion which puts Marc beyond the power of the secret police for ever;

> Mae Iris yn galw arnat, Marc[.] Hi a'th ddanfonodd di atom ni. Hi a roes ei bywyd drosot ti, i'th gadw di rhag drwg. 'Ddar'u hi ddim dianc rhag poen. Fe ddewisodd ei phoen, ac fe wyddost ti hynny; fe yfodd ei chwpan i'r gwaelod er dy fwyn di, er mwyn dy gael di gyda hi am byth. Rhaid i tithau'n awr fyw, a'th fywyd di ar ben, nid dy fywyd dy hunan, ond bywyd Iris.

> Iris is calling to you Marc. She sent you to us. She gave her life for you, to keep you from harm. She didn't escape pain. She chose her pain and you know that; she drunk her cup to the dregs for your sake, to have you with her for ever. Now you must live, even though your life is over, not your life, but hers.

As Calista gives Marc the rosary and tells him what to do with it,[8] reminding us of Iris's action at the end of the first Act, by now so far behind us, the focus shifts once again onto Marc himself. The rosary, she reminds him, is Iris's gift to him — a gift to replace herself — and she offers it to him in exchange for the cigarette case. Marc takes it and with it accepts her counsel and Iris's faith. From this moment on his path is clear before him. Nothing remains of his life that can be measured in terms of emotional fulfilment, of course. In this sense, as he says, his life is over. But he had earlier promised, in the event of failure, to devote his life to revenge; now in working with Phugas and serving the Church he finds a practical use for his new faith.

> Marc: Be' wna'i 'i llaswyr hi?
> Calista: Gwna fel y gwnaeth Iris, dyro gusan i'r groes.
> Marc (gan syrthio i'w liniau a chodi'r llaswyr at ei wefus): Iris, Iris, gweddia drosof i.

> Marc: What will I do with her rosary?
> Calista: Do what she did kiss the crucifix. Marc (falling to his knees and raising the rosary to his lips): Iris, Iris, pray for me.

These closing words mark the climax of the Act and the play and the beginning of Marc's own spiritual journey. Where it will lead him we may not know, but the fact that it has begun is the triumph of love; and our understanding and acceptance of that is the triumph of the dramatist.

3. *Brad*

The origins of *Brad* are to be discovered in the period immediately before and during the 1939-45 war in the series of weekly articles Saunders Lewis contributed to *Baner ac Amserau Cymru* between January 1939 and July 1951. The enormous task he set himself here was to develop, in almost total isolation for much of the time, an independent criticism of the European political situation. He began with the assumption that European politics during the years following the Versailles Agreements was dominated by the continuing struggle for economic supremacy between Germany on the one hand, Britain and France on the other. From this standpoint the efforts of both parties seemed equally legitimate, their propaganda equally biassed. In the hectic atmosphere of the last few months before the war Saunders Lewis tried again and again to disperse the clouds of misinformation, emphasising what he saw as the fundamental truth of mutual self-interest among the embattled states:

> Amddiffyn y sefyllfa bresennol yw polisi Lloegr; nid oes neb yn amau hynny hyd yn oed yn yr Almaen a'r Eidal. Pwynt ateb y gwledydd hynny yw bod y sefyllfa bresennol yn golygu cyflwr parhaol o anfantais iddynt hwy ac yn annioddefol iddynt; gan iddynt fethu ym mhob cais i newid y sefyllfa anfant[e]isiol honno drwy berswâd, rhaid iddynt geisio ei newid drwy rym; y mae Lloegr a Ffrainc yn gwrthod newid dim ar y sefyllfa ac yn barod i geisio rhwystro'r cais i'w newid drwy rym. Gan hynny, y mae rhyfel yn anochel.

> England's policy is to defend the status quo; no one doubts that, even in Germany and Italy. Those countries reply that the status quo represents a continuing state of disadvantage for them which is insufferable. As they have failed in every effort to change that disadvantageous situation by persuasion, they must try to change it by force. England and France refuse to change the situation in any way and are ready to try to resist the attempt to effect change by force. Consequently war is unavoidable. [6]

Nothing, he argued, should be allowed to conceal the fundamental economic nature of the conflict. Neither Danzig, nor Poland, any more than Czechoslovakia, was an appropriate cause of conflict. Nor should the clouds of moral outrage emitted by the British Press and the Government conceal the similarity of aims and methods employed by the major powers:

> Os yw Lloegr yn dal na ellir gwneud heddwch heb i'r Almaen wneud iawn am ei hanghyfiawnder yn y gorffennol i wledydd bychain, yna y mae'r un mor iawn i Loegr hithau ddechrau ar yr un llwybr. Gellir tybio y bydd ei hen gownt hithau yn ddigon uchel iddi arafu ei phrysurdeb i godi'r mater hwwnw. Yn ail, ofer hollol yw i unrhyw wlad a arwyddodd Gytundeb Versailles ddannod i'r Almaen iddi dorri ei gair. Paham na ellir am unwaith gael cydnabod y gwir — wrth gwrs fod Hitler wedi torri ei air; ni byddai ef na'i wlad yn y sefyllfa y maent oni bai am hynny. Mewn gwleidyddiaeth grym y mae pob llywodraeth yn torri ei gair pan fo hynny'n fanteisiol iddi. Gwnaeth Lloegr hynny ddegau o weithiau er 1919, felly Ffrainc, felly yr Almaen, felly Rwsia. Tinddu meddai'r fran wrth y wennol.

> If England maintains that peace may not be made until Germany makes up for her past injustice to smaller nations then by the same principle she should begin to tread that path herself. One may suspect that her own account may be sufficiently weighty to discourage her from hastening to raise the matter again! Secondly it is entirely pointless for any country which signed the Versailles Agreement to reproach Germany for breaking her word. Why may we not recognise the truth for once? — of course Hitler has broken his word; neither he nor his country would be in their present situation had he not done so. According to the politics of force every country breaks its word when it is advantageous to do so. England has done that dozens of times since 1919, so has France, so has Germany. And the pot calls the kettle black! [7]

The most frequent emphasis in this series of articles arises from the necessity of persuading his readers to dissociate themselves from the British tendency to "hypocrisy as a political method". This followed from a deeper conviction regarding the nature of European political life which sets him apart from others who might have shared the same aim. He saw contemporary conflicts in the context of the historical development of European society from the point at which the Christian ideal of human society as a reflection of the eternal City of God first rooted itself in the receptive soil of Roman civilisation.

Without reference to the spiritual dimension it is all too easy to misunderstand Saunders Lewis's view of European history. In particular, his constant reference to the multi-national Roman Empire as the starting point of distinctly European civilisation may see incompatible with his insistence on the ideal of the nation which motivated his own political activity. Saunders Lewis, however, never presented the Empire as the embodiment of a fully realized political ideal. Its relative importance derived from two factors: firstly, in that it introduced the concept of a long-term political order, allowing for social and cultural development and change; secondly that it provided a framework through which the Christian idea that human society proper should reflect Divine law could be disseminated. In his own day Saunders Lewis thought he was witnessing the final consequences of the abandonment of that ideal. All the peoples of Europe shared responsibility for what was happening in the degree to which they had failed even to attempt to order their affairs according to moral principles deriving from spiritual law. Even his own people shared that responsibility, though they might have claimed to be helpless, on the periphery of European politics and under the domination of another nation. So, in 1939, he told them:

> Cymry ydym ni, ac wrth ystyried achosion y drwg a'r drygau presennol yn Ewrop, yr unig agwedd sy'n gweddu inni yw cydnabod ein cyfrifoldeb ein hunain am lawer iawn o'r erchylltra, yn gymaint ag na cheisiodd y genedl Gymreig erioed er 1918 sefyll yn annibynnol dros gyfiawnder cydwladol yn Ewrop.

> We are Welsh and in considering the causes of the evil and the evils of the present situation in Europe the only fitting attitude fitting for us is to recognize our own responsibility for many of the horrors, in so much as the Welsh nation never sought at any time since 1918 to make an independent stand for international justice in Europe. [8]

The abandonment of this responsibility by the major European powers and the adoption in its place of various ideologies designed to justify their common economic imperialism was the fundamental cause of the political conflict, Saunders Lewis argued. Nor was this conflict merely a temporary phase, an inevitable part of the cycle of development in which different European nations exercised temporary dominance over the others. By 1939 a process of deterioration had set in which had released terrifying forces, the ultimate result of which would be the destruction of Europe altogether.

Hitler himself was one of these forces. Saunders Lewis was fascinated by his destructive capacity and his apparent invulnerability. The universal adoption of *Real Politik*, combined with the obvious injustice of Germany's treatment at the hands of her victorious rivals in 1919, provided Hitler with an opportunity. He appeared to Saunders Lewis as an angel of destruction. In March 1940, in a long report of Hitler's speech in Munich in which he celebrated his escape from an attempt on his life, we discover the seed from which *Brad* was to grow. Here Saunders Lewis refers to Hitler's claim to Divine inspiration and protection:

Y mae saint mawrion megis Siân o Arc wedi honni pethau tebyg. Y mae doethion pur ac aruchel megis Socrates wedi hawlio profiad o'r un natur. Nid yw'n annichon o gwbl fod Hitler wedi cael profiad a ymddangosai iddo ef yn oruwchnaturiol. Ers pum mlynedd y mae ef wedi byw gydag angerdd hollol eithriadol. Y mae dau beth y gellir eu dweud am honiadau fel hyn.Un yw bod gwr a gafodd brofiadau fel hyn yn ddyn peryglus dros ben y cyffredin o ddynion. Dyry'r profiad nerth ac egni ac ymwybod o ddiogelwch a sicrwydd personol iddo a'i gwna'n elyn ofnadwy. Yr ail beth yw bod y cyfryw brofiad yn rhagdybio byd ysbrydol; ond geill byd ysbrydol gynnwys ysbrydion y Fall yn gystal ag ysbrydion y Goleuni. Nid yw profiad goruwchnaturiol ynddo'i hun yn brawf o gwbl o arweiniad Rhagluniaeth. Gall fod yn gwbl fel arall. O gwmpas Hitler y mae Ewrop oll heddiw yn rhyfela, Rwsia anferth ac ymerodraethau enfawr Lloegr a Ffrainc, a'i ymerodraeth newydd wancus a nerthol ef ei hun. Awgryma ei eiriau ef, a'r cwr llen a gododd ef ar brofiadau ei enaid, fod nerthoedd mwy Titanaidd hyd yn oed na'r rheiny hefyd yn ymgodymu o'i gwmpas.

Great Saints such as Joan of Arc have asserted similar things. Wise and sublime sages like Socrates have claimed experiences of the same nature. It is in no way impossible that Hitler should have experienced something that seemed to him supernatural. For five years he has lived with wholly exceptional intensity. There are two things which may be said about such claims. The first is that a man who has had experiences like this is dangerous beyond the common run of men. The experience brings him strength and energy and awareness and confidence and personal security which make him an awful enemy. The second is that such experiences assume a spiritual world; but a spiritual world may contain the spirits of Hell as well as the spirits of Light. The fact that an experience may be supernatural is no guarantee of Providential guidance. It may be quite otherwise. Round about Hitler the whole of Europe is at war, gigantic Russia and the mighty empires of France and England and his own new, greedy and powerful empire. His words, lifting a corner of the curtain which conceals his soul's experiences, suggest that powers even more Titanic than those may also be exerting themselves about him'.[9]

To destroy such a creature, even in disobedience to the laws he had twisted to serve himself, could be no treason, though its failure might be treated as such and punished with truly devilish rigour. The failure of the inevitable attempts to assassinate him constituted an intellectual problem which his eventual suicide in the Berlin bunker in 1945 served only to increase. After the war Saunders Lewis read and studied the various accounts of the conspiracies against the Fuhrer, from H.B. Gisevius's *To the Bitter End* (English translation 1948) to Wilhelm von Schramm's account of the 1944 bomb plot, whose appearance in English could not long have pre-dated the composition of *Brad*. This last conspiracy was the best organized of them all, involved a large number of the highest ranking serving officers and must have appeared almost certain of success. Its failure was at once remarkeable and disastrous because it concluded with the complete demoralization of the officer class and the destruction of the few institutions which embodied some of the remaining elements of Christian civilisation. Not that Saunders Lewis in any way idealized the Prussian Officer Corps. On the contrary, a proper appreciation of *Brad* depends precisely on an understanding that the disastrous collapse of the Corps resulted from the fact that they had for too long compromised with those tendencies in recent German history of which Hitler himself was the product. Nor in this repect were they exceptional. Saunders Lewis's whole analysis of modern European politics rests on the assertion that Germany is typical rather than exceptional and that neither the eventual destruction of Hitler nor even the long series of grotesque trials which followed the German defeat could truly disguise the spiritual collapse which *Brad* was designed to reveal.

Twelve years after composing *Brad* Saunders Lewis returned to the subject of the conspiracies against Hitler with his television play, *1938*, where he presented not only General Beck, the originator of the 1944 plot, but Hitler himself. The earlier play, however, does not present these central characters. *Brad* deals with a relatively peripheral but uniquely self-contained situation of the Staff Officers in and around Paris. The conspirators in Germany itself might claim to some degree to have been defeated by circumstances, but those involved in the attempted *putsch* which took place in France after the announcement of the supposed assassination of Hitler had no such excuse. Their failure was their own, a moral failure quite unmitigated by circumstances, which reflects not only on themselves and the exceptional circumstances of conspiracy and revolution but on the normal unexceptional world which had produced them and in which they lived. Saunders Lewis referred to the play as 'Trasiedi Hanes', a phrase which has a certain ambiguity lacking from the descriptive term, 'historical tragedy'. It implies rather, 'the tragedy of history', a kind of play where the characters, though free to act and react to circumstances to a degree which ensures their moral responsibility, are nevertheless implicated in an action which transcends their fate as individuals and to which, because of what they are, they are doomed to contribute.

With two exceptions all the characters of *Brad* are high ranking staff officers of the German army, highly conscious of the duty they owe to the Corps and committed to upholding its traditions and values. When the play opens we see them involved in the more or less desperate attempt to maintain a front in Normandy against the advance of the American and British forces. None of them have any illusions concerning their ultimate inability to withstand this advance, particularly because Hitler, having taken responsibility for the overall conduct of military operations into his own hands, refuses to allow the redisposition of forces allocated to the defence of Southern France. All of them know that Germany faces defeat now that Stalingrad has fallen and Russian troops are pressing forward on the Eastern front. With the precedent of 1918 at the forefront of their minds, they know that Hitler now stands in the way of a conditional surrender which could preserve German territory intact. At the very least a speedy resolution of the conflict in France would allow the advance of the Western allies to overtake that of the Russians and prevent the dismemberment of Germany.

Knowing this, several of them have become deeply involved in the plot to assassinate Hitler, namely General Stuelpnagel, the Military Governor of France, Colonel Linstow, the Chief of Staff in Paris and Colonel Hofacker, a member of the Governor's Staff. This conspiracy has proceeded with the knowledge of Germany's most charismatic and successful soldier, Marshal Rommel, who is prepared even for independent surrender in France. Rommel, however, shortly before the assassination attempt, is wounded and hospitalized. His authority as General in Charge of Western Forces has passed to Field Marshal von Kluge, who is unaware of the details of the conspiracy but has conceded his willingness to accept the authority of General Beck when he hears that Hitler is no longer alive. He is aided by his Chief of Staff, General Blumentritt, who is also uninvolved in the conspiracy.

The play begins on the afternoon of the day when the assassination attempt is to take place. It comprises three Acts, the second of which is set on the night of the same day and the third on the morning of the third day after the attempt. During the first part of Act I the conspirators learn of the supposed success of the plot; then, without the authority of Kluge, who is engaged on the Normandy front, they put into operation the projected plan to arrest the Gestapo and S.S. troops as a preliminary to accepting the authority of General Beck in Berlin and proceeding to sue for immediate peace in France. In the second Act, during a meeting between Stuelpnagel, Hofacker and Linstow and Marshal Kluge, they learn that the plot has not in fact succeeded, that Beck is dead and the Nazis firmly in power in Berlin. All concerned are aware that the consequences for the Armed Forces will be disastrous and that there will be a merciless and immediate execution of anyone even suspected of complicity and a final destruction of the last remnants of the independence and integrity of the Officer Corps. Because of Stuelpnagel's prompt and decisive action in arresting the Gestapo, however, the situation in France is by no means desperate. The way is open for Kluge, as military head in France, to seek for peace on his own initiative. This would save many lives, prevent the decimation of the officer Corps and protect the real interest of the German nation. A precedent exists for such action in the behaviour of General York who, during the retreat of the Napoleonic armies from Russia in 1812, agreed a new alliance with the enemies of France against the express command of his sovereign. Rommel would certainly have accepted this precendent and acted in the true spirit of the Corps. Kluge refuses to do so, preferring to keep to the letter of the code, arguing that he is bound as an officer by his oath of allegiance to the Fuhrer. He orders Stuelpnagel to release the Gestapo and deprives him of his command and in doing so condemns to death not only the conspirators and those associated with them but thousands of the troops under his command. This is the central act of treachery referred to in the play's title. His formal refusal to betray Hitler barely conceals, even from himself, the substantial betrayal of his caste, his subordinates, his country and, as Hofacker clearly observes, the cause of Europe as a whole.

In the third Act the title takes on new implications as we witness betrayals of a different kind. The focus of the play changes so as to permit the development of the more private relationships introduced in the first Act. Here two characters who were not modelled on the personages of the historical drama are given the opportunity to act more freely than before. They are Stuelpnagel's secretary, the Countess Else von Dietlof and the head of the Gestapo and the S.S. in France, General Karl Albrecht. Else shared little with the Countess Podewils, who played the same role in real life. Albrecht, Saunders Lewis said, was a "synthetic" character, the "picture of a type and the ideas of the type." The dramatist needed them so as to develop the inner dimension of the public action and to convey to his audience the full extent and kind of the corruption which has penetrated every aspect of the world in which his characters live. Both Else and Albrecht take part in the public action of the play, but in relation to the central character, Hofacker, they also contribute to an action which at first appears subordinate but which later comes to seem the main plot of the play.

We become aware that Hofacker is indeed the central character when we learn that he and Else are lovers. Up to this point, which occurs midway through the first Act, the situation presented in the play has a certain openness about it which is lost from then on. Until then although the characters are in a state of tension, not knowing whether the plot has succeeded or not, the audience are not, for they already know that it has failed. This knowledge must also affect their response to the debate between Albrecht and Hofacker and Stuelpnagel in which the ultimate issue of the action is bluntly presented:

> Albrecht: Mae'r dydd yn agos y bydd y fyddin i gyd, corps y swyddogion hefyd, dan awdurdod Himmler.
> Stuelpnagel: Y dydd hwnnw bydd traddodiad Corps y Swyddogion ar ben.
> Albrecht: Y dydd hwnnw bydd brad ar ben.

> Albrecht: The day is at hand when the whole army, including the Officer Corps, will be under the authority of Himmler.
> Stuelpnagel: When that day comes the tradition of the Officer Corps will be at an end.
> Albrecht: When that day comes treason will be at an end.

The audience must be aware of the irony which arises from their knowledge that what Albrecht predicts and Stuelpnagel fears will actually come about. This irony, of course, is complicated by that arising from the conspirators' momentary expectation of the news from Berlin which will be the signal to take the action against Albrecht which eventually brings the Act to a close. However, the audience have as yet no means of understanding the deeper meaning of Albrecht's words, which is quite beyond his own understanding and will remain so. When the Gestapo triumph treachery will indeed be at an end, because there will be nothing left to betray. By that time the forces already at work in the world will have worked themselves out quite thoroughly. There will be nothing left but to face desperation in whatever way possible, with those few scraps of dignity which invest tragedy with meaning and increase its pain.

It is in the conversation between the two lovers that the audience begin to be aware of the inner meaning of the circumstances. Their mutual love makes them particularly vulnerable and in dramatic terms, particularly interesting, in much the same way as Marc and Iris in *Gymerwch Chi Sigaret?* Sharing the same excruciating sensibility that love brings, they also seek some kind of protection from circumstances. Fearing the worst, in spite of all the care and caution that has gone into the planning of the assassination attempt, Hofacker tries to persuade Else that she must stifle her feelings and banish him from her thoughts. Her reply is unanswerable: "I don't think about you, you silly fool. You are my thoughts".

Even when we first hear these words, of course, we know that Hofacker's worst fears will be realized. This makes it easier to recognize in him one of those exceptional characters endowed with the ability fully to reflect on their own experience even as they live it. It is the level of his awareness of what is happening to them which adds the inner dimension of tragedy to the public events. In a sense whether the plot succeeds or fails is irrelevent to Hofacker; the mere fact that it could fail is enough to make him realize that love, under the conditions in which they now live, is a weakness which threatens the last vestiges of civilized life. For love may undermine the will, consenting to any humiliation in order to preserve illusion. In a world in which all choices were open this would not be so. In such a world Luned of *Gwaed Yr Uchelwyr* might preserve her love and the dignity of her family, Marc might delay the moment of his commitment indefinitely without harmful consequences. As Hofacker is quite aware, however, their world is increasingly restricted, a world in which one choice cancels out another and in which the overall, inescapable commitment to risk everything in the name of patriotism and honour has already deprived them of the freedom to love. "I had to take the chance", he tells Else, "though there is scarcely a hope of success". That remaining

ray of hope, in fact, is irrelevant, because it is unreasonable. The choice
he has made would have been made even had no hope existed. It is
made on the understanding that the individual may not in the final
analysis be able to affect the nature of the world in which he lives and
will have to find some way of asserting his independence of it. Love is
an acknowledgment of the world and needs the world for its fulfilment.
Where that world is irremediably corrupt reason demands a total
withdrawal because that is the only remaining form of freedom and
the only remaining way to acknowledge the meaning of love.

Hofacker refuses to contemplate suicide in the event of defeat. To
escape from the world would be to acknowledge its power; he chooses
to remain in the world on his own terms. The price he must pay for
this decision is twofold: the deliberate denial of the demands of love;
and the exquisite physical and mental pain of torture, followed by slow
and certain death in the cellars of the Gestapo. In the event he is also
obliged to suffer the pain of what he sees as Else's betrayal of him, the
final betrayal of the play.

What Else does is quite natural and quite consistent with her love for
Hofacker and nevertheless a betrayal of that love. In the final Act of
the play Albrecht proposes a bargain; if she will willingly spend the
night with him he will authorise a pass which Hofacker may use to
escape the consequences of the conspiracy. The point at issue here is
not whether such a sacrifice on Else's part is too light or too heavy a
price to pay for the preservation of the man she loves. Such a mortifi-
cation of the flesh would disturb neither Hofacker nor Saunders Lewis,
were it possible thereby to attain a good end. The point is twofold:
first that Hofacker, having consciously rejected the world, is simply
not there to be saved in the flesh; and that to accede to the bargain
offered by Albrecht is not only pointless but positively harmful,
consisting in an acknowledgement of his terms rather than her lover's.

In this third Act the character of Albrecht undergoes considerable
development, to the point at which he can be seen to stand over against
Hofacker. In the first Act Albrecht had functioned rather as the type
of the Gestapo officer, representing everything that truly civilised man
might be seen to reject. Saunders Lewis takes advantage of his absence
from the stage in the second Act and the traumatic events which have
taken place in the interval to motivate a considerable change in him.
When Albrecht presents himself at the beginning of the third Act his
confidence has deserted him. By now he too feels betrayed and
abandoned. Saunders Lewis allows him a long speech in which he

fleshes out the skeleton of the Nazi type, whose loyalty to Hitler and National Socialism was bred in the gutters of the Weimar Republic and fuelled by the humiliation and starvation of the bitter post-war years. Obliged at last to recognize the inevitability of defeat and the disintegration of the solid world which Hitler had created, Albrecht, too, must decide what to do. Like Hofacker he must exercise his human freedom, though in the bitterness of defeat.

The choice he makes is diametrically opposed to Hofacker's. A creature of the material world, he chooses destruction within it. "Well, as there are only a few days left," he tells Else, "I will insist on getting revenge...revenge and pleasure together, together, Else." In a very real sense Else's acceptance of the bargain is an acceptance of him and a rejection of Hofacker, for the point at issue between them by this time is quite clearly the one which was at issue earlier between Else and Hofacker. At that time she avoided choice, playfully, but by now choice is unavoidable and when she chooses our memory of her words in that earlier scene should help us to understand the deeper implication of her action.

Hofacker had put the issue quite bluntly to her in the first Act: "Else, if not for your own sake, then for mine..." For his sake she tells him, she would endure the torture of the Gestapo, or even the worst torture of Albrecht's bed! But when she eventually agrees to that sacrifice it is not for his sake at all, but rather so as to avoid facing the reality of the choice which he requires of her. This is a betrayal of their love, which her last despairing embrace of his body does nothing to mitigate.

Else's bargain turns out to be doubly pointless. Hofacker would never have used his pass; but in any event, circumstances prevented it. Else comes in to give it to him as Albrecht, having by now received formal instructions from Berlin, is arresting him:

Iarlles: Cyrnol von Hofacker, dyma'ch pass chi i fynd i Berlin.
Albrecht: Frau Iarlles, mae'r Cyrnol yn mynd i Berlin a 'does dim angen pass.
(Mae hi'n estyn ei dwylo i'w rhoi am wddf HOFACKER, ond yn syrthio ar hyd ei gorff ef i'r llawr. Nid yw yntau'n agor ei lygaid. 'Does neb yn symud. Mae'r llen yn disgyn.)

Countess: Colonel von Hofacker, here is your pass for Berlin.
Albrecht: Countess, the Colonel is going to Berlin and has no need for a pass.

(She reaches out and puts her arms around HOFACKER's neck, but sinks to the floor, still holding on to him. He does not open his eyes. No one moves. The curtain descends.)

This final tableau fixes the relative positions of these three characters with remorseless clarity, ensuring that we are left with the clearest memory of the personal implications of the action. We must also remember, however that *Brad* is a tragedy of history rather than a personal tragedy. Right through this last scene, even up to the final moments, we have been aware of the debate which the central characters carry on among themselves, often angrily and with bitter conviction. Albrecht, for example, is quite aware of the moral and philosophical stand taken by Hofacker: his bargain with Else is also consciously an argument against her lover; and he refers to this debate even in his last words to Hofacker: "Romantic fool! Do you think that pain is meaningful?"

Nowhere in the play are we able to escape from the knowledge of how intimately the personal and the public are intertwined. What we learn from the painful developments of the final Act is how the struggles of the individual may dignify the destructive workings of history so as to raise it to the level of tragedy. The play is designed, however, to ensure that Hofacker's denial of the world reinforces our awareness of the nature of the historical process. *Brad* contributes to the age old debate concerning the relationship between man and the world he lives in. It raises two fundamental questions which are linked together: are we free to decide our own destiny?; and is our experience ultimately meaningful? Albrecht, of course, would answer no to both questions. Hofacker could answer yes to neither and yet insists on behaving as if it were not possible to do so. By means of his painful struggle he does create a measure of the freedom in which he finds it so difficult to believe and in doing so invests the action with the dignity of tragedy. Saunders Lewis has great admiration for him. Yet he presents him as a creature of the world he lives in, compromised by it and so implicated himself in the web of treachery in which he struggles.

In order to understand where Saunders Lewis himself stands we must go back to the end of the second Act, to the point when the officers, bitterly disgusted with Kluge's cowardice, leave the stage. At this point, of course, the audience's appreciation of Kluge's treachery is complete. Watching Stuelpnagel, Linstow and Hofacker leave, to face certain death, they are painfully aware of what Kluge's action

means. This is a dramatic moment which Saunders Lewis might well
have chosen to end the Act, leaving us free to reflect on the historical,
public action on which the play is based. However, he chose to
continue after the officers have left, giving us a short scene between
Blumentritt and Kluge in which the latter reveals the personal factors
which have motivated his treachery, namely the financial debt from
which Hitler had rescued him some time before. The most striking
thing about this scene is that although it is anti-climactic it also seems
completely natural. It is not actually a part of the action as it has
developed up to this point because it adds nothing to the sum total of
treachery nor has implications for the other characters. But of course,
it satisfies a demand which must have been growing in our minds
throughout the preceding scene, that is, the demand for an explanation
of behaviour which is almost impossible to accept. This short scene,
where we learn why Kluge has betrayed his colleagues, his caste, his
responsibility as an officer and a patriot confirms a suspicion which
must have been present in our minds throughout the dramatic scene
which precedes it. It must also oblige us to reflect on something which
we might not have noticed earlier, namely our intense disappointment
at the fact that the officers accept Kluge's treachery and in doing so
allow themselves to be implicated in it, in spite of their bitter recognition of what it is. Later on Linstow exclaims that they should have shot
Kluge then and there. That is in fact precisely what they were bound
to do according to the logic of their own arguments and their interpretation of their oath as officers. Each one of them had accepted a much
more serious act, the assassination of Hitler, but of course that murder
was to be committed at a distance and did not involve someone whose
authority they accepted. They could argue that the oath to Hitler had
been extorted from them. Nevertheless we must notice that the essence
of their position is that any oath which impedes their fulfillment of the
higher duty to their fellow Germans and their fellow men should be
set aside. The astonishing thing is that none of them see at the time
that this applies to the oath of obedience within the Corps.

If they fail to see this it is important that we should not, for their
failure to act against Kluge is as much a treason as his refusal to accept
authority. Not that they share his moral cowardice. It is merely that
they do not understand the full range of their own responsibility. Not
one of them, including Hofacker, believes that it is open to him to take
the responsibility which Kluge abrogates. Rommel, of course, might
well have done, but Rommel, in Albrecht's terminology is a Romantic,

that is, someone who is in no way compromised by the materialistic view of the world of which the Gestapo chief is merely the most outspoken representative. Albrecht insults Hofacker with this abusive title, as we have already seen, because Hofacker refuses to accept the ultimate consequences of the materialistic view. Yet Hofacker's problem is that he is in fact insufficiently Romantic; he too is compromised by the world.

Rommel, of course, was struck down by bitter chance the moment before the conspiracy matured, his fall demonstrating quite indisputably that man is at the mercy of accidents in the material universe. Saunders Lewis's main point is that he remains free in the human world, even though he may deny his own freedom. The tragedy of this particular period of history, which the circumstances of the bomb plot dramatically reveal, is that European society has been so deeply penetrated by materialism that even the very best of men have lost confidence in themselves. The world of *Brad* shares much with that described in W.B.Yeats' poem, 'The Second Coming':

> Things fall apart; the centre cannot hold;
> Mere anarchy is loosed upon the world,
> The blood-dimmed tide is loosed, and everywhere
> The ceremony of innocence is drowned;
> The best lack all conviction, while the worst
> Are full of passionate intensity.

Hofacker recovers some conviction, of course, but only by means of abandoning the world. In the second half of the play Saunders Lewis introduces the character of Blumentritt in order to ensure that we understand exactly what he is saying about history. Blumentritt, increasingly involved in the public world after the failure of the *putsch*, develops as a foil to Hofacker. He is an indisputably honourable man, morally sensitive yet capable of action, committed to the world as it is, essentially sane. During the aftermath of the *putsch*, while Albrecht and the Gestapo are riding high, he does what he can to reduce the consequences of his colleague's treason, but this is pathetically little. In the final analysis Blumentritt is powerless to do anything but co-operate with Albrecht and hope for the best. As Linstow puts it, Blumentritt succeeds in doing no more than dignifying their shame, in which himself he is fully involved. Blumentritt is a reliable man, but quite ineffective. The circumstances in which he finds himself require something more, of which he is quite unaware. Against his innocent ineffectiveness, which can do nothing to save the world, the bitter intensity of Hofacker's passionate rejection of it derives greater force. Nothing can save this world but the passionate search for another kind of freedom, ultimately attainable only through death.

4. Esther

Two main Biblical versions of the story of Esther exist, in Hebrew and in Greek. The former, a shorter version, is that included in Protestant Bibles, the latter, part of the Apocrypha, is included in the Bible by the Roman Catholic Church and is the version which Saunders Lewis used. Set in Persia in the Fifth Century B.C., it tells the story of how King Ahasferus of Persia gives a great feast, at which he sends for his Queen, Vashti. Angered by her refusal to come, Ahasferus follows the counsel of his ministers and abandons Vashti. Then, to replace her, he orders that beautiful girls be selected from throughout his realms. From among them, unaware of her race, he chooses the Jewess, Esther, who had been brought up since her parents' death by her cousin, Mordecai. Through Esther Mordecai is able to warn the king about a plot against his life by two of his ministers. Shortly afterwards Ahasferus elevates Haman to the rank of chief minister and because Mordecai refuses to bow down before him Haman persuades the king to authorise a massacre of all the Jews in his realms, arguing that their particular religious customs make them a danger to the state. Mordecai then goes to Esther and begs her to intercede for her people, though it is forbidden on pain of death to approach the king without being summoned and Vashti's fate is a clear warning of the likely punishment for disobedience. Braving the danger Esther is forgiven. She invites Ahasferus to a feast, with Hamam, and then to another one. Still angry with Mordecai, in spite of the honours lavished on him, Haman determines on his immediate destruction. On the advice of his wife and his friends he has a high gallows built for the purpose and intends to asks the king's permission to hang him the very mext morning.

In the meantime, however, unable to sleep, the King is reminded by reading the Chronicles of his reign of Mordecai's valuable service and asks his chief minister's advice as to how he should honour him. Haman, having mistakenly thought the honour intended for himself endures the bitterness of administering it to Mordecai. Returning home, he is warned by his wife that he is likely to meet further discomfiture at Mordecai's hands. Then, going straight to the second feast, he is denounced by Esther as her persecutor. Angry, the King goes to the garden to reflect, returning to see Haman huddled across the couch where Esther lies. Infuriated, Ahasferus orders his immediate execution on the gallows he had run up for Mordecai. The royal favour passes to the Jews, the proclamation is reversed and bloodily implemented against Haman's family and other enemies of the Jews. Mordecai, in gratitude for their deliverance, institutes a special feast.

Like many ancient narratives, the Book of Esther gives us detailed accounts of the behaviour of its characters but tends to be vague about their motives. So much of its 'meaning' has disappeared with the original audiences who could be relied upon to interpret it correctly. The Hebrew version is particularly inexplicit and the Greek redactor, who was writing for a particular audience, evidently felt that it left too much room for doubt concerning some important matters, like Mordecai's refusal to bow to Haman and Esther's response to Ahasferus.[10] Consequently he attributes to them long prayers in which Mordecai makes it clear that his reason for refusing to bow to Haman is respect for the Almighty – "I will not bow down to any but to you, Lord" – and Esther states that she hates "honours from the godless" and loathes "the bed of the uncircumcised." This leaves her position quite clear as one of the Jewish heroines, like Judith and Jael, whose awareness of the demands of the world are swallowed up by their sublimely confident faith. A problem remains in relation to Mordecai, however, because his respect for God does not prevent him from paying respect to Ahasferus.

When Saunders Lewis came to adapt the story he overcame this difficulty by attributing Mordecai's stubbornness to his knowledge that Haman was involved in the plot against the life of the king. He then had to explain why Mordecai kept this knowledge to himself instead of sharing it with Esther and later, when questioned by Ahasferus, confessing it openly and so defeating his enemy. Typically he saw in this difficulty an opportunity for developing the character of Mordecai and taking the action of the play in a new direction. Within the quite unambiguous framework established by the Hebrew author and without adding anything beyond the detail provided in the Greek version, he saw an opportunity for asking and answering those central

questions concerning human character and civilisation which had
preoccupied him for a number of years.

The striking combination of certainty and uncertainty presented by
the ancient text was something which had attracted the dramatist's
attention several times before and was to do so again. In this case,
however, we have to consider another text which must have mediated
between the Biblical story and the Welsh play. It is inconceivable that
Saunders Lewis would have been unaware of Racine's version of
Esther's story, which had marked his return to the theatre in 1688,
after an absence of twelve years. Racine's *Esther* is one of two plays
based on Biblical stories which he composed for performance by the
female pupils of the school established by Louis XVI's second wife,
Madame de Maintenon. Like its companion piece, *Athalie* (1691), it
betrays its purpose in its form and substance. In introducing a strong
choric element Racine saw an opportunity to display the graces of a
wider cross section of the young ladies of Saint Cyr than would have
been possible without it. In doing this, however, he was doing no more
than expanding a suggestion clearly made in the Hebrew story, where
Esther refers to her maids fasting with her in preparation for the
attempt to gain her husband's favour. He also took up other points in
the text which might have been intended as hints to a dramatist. The
Hebrew author's mention of Haman's wife, Zeresh, for example,
provided the basis for the introduction of a French version, renamed
Zarès, who acts as Haman's confidante, giving us the opportunity to
share his thoughts during the moments immediately before Esther's
feast. Where necessary, however, Racine was prepared to invent a
character quite without precedent in the original. So he equipped
Esther with her own bosom friend, Elise, whose six month separation
from her gives Racine an excuse to begin the play with a reunion and
immediately off load onto the audience a good deal of information
about recent events.

The primary emphasis in Racine's play is devotional: it celebrates
Divine Providence, which works even through human wickedness.
Racine accepts the traditional identification of Haman as a descendent
of the Amalecite king, Agag, killed by Samuel because he opposed God
through His chosen people, Israel. His Aman, however, is motivated
by overweening pride rather than racial hatred. Racine makes no
attempt to explain the Jew's refusal to bow to Aman; this aspect of the
story is absorbed by his preoccupation with Divine Providence. In
God's eyes, Mardoche tells Esther, the whole universe is as nothing;

And weak mortals, helpless toys of Death, / In his eyes are as if they were not."[11]

Racine's secondary concern was to compliment the King by associating Saint Cyr with Israel, and Louis with Ahasferus. This involved some difficulty because he had accepted from the Greek text the suggestion of Esther's revulsion from pagan practices, but he overcame it by incorporating into the text the traditional attribution to Ahasferus of responsibility for continuing the rebuilding of Jerusalem, interrupted since the days of Cyrus.

Saunders Lewis follows Racine in adopting these two important points, but he developed them much farther than Racine. In fact his reading of Racine must have sent him straight back to the Old Testament, where he gathered evidence to sustain his interpretation of the clash between Mordecai and Haman as an example of the ongoing struggle between the long suffering Jews and their implacable enemies. The confrontation between the Jew and the Amalecite, determines the frame of the drama; it begins with Haman's proclamation and ends with the elevation of Mordecai and Ahasferus's promise to rebuild Jerusalem. However, Saunders Lewis takes care not to confine the dramatic action within this framework. His play is by no means a simple demonstration of the workings of Divine Providence. Significantly the element of irony, so highly developed in previous plays, is relatively undeveloped here. This is because he is reading the story against the background of contemporary events. Esther saved her nation from the pogrom threatened in Ahasferus's Persia; no such heroine had emerged to lead the chosen people out of Hitler's gas chambers.

Throughout *Esther* we are reminded of how evil had so recently triumphed in the world. Evil, Saunders Lewis suggests, is the logical consequence of the human condition considered merely in itself. It can only be overcome by realising God in the world and this in turn depends on our ability to conquer the strongest principle of human nature and cast out fear. The unique importance of the Jews is that they are aware of themselves as the children of God and so believe that steadfast faithfulness to their own ways is the way to salvation. The strength of the Jews does not derive from pride or from a conviction that they are specially endowed, but rather from the fact that they are prepared to suffer. Their recognition that, as Mordecai puts it to Ahasferus, "Israel is the altar of the world," is what sets them apart. "We are ready to die," Mordecai says, "Ready for the concentration

camps till the end of time". This is the basis of Mordecai's own heroi
nationalism, which transcends selfishness and sentiment. "Do yo
understand what the Proclamation means?" he asks Esther and he
answer expresses the lively horror which characterised the humani
response to Nazi atrocities: "Death climbing in at our windows t
destroy the little ones? Yes, I understand". But Mordecai dismisse
her response: "That's happening all the time, in every part of the worl
Wherever there are men little children and babies are killed." What i
different this time is not that it is happening to them, but that Hama
is threatening their existence, as the witnesses of God: "That's ou
function, our task on earth to say that He exists. The Proclamatio
abolishes that".

Mordecai's strongest conviction is that man is present on the eart
not to avoid suffering but to act out his responsibility as an agent c
God. Esther accepts the same view and explains it to Ahasferus whe
he protests that the Proclamation cannot reach her in the palac
because her nationality is subsumed in his. "Today is the day of th
people's suffering. Because of that I am an Israelite...I am responsibl
for them". "Who taught you this?" Ahasferus asks her and her answe
is stunningly simple — "Cain".

For Racine the immediacy of dramatic performance was a means o
celebrating the workings of Providence through history and at the sam
time emphasising the differences between the historical and theologi
cal circumstances of Ahasferus and Louis. So he was concerned t
accentuate our awareness of historical differences. Saunders Lewis, o
the other hand, deliberately obscures our sense of the differenc
between the old and the new dispensation. For the Covenant betwee
God and man is unchanging throughout history: only mankind'
awareness of it develops. What was true for the Jews in ancient Persi
is now true for all men. Their dual responsibility to God and to thei
fellow men was still to be implemented through the medium of thei
own distinct culture and language. He emphasises this by deliberat
anachronism. The condition of the Jews throughout history is severa
times explicitly related to the position of his own nation in th
Twentieth Century. So Haman, at his most confident moment an
quite unaware of Esther's nationality, tells her that it is obvious tha
she does not belong to a subjected nation: "Every nation like tha
they're cowardly to the marrow of their bones. They will go to thei
destruction like sheep. You can drown their country under water an
they'll weep and take your charity". And in a different key he builds

number of New Testament references into Esther's central scene with Ahasferus. This gives us the impression that Esther is anticipating the Christian revelation by virtue of the heightened awareness that results from her having overcome fear.

The shape and substance of Saunders Lewis's play are determined by his and our historical perspective. If the central truths of Revelation are always with us, we rarely succeed in grasping them firmly. *Esther*'s success is exceptional. *Brad* had reminded us of more recent failures. In *Esther* he needed not only to dramatise the triumph of love and faith, but also to relate it to the world in which, so recently, the forces of evil had freely indulged in the most grotesque orgy of destruction against the very people whose survival the Bible story was composed to celebrate.

The action of *Esther* is developed through a series of debates between characters whose different attitudes represent different aspects of the human condition. Beneath the surface, however, the dramatist develops two largely independent sources of dramatic interest which reflect his awareness of both aspects of his subject. The first of these is the clash between Haman and Mordecai, where the problem of evil is defined in terms relating to the social and political world in which we live. The second is the relationship of the two lovers, who achieve a different level of experience, at which evil becomes in the first instance irrelevant and in the second ineffective.

The confrontation between Mordecai and Haman is the original source of the action and absorbs our attention at several important points. However, as Saunders Lewis presents it, the main factor in the development of the play is the love between Esther and Ahasferus, which is quite original to his version. This is in no way confined within the action arising from the original confrontation but represents an independent movement in itself and one which largely subsumes the other as the play goes on. In the third and final Act they are brought together, but hardly to be reconciled. At the beginning of this Act the action which began with the Proclamation is largely resolved; certainly at the point when Ahasferus goes out into the garden Mordecai's triumph is to all intents and purposes complete. Yet the most important scene of the drama remains, when Haman confronts Esther and begs in vain for her mercy. At this point a new dramatic focus is defined in the figure of Esther herself. In the calmness of her triumph she absorbs the energy of the debate which has developed in the course of the play.

The play begins with Harbona's reading of the Proclamation to the assembled messengers. The audience are likely to be struck immediately by the horror of its contents and the casualness, indeed, enthusiasm of its reception and to draw the obvious conclusion with reference to recent events in Germany. There is one element, however, which they may well fail to notice until Harbona mentions it to Haman a few moments later, which is that the Proclamation is deliberately cast in the very terms which Samuel used in his original invocation to Saul to destroy Amalec: "put him under the ban with all that he possesses. Do not spare him, but kill man and woman, babe and suckling, ox and sheep, camel and donkey." (1 Samuel XV, 3) We can hardly fail to notice Haman's savage irony and reflect on the horror of Samuel's unrelenting vicious revenge:

> Then Samuel said, 'Bring me Agag the king of the Amalekites', and Agag came to him reluctantly. 'Truly, death is a bitter thing' he said. Samuel said: 'As your sword has made women childless, so shall your mother be made childless among women.' Then Samuel butchered Agag before Yahweh at Gilgal.[12]

In this way Saunders Lewis is presenting us with questions similar but more absolute than those we encountered in *Gymerwch Chi Sigaret?* and *Brad*. How may we come to terms with brutality and destruction, when we find them in others or in ourselves?

Haman has answered this question to his own satisfaction by taking on the thing which frightens and disgusts him. Through the medium of his conversation with Harbona, Saunders Lewis presents us with two conflicting principles. Harbona's whole character is a development of the opportunism encapsulated in the one brief contribution permitted him in the Biblical story. Harbona's attitude to life is superficial, but is founded on a frank acceptance of human limitations. By contrast Haman seems to possess greater depth and intensity of feelings. The discussion between them quickly comes to turn on one point; whether the past has authority in the present. Harbona protests, "...nobody revenges a five hundred year old offence...Five hundred years ago not even the Persian empire existed". Haman's reply has apparent authority: "Agag existed. Samuel existed. The Jew exists today. I exist, too". In conversation with the cooly uncomprehending Harbona, however, Haman soon reveals that he is adopting the past as a means of rationalising the present. The fondly preserved image of

Samuel, "with the foam and the lice on his beard, butchering Agag in Gilgal" is actually no more than a way of relating to the reality of Mordecai.

At this point Saunders Lewis brings Mordecai on stage. Clothed in sackcloth and ashes, he climbs the stair that leads to the palace antechamber, pauses and looks at Haman. In the conversation which follows we are given the key to Haman's hatred, though we are unable yet to appreciate it as such. For Harbona Mordecai is the man who saved the King's life by revealing the plot against him, Haman the judge who disposed of the conspirators with suspicious haste. Harbona has no interest in Mordecai's motive in refusing to honour Haman, but accepts it unquestioningly as a justification of his desire to revenge himself against the whole Jewish nation. He is quite unable, however, to understand the perverse desire behind Haman's vengefulness. Haman's ruling passion is the desire for that illusion of power which alone can compensate for his own human weakness. For Haman ruling the human world, which is the art of politics, provides an opportunity for rivalling God himself, whom he is capable of perceiving only as the instrument of death. Death for Haman is the ultimate reality, and he is conscious of power only in so far as he can administer it to others.

Through Haman's meglamanic speech Saunders Lewis reminds us of Auschwitz and Belsen, of Hiroshima and Nagasaki and looks forward to the ultimate horror of nuclear combat:

> Mi fedra'i ddychmygu y daw dydd rywbryd y gall rhyw un dyn, prif weinidog neu gadfridog, gymryd pelen o dn yn ei ddwylo ac yna, o'i thaflu hi, ddifa'r ddynoliaeth i gyd, rhoi'r byd ar dn. Pan ddaw hynny, Harbona, dyna ddiwedd y byd. Oblegid 'fedrai neb dyn wrthod y demtasiwn...y profiad o fod yn Dduw.

> I can imagine that a day will come sometime when one man, a prime minister or a general, will be able to take a ball of fire in his hands and then, throwing it, destroy all humanity, setting fire to the world. When that happens, Harbona, that's the end of the world. Because no one could resist the temptation...the experience of being God.

This is not so much a phrophecy as a reflection on past events and on human nature itself, which is strengthened by Harbona's response. He accepts it quite calmly as a neurotic symptom in one whom it will be much to his advantage to please and offers the solace of an immediate execution of Mordecai, which will remove the irritation, leaving nothing but pleasure behind. He also hints quite clearly this time that he understands the clearly related matter. Hanging Mordecai will be a means of burying the secret of the conspiracy against the King.

Within moments of Haman's exit to order the erection of the gallows Esther enters and a new phase of the action begins. We are prepared for her entrance by the interest and irony generated within the discussion between Haman and Harbona. Here we are already permitted to sense what the play will make abundantly plain, that Haman's brooding violence is far from being a form of strength. Harbona's apparently simple adherence to the pleasure principle, far from being merely the innocence of youth, represents the stuff from which human strength may grow. Harbona himself, sensuously aware of Esther, intuits the passionate strength we are later to discover in her, which permits no recognition of the perverted weakness of the wicked.

To begin with, the second half of this first Act seems to balance the first, as we become aware of the inner meaning of the contrast between Mordecai and Haman, the servant of God over and against the man who would rival Him. Mordecai is willing to accept his own and his nation's weakness. His faith in God swallows up his pride and his instinct for self-protection. The particular form of Revelation permitted to the Jewish nation is the fountain head of his passive strength and active determination. He will not act to save himself, but only to implement the will of God as revealed in the Covenant between God and Abraham and the prophets.

Mordecai's response to Esther's suggestion that it might be possible to seek reconciliation with Haman fixes our impression of the two men locked in irreconcilable conflict: "Reconciliation is impossible between him and the God of Israel. Reconciliation is impossible between him and me...Bowing to him would be treachery". It would be natural to expect that we should go on from here to explore the conflict more fully, especially as Mordecai's attitude is not entirely consistent, but we have to wait a good while for the information which resolves the inconsistency. Esther's reply to Mordecai effectively shifts the focus onto herself and there it remains for the rest of the Act. Appropriately she answers him with a quotation from the fifty-seventh Psalm, which corresponds to the quotation from Jeremiah, with which he began the conversation, warning her of the danger which threatened them over the head of the uncomprehending Harbona.

In what remains of the scene the action takes a new direction. We are expecting Mordecai's request that Esther go to Ahasferus and beg for the repeal of the Proclamation: so far we have no reason to think of her as anything other than an instrument in his hands, willing or unwilling. Suddenly, however, we are forced to see her differently. The experience of isolation has in no way weakened her sense of responsibility to her nation but it has changed her awareness of herself. Esther has been prised just far enough away from her own race to be exposed to a danger which Mordecai had not anticipated — she loves Ahasferus, in spite of the fact that love has no place in the court of a Persian king. And even now, as Mordecai begs her to go unannounced into Ahasferus's presence, she is suffering the agonies of doubt which follow his unexplained, month long absence from her. She cannot face the thought that the king may not extend his sceptre towards her in forgiveness and she fears this more than the death of her people, more even than the frustration of God's will. For Esther love has brought a new kind of living, which Mordecai knows no more of than Haman, but which the cynical Harbona, preoccupied with physical pleasure, would be more likely to understand. Rejection by Ahasferus would end this new life with a second death: "The death of the heart, the death of the soul, the disappointment which is a living death..."

When Esther agrees to go to Ahasferus it is not in order to save the Jews, but to prove his love. Her family, her nation, the debt to Mordecai, are all aspects of her love, attributes which she offers almost sacrificially. Mordecai plays on the sheer improbability of Ahasferus's love to sting her into action: "You're saying that to comfort yourself and convince yourself. And you don't believe it." And of course, at this point he is right. Esther can only say that it is true because it must be true: "My life depends on its being true." Mordecai is still a good way from understanding her. For him the other considerations still bear weight "The life of your nation, the promise made to the world, the sole hope of humanity, all depend on its being true." In the passionate intensity of her doubt he sees the chance to save all these — "I challenge you to prove that its true...You're lying to your own heart. There is a proof. You know there is. Love or death."

Mordecai's skilful manipulation brings Esther step by step to the climactic moment of rejection and commitment — "Shut up, you blaggard. Don't blaspheme. I'll go to him. I'll throw my life at his feet...And if I perish, I perish." Yet in dramatic terms Mordecai's rôle is subordinate to hers; he plays Iago to her Othello, Mephistopheles to Esther's Faust. The fact is that her weakness represents a kind (strength that neither he nor we have any notion of. Her doubt itse represents a kind of daring which has transformed the situation.

As Mordecai understood it, there was ultimately no danger becau it was inconceivable that God should fail to fulfil His own promise The meaning of faith is precisely that man can depend on God. Esthe however, forced into a dimension of experience for which Mordecai teaching has not prepared her, has unknowingly anticipated the Chri tian Revelation — she has put her faith in human love. And the strengt of her commitment is such that she drags Mordecai with her, althoug he doesn't understand that. "Love or death" he tells her. "Death is th law", she replies, summarising the basic tenet of Jewish and Christia teaching. But, Mordecai insists, "love doesn't come under the lav Love is free of the law". The law he refers to here is the Persian law but the form of his words must recall to our minds the teaching of th New Testament relating to Jewish Law, from which humanity has bee freed by the love of Christ. In the last moment before her surrend Esther protests, "I have no right to gamble on his love" and her wor remind us of Marc's desperate gamble in *Gymerwch Chi Sigaret?* an Phugas's advice to him there: "You've already lost everything exce your life. So throw your life on the table and bet that God exists' Esther's courage is greater than Marc's. She defies her fear and i doing so wins exactly that reward which Iris had desperately hope her husband might win for them.

The Second Act begins from a quite different position, developin the same debate which had begun in the conversation between Har bona and Haman. Harbona and Ahasferus, because they are so fa removed from each other, find it easy to discuss their innermo preoccupations. Ahasferus, his self-confidence badly shaken by Fasti disobedience, is racked with doubt and can envy Harbona's simple self-sufficient pleasure seeking. The idea of jealousy is the key to thi conversation, as to the earlier discussion between Harbona an Haman, as it reminds us of the essential isolation of each human being from which the love that Ahasferus longs for is the only means (escape.

Fear and doubt provide the link between this opening movement an the next scene, which returns our attention to the fundamental oppc sition between Mordecai and Haman. Sleepless, Ahasferus has bee reminded by reading the Chronicle of his reign of the plot against hir and of Mordecai's service. He calls for one of his officers to discus

ith him how he should reward Mordecai and it is Haman who
answers, entering with the intention of persuading the king to permit
im to hang Mordecai immediately. It is ironical that the more he
isists on the danger from the Jews the more aware Ahasferus will
become of the danger from which, due to Mordecai and Esther, he
as escaped. The working out of this irony provides the framework for
ie remainder of the Act. It is deepened by Haman's impression that
e is to be the recipient of the honours concerning which Ahasferus
uestions him. This conceals from him the fact that his insistence on
ie danger that surrounds Ahasferus will weaken his own position in
everal ways, of which we are becoming increasingly aware. Step by
ep he builds up his case for executing Mordecai, resolutely turning
very twist in the conversation back to the fact that the king is in danger
ntil he wrings from him agreement: "Very well, choose your Jew.
Vhich Jew?"

In the moment of Haman's triumphant reply — "The leader of the
ews in Susa" — Esther's approach dramatically breaks across the
ourse of the action, though the irony is sustained until the very last,
ith Ahasferus's defiant order: "Open the antechamber wide. Let the
ews come!" Of course, they do, in the person of Esther, but with her
ntry the irony lapses for a while. During the scene which follows we
orget the Jews' struggle for survival and enter the charmed circle which
urrounds the lovers. We have been prepared for Ahasferus's reaction
o Esther's entry by his earlier reflection on the fact that he owes his
fe to Esther: "Perhaps I've been losing sleep needlessly". We have
ess reason to anticipate the fearless devotion with which she wins the
omplete trust of her husband. Not that there is no precedent for this
1 the Bible; for Esther's attitude is precisely that of the bridegroom
1 the Song of Songs, who tells her lover; "For love is strong as
)eath,/...The flash of it is a flash of fire,/ a flame of Yahweh himself".
)nce again, however, Saunders Lewis draws on the New Testament
1 shaping the words with which his heroine calms her lover's anxiety:
Love casts out fear" (I John,4,18). Ahasferus's reply draws on the
sridegroom's speech from the Song of Songs again "Set me like a seal
n your heart,/like a seal on your arm". (VIII,6) The words with which
sther acknowledges this represent the most striking anachronism of
ie play, for she answers with a phrase from the closing sentence of
ie Hail Mary, from the Catholic Mass: "Holy Mary, Mother of God,/
ray for us sinners,/ now and in the hour of our death".

The basis of Esther's triumph is humility, a selfless and fearle
commitment to love. In following the strongest demands of her ow
nature she has transcended selfishness. The basis of her achieveme
is the courage with which she acknowledges and defies the existenti
anxiety which in the first instance love accentuates to the point of pai
Love is the greatest exposure of the self because it represents a tot
dependence on another person. In this sense love is an acknow
ledgement of the possibility of death, which in itself is intensely painfu
At the same time it is the most complete fulfillment of human natu
and the thing which human beings most fear. It is also, Saunders Lew
argues, the door through which we may approach God. This is wh
he makes his lovers play out for us the Divine Comedy buried in th
Scriptures. When Ahasferus adopts the words of the Bridegroom he
reminding us of the eternal act of surrender in which human natu
reaches fulfillment. And in adopting the words of the prayer to Mar
Esther is identifying her act of love with the fearless self-abandonme
of the Mother of God. Through them both the dramatist is celebratir
the union between the human soul and God.

What follows immediately is a return to the 'casual comedy' o
human conflict. Only gradually, beneath the sychophantic humour o
Harbona and Haman, we become aware again of the irony whi
accompanies the clash between the human and the Divine wi
Haman's dreadful lesson to Esther begins this process — "Mercifulnes
is the beginning of your fall". Her reply, which clearly foreshadows th
ending of the play, is anything but a comfortable irony: "I w
remember the Chief Minister's lesson. When it's a matter of politics.
won't go on my knees as I did today to beg for mercy". Ahasferu
breaks across this conversation, bringing momentary relief, and th
lighthearted exchange which follows serves to bring us back to th
main action which determines the framework of the Act. Amidst th
general rejoicing Mordecai's name will arise naturally as the savio
of the King and as the proscribed leader of the Jews and this coir
cidence will draw Ahasferus's attention for the first time to th
desperate conflict of which he has so far been kept unaware. Befo
this can happen, however, Saunders Lewis ensures that we understar
how strongly circumstances are working against Haman. Rememb
ring Esther's part in the defeat of the plot against his life, Ahasferu
picks up his earlier conversation with Harbona to remind us that h

has gained so much in Esther's love that nothing can weigh against it in the scales.

In fact Haman has already lost the battle against Mordecai and the audience must be strongly aware of this as they catch the scarcely concealed mockery of Esther's address to him: "And Haman, my lord Haman, Haman the Agagiad, the man whom the King honours before all, the King's hand maiden also honours you". Already she is assuming control of events, bringing his thoughts carefully back to Mordecai: "The man whom the King honours! Thanks for that word Esther. I had almost forgotten". The irony of the conversation which follows, as Haman complacently describes the honours which he assumes are intended for himself, emphasises the weakness of his position. This is revealed to him only gradually, but we must be waiting all the time for the King's realisation that the man whom he is discussing with Haman is the same as the Jew to whose immediate execution he has already been persuaded to assent.

At this point in Racine's play he took care to maintain dramatic suspense by having Ahasferus remind us that his recognition of Mordecai's service in no way affects the edict against the Jews: "No less for this will I condemn this hated people".[13] So his Esther is left with a good deal to do before the security of the Jews can be assured. Saunders Lewis works quite differently. His Ahasferus clearly foreshadows his later rejection of Haman before sending for Mordecai: "I have no wish to judge rashly...There may be some mistake. I must hear your report on the Jews again...Harbona, where is this Jew?" In this way the dramatist frees the audience to accept the final movement of the Act on its own terms. For the first time Ahasferus is faced with the reality of Judaism. In the person of Mordecai he confronts exactly that humility, the essential selflessness which he has already recognized in Esther.

In one important sense Ahasferus and the audience are at one in the scene which follows, understanding so much and accepting more. Mordecai is still in some measure an unknown quantity to both. Ahasferus has already prepared us for the action of the final Act, which is to reveal Esther fully rather than resolve the conflict between Haman and Mordecai. In this last action, which is to order the ritual annointing by which Samuel identified Saul and David as chosen by God, he acts as King, the agent of Divine authority, whom Esther has seen in his glory as the angel of God. His words not only order the elevation of Mordecai but also foreshadow the annointing and the Crucifixion of the Son of Man. Everything done to Mordecai here in the Persian court was again to be done to the Messiah, "the annointed one" in course of time. Only then would the revelation foreshadowed here be complete, in the paradoxical union of pain and joy.

The third and final Act of Esther begins with the sensuousness of the Song of Songs. This is a direct reminder to the audience of the fact that Esther's spiritual achievement is rooted in her sensuous nature. It also gives Saunders Lewis an opportunity to develop our awareness of the interdependence of the spiritual and the physical. The different ways in which Haman, Ahasferus and Esther respond to the song and the dance of the maidens in the sensuous setting of the moonlit palace gardens establishes a scale of responsiveness in which the spiritual and the sensuous become more intense in relation to each other. Haman's response is coarse in the degree to which he sees sensuous indulgence as a relief from the bitterness of man's experience. Ahasferus is at once subtler and simpler. If Haman's reponse represents the relative crudity of romantic poetry his master's vision corresponds to the classical aesthetic of Welsh poetry as Saunders Lewis had described it himself: "Pattern in movement, weaving the waves of the sea into intellectual ceremony and order, complexity becoming cynghanedd,[14] a kingdom many and yet one". Esther, however, suggests an aesthetic of sensuous self-abandonment, yet more refined. For her, again with deliberate anachronism, dance is a form of worship, one with the physical coupling of lovers and the Catholic Mass: "Worship. A king playing naked in the presence of God. Man and wife worshipping each other in the flesh. That's what dance is, a mass."

Esther makes this statement a means of moving on towards the revelation of her race and the discomfiture of Haman. Ahasferus asks her, "What kind of worship was tonight's dance?" and answering, "My worship for you..." she has the chance of saying it is also her farewell and of explaining why. "Today", she tells Ahasferus, "I was condemned to hang." In fact Esther has one serious difficulty left to overcome. In becoming Ahasferus's queen does she not abandon her own people? If so, how can the edict affect her? Ahasherus tells her "You have no nation but me". She answers by explaining that her responsibility to her people is another aspect of the confident self-possession which underlies her abandonment to Ahasferus. So she tells him that it is because the Proclamation condemns the Jew for that irreducible element of identity that she will stand with her nation

[T]his Proclamantion hangs the Jew for one crime only, that he is a Jew. And I, your Queen, am a Jew. I will die with my people."

Although not explicitly, the next scene will contain a proof of Esther's humility, of which she will be quite aware. Haman, meanwhile, is openly on trial and as the King presses him the only line of defence which is open to him leads him irresistibly to his downfall. Haman seizes on the one point of weakness in Mordecai's conduct, the fact that he has disobeyed the King in refusing to bow to his chief minister. And as he does this Esther leaps intuitively to the only possible explanation for his conduct that Mordecai knows of Haman's unworthiness, though he is unwilling to publish it and so destroy him now that he knows the King is safe. From this point on Esther hounds Haman, becoming indeed the tigress which Harbona sensed in her. Two traitors hanged without calling witnesses, without being quesioned, without torture to explore their motives, without an official record of the trial". She taunts Haman mercilessly, hardening the suspicions of the King with the very words Haman has chosen for his defence. Who would have replaced the King were the plot to have succeeded, she tells Ahasferus, but he whose thoughts are moulded by, "The welfare and interest of the kingdom...nothing personal".

In the scene which follows the allegorical element which Saunders Lewis borrowed from the Song of Songs, comes closer to the surface of the action. Ahasferus, as King, stands more obviously in place of God than before and the other characters reveal in relation to him different aspects of the relation between man and his Maker. Ahasferus sends for Mordecai, asks him to reveal what he knows about the background of the plot and threatens him with torture if he refuses. Later he asks Esther why she did nothing to protect Mordecai from his threat and she tells him; "I knew it was I who was on trial". What is being tested here is the truth of her total dependence on Ahasferus and her own statement that she will act only on the principles she has announced. She will accept casual suffering gladly and will take arms only against that which threatens her essential selfhood and the love for Ahasferus which is its highest expression.

Mordecai's behaviour reveals a different stance. In fact the contrast between Esther and her uncle reflects partly the contrast between the Old Testament dispensation and the New. It also, more immediately reflects the contrast between the Calvinist tradition in which Saunders Lewis had been brought up and the Thomistic Catholicism he had adopted. Mordecai will act in reference to the world only in so far as it is possible to implement the will of God. Otherwise his freedom of action is limited by the injunctions of the law. To reveal Haman's complicity in the plot against Ahasferus is uneccessary: Ahasferus is already safe and thereby the rebuilding of Jerusalem, which according to prophecy he is to initiate, is secured. To implicate Haman would lead to the latter's certain death and Mordecai has no reason to undertake that responsibility, the salvation of the Jews being assured through Esther. To his own fate he is indifferent because it lies in the hands of Yahweh.

Mordecai's stubbornness, interpreted by Esther as, "a form of loyalty", contributes directly to the action in strengthening the impression which Ahasferus has formed by now of the integrity of the Jews. By contrast Haman's protestations of loyalty and innocence must sound false and by the time that Ahasferus goes out into the garden to reflect on the situation it is clear to the audience what decision he will come to. So although the last scene, which presents the consequences of his decision, completes the action on which the play is based, it is not the climax, which is reached a few moments earlier, in Esther's devastating triumph over Haman.

As Haman pleads with Esther for his life the contrast between them becomes more and more striking, until in the end she is left quite alone, the centre of attention. The basis of this contrast is that she is totally in possession of herself and he is remorselessly driven to realise that he is not. The basis of his weakness — and gradually we realise, the basis of his wickedness too — is his refusal to concede vulnerability. Like Dennis, the hangman in Dickens' novel, *Barnaby Rudge*, Haman cannot believe in his own death: "Hanging is something that happens to other people. No one in his right mind can imagine himself being hanged". [15] But of course both Mordecai and Esther have been prepared to contemplate their own end and have found greater strength in doing so. Haman's mistake throughout has been that he has stifled his own imagination, which in consequence has become fixed on the image of Mordecai in the image of Samuel. This image has obsessed him, governing all his actions. Confronted with the certainty of defeat and death, Haman destroys himself, collapsing into grotesque assertiveness, comic in spite of the disgust and horror it arouses: "Save me from hanging, Esther. Do you see, they can't hang me, they can't...'

By this time the drama is more or less over. The King returns to find Haman at Esther's feet, calls Harbona and orders Haman's immediate execution on the gallows he has erected for Mordecai. The latter is summoned and offered the post of Chief Minister and accepts it on condition that he is allowed to take part in the rebuilding of Jerusalem and that the Proclamation against the Jews is immediately revoked. Saunders Lewis in fact brings the action to an end far more abruptly than the authors of the Biblical story. Both the Hebrew and the Greek version give considerable detail about the reversal of the Proclamation and the Jews' revenge on their enemies. Racine avoids this but ensures that the main focus is firmly on the King as he explains the reversal of his decision: "Your king is no longer a prey to the counsels of the wicked. The veil has been removed from my eyes, crime is confounded..." [16]

By contrast in the Welsh version the focus of attention is kept firmly on Esther herself, a point of stillness amidst the flurried action. By now Esther occupies a position above that of the audience themselves. The laughter with which she replies to Haman's frenzied plea and the supreme confidence in her own intuition which is revealed in her explanation of how she knew of Haman's implication in the plot puts her just a little beyond the audience's sympathies. But this is in the nature of things. Esther has achieved a purity of emotion beyond the range of the audience. Sympathy directed to Haman is wasted, suggesting that we share his blindness to some degree. "Mercy, Esther, mercy!" Haman screams, failing to see that such appeals may only be made to the God whom he has despised. Evil and suffering are not at Esther's disposal, though they have been at his. In his defeat he is farther from understanding her than ever and though we have a measure of wisdom ourselves, won through sympathy and concern, it is beyond the reach of art to teach us the confidence and objectivity which are won only by conquering fear. Esther is truly a heroine in the Jewish tradition, the stream from which flowed a great river, essentially human and yet, like Mary, exceptionally privileged in her faith.

5. Cymru Fydd

The title, *Cymru Fydd*, invites us to interpret the play as a political allegory. The term is ambiguous. It refers to the movement founded in 1886 to revitalise Welsh life and culture, which foundered ten years later on the sands of political division.[17] So it is a reminder of the disappointment of idealistic dreams. When Dewi Rhys, who in one sense is the play's central character, applies this phrase to himself he implies a bitter criticism of contemporary Wales.

Long before the action of the play begins Dewi, the son of a Nonconformist minister and a successful student of philosophy, has lost his faith in religion and in everything else. Dewi is unusual only in his nervous sensibility and his sensitivity to moral and philosophical issues. As his father remarks, nine out of ten people in Wales now share Dewi's inability to believe in anything. He differs from them only in being unable to distract himself from the consequent preoccupation with emptiness.

Dewi suffers from a quite literally fatal tendency to consistency, which arises in reaction to his own inconsistency. Isolated from others and with nothing to hold on to outside himself, he is unable to grow beyond the emotional dependency of the child. The same self-preoccupation which leads him to question the basis of religious faith in his own experience also prevents him from working through this stage with the help of his parents. For he is aware at one and the same time of a desire to challenge them and a desperate need for their approval. Consequently, after losing his faith, he continues to attend chapel with them and the resultant loss of self-respect gradually undermines his faith in himself and in them.

In Dewi's mind logical consistency, finely developed during his period of university study, grows side by side with emotional confusion. Step by step Dewi loses his grip on everything outside himself, ending in a fierce and defiant state of alienation. The last step in this process is taken as a result of his following his girlfriend, Bet, to a Welsh Language Society demonstration where she and her friends are physically maltreated by louts in the crowd, with the passive consent of the police. As Dewi later tells Bet, he went there to see if political commitment could give him anything to replace what he had already lost, "to see if Wales could put excitement in my life", but the reality of Wales, a people without respect for their country or their language, or themselves, sent him away cursing everyone and everything. "And the following Sunday night", he tells Bet, "I broke into a garage and stole twenty pounds".

Dewi has no respect for truth to the extent that he thinks it exists at all. He is consistent only to the mood of the moment, wilful and childish in asserting what he wants himself to believe or others to accept. From the opening moments of the play and from the reaction of his own mother we learn that we must treat his assertions with scepticism. Yet on the other hand his view is severely logical and has a certain authority which is difficult to resist. Bet has little defence against his nihilistic assault on the beliefs on which her life is founded.

> Duw, crefydd, eglwys neu gapel, Cymru, yr iaith Gymraeg, dyna dy fyd di. Cred di fi, mae Capel Celyn dan y dwr yn ddameg o dynged Cymru a'i holl gapeli.

> God, religion, Church or chapel, Wales, the Welsh language – those things are your world. Believe me, Capel Celyn under the water is a parable of the fate of Wales and all its chapels. [18]

In fact much of Dewi's negative vision is shared by his creator. *Cymru Fydd* is founded on the mingled sympathy and pity of the author for a character who has seized with blinding clarity of mind on only one aspect of the truth. With neither past nor future, nor any resources but those he finds within himself, Dewi argues, he is left to create his own meaning. Consequently his choice must be to derive from the external world the most effective form of self-stimulus:

> Rhaid imi ddewis, a thrwy ddewis sefyll fy hunan yn wyneb byd a chymdeithas, troi byw yn sialens ac yn wefr. Herio cymdeithas, herio cyfraith a barn, dewis bywyd troseddwr a herwr. Dyna'r ateb i argyfwng gwacter ystyr.

I must choose and in choosing set myself up against the world and society, turn living into a challenge and a thrill. Challenge society, challenge law and judgement, choose the life of a criminal and an outlaw. That's the answer to the crisis of the emptiness of meaning.

Dewi is quite aware of where his path will lead him. He compares himself with Hitler, who had a nation and a country to play with, "and to give him the thrill of living and afterwards to die at his own hand".

Unlike Hitler, however, Dewi has only his own life to play with, so although the game will conclude in the same way, it will be easier to respond to the fundamental pathos of the player's situation. Because his 'philosophy' is a protest against emotional vulnerability rather than being based on its acceptance, Dewi lacks the strength to endure the world's rejection of him, he cannot accept imprisonment, nor work through his suffering to calmness of mind. Consequently he escapes from prison at the first opportunity, robbing and assaulting a traveller in the process, and sneaks back home. His return in these circumstances can be nothing but a spiteful gesture towards those whose continuing love frustrates and torments him. His mother understands this from the very beginning, when he slips in through the window from the darkening garden. Younger and stronger, Bet takes longer to understand and fights harder against it. The duration of the play is determined by this painful process, from which, in a sense, Dewi's suicide releases her and ourselves.

Though he sometimes claims to have deceived himself and even persuades Bet to do the same, Dewi is quite aware of the situation and even of the political dimension which the comparison with Hitler revealed. So he tells Bet, with spiteful playfulness, he is, "Cymru Fydd", suggesting that his doomed self-preocupation is an emblem of the state of Wales. The disintegration of the national movement and of Welsh Liberalism at the end of the Nineteenth Century, Saunders Lewis would argue, resulted from just that alienation from the past which Dewi viciously boasts. His life is thus a fulfilment in the individual sensibility of the drama played out in the political arena between 1886 and 1894. It is also an image of what lies ahead even for those, who, like Bet, so far cling to what he calls the "shibboleths": "Father, mother, country, language, love...", Dewi tells her in his final speech, "They're all claptrap". Only self-deceit, complacency and hypocrisy, Dewi says, protect Bet and the national movement from reality, and only the itch of lust distracts them from the bitter knowledge which is destroying him.

Bet's name, Saunders Lewis confessed, is a deliberate reference to the Pascalian wager which Phugas had urged on Marc in *Gymerwch Chi Sigaret?* "The unanswered prayer of the Christian", he had suggested in the Preface to *Cymru Fydd*, was a more reasonable alternative to the "hopeless faith" of the Marxist which Dewi rightly rejected. Bet's attitude is not only more reasonable, but more realistic than that of her lover, from whatever viewpoint it might be considered. While Dewi denies the reality of the past and consequently its influence on the individual, Bet acknowledges its existence in her. The individual moulded by the world, Bet would argue, can hardly claim to exist in total separation from it, though she puts it in a different way. "Can you believe in that stuff?" Dewi asks her, referring to religion, and her reply is simple and direct: "I can't do otherwise. It's in my blood".

With the same selfless selfishness which motivated Iris in *Gymerwch Chi Sigaret?*, Bet struggles to save Dewi from himself. Putting aside his childish project of escape to America, she offers him a future which can be gained only by accepting the past. That is, she urges Dewi to give himself up to the police, serve the lengthened prison term which now awaits him and come out of prison to start a new life with her. Dewi accepts this offer, but demands the compensation of sleeping with her that night. Bet agrees and comes down the next morning to phone the police in his name. When Dewi comes down, wakened by the noise of their arrival and learns that she has done this, he turns on her viciously in a way reminiscent of Pinkie's behaviour in Grahame Greene's Catholic novel, *Brighton Rock* (1938). At the end of this novel Pinkie's wife, expecting to receive his last message of love, walks away to listen to the gramophone record on which he has recorded his bitter rejection of her and of life itself. Typically Greene wanted us to be aware not only of her innocent suffering, but also of the perverted innocence of her husband, Saunders Lewis's aim is similar. It would not be unfair to look on *Cymru Fydd* as a transposition of the situation explored by the Catholic novelist to a Welsh setting and a dramatic medium.

The accepted reading of *Cymru Fydd* rests on the assumption that the ending of the action leaves Bet pregnant with Dewi's child and that this child, educated in the light of his mother's suffering, will indeed represent a different future Wales. This would represent, or at least imply, a new nationalism, drawing strength from the two streams of religious tradition native to Wales and would guarantee the continuation of the fight for a distinctively Welsh civilisation which Dewi himself had given up.

We have, in fact, no assurance in the play that Bet is pregnant, so we have no guarantee as to the future, but there seems little to undermine the restrained optimism of this allegorical interpretation. In a sense, however, although the presence of a political debate and an allegorical dimension is undeniable, it is almost peripheral to the play as such. The main dramatic focus of *Cymru Fydd* lies elsewhere. Dewi himself, though he initiates the action of the play and ends it with his suicide, is not really the central character. By the end of the play we have come to see that his childish refusal to face reality has reduced his status in dramatic terms to a level not far above that of the police Inspector who comes to arrest him. The play's main focus is on the state of mind and the suffering of his mother and father and Bet. Their rôle is of course far more passive than his — they have little to do other than suffer the consequences of their love and his defiance. Because of this *Cymru Fydd* is constructed in a way quite different to the two major plays which preceded it. The striking dramatic effect of *Cymru Fydd* derives from the way in which positive, almost melodramatic, action is off-set and pushed from the centre of the audience's attention by their awareness of its implications for characters other than those who initiate it.

The play begins with a phone call which we have insufficient means of interpreting at the time, though later we may assume that it follows from Dewi's escape from prison. All we know at the time is that the minister's wife is arranging an appointment for him with an unidentified caller later that evening. Immediately after this Dewi enters the room through the window and we receive our first positive piece of dramatic information. We may well fail to register it consciously at the time, because we are preoccupied with Dewi's dramatic entry, but at some level of consciousness we must notice the quality of his reception. A little later on Dewi himself will draw our attention to this, when he asks his mother; "Haven't you got a kiss for me? No word of welcome. Only Oh Dewi!" If anything Dora is slow to realise consciously the implications of Dewi's behaviour, as we see when she offers to put the light on and is rudely stopped by her son. But on another level she has learned her lesson well; she knows by now that there is no room in her relationship with Dewi for natural feelings. What has taken their place is the impersonal resentment which has grown from the discovery of a bitter enemy in the deepest recesses of her own heart. Though he understands so much, Dewi seems not to understand this. "It's a bit late to start worrying about your father", she tells him when he asks whether he is still in the Church: "Was it to prove your godliness that you came in through the window?" Dewi misinterprets her sharpness as an example of her characteristic wit. It certainly is that, but for Dora, it is a sign of a different, more instinctive feeling of revulsion, from which Dewi is only too glad to turn away: "Vomit isn't wit", she tells him.

This bitter remark concludes the first movement of the play, which has introduced Dora's problematic response to her son. The next phase of the action turns around another phone call, this time unanswered, because Dewi assumes it will relate to his escape. The conversation between Dora and Dewi turns to the question of how and why he has come home. In this conversation both Dora and the audience are deceived by his initial explanation of the circumstances – Dewi says nothing at this stage about his attack on the traveller and theft of his car and wallet. This is important for several reasons. First, because we share Dora's experience of Dewi and so are prepared to reassess our interpretation of her reaction later on. Secondly because it leaves us unprepared to assess correctly Dewi's reaction to his mother's urging him to give himself up. The severity of her logic has an ironical implication which we will come to understand only later, towards the end of the Act.

What is likely to strike us most forcefully in the first half of this scene, before the telephone rings, is the fact that Dewi is so sensitively aware of the implications of what his mother urges on him. "The way of the Cross, is it?" is his response to her which, of course, has implications for the Catholic Christian and for an audience aware of Catholicism which it cannot have for either character on stage. Dora's response to this is a powerful realistic argument, based on strong emotion:

> Mae hi'n ffordd dreng, nid i ti'n unig. Ond dyna'r unig ffordd. Rydw i'n fam iti. Ti yw unig ffrwyth 'y nghroth i. Mae dy dad wedi crymu ei ben fel hen wr ac yntau prin iawn yn ganol oed. Rydw innau...fel y gweli di. Ond mynd yn ôl i'r carchar, dy roi dy hun i'r plismyn, dyna ydy'r unig lwybr i ryddid, heno nesa.

> Its a rough path, not only for you. But its the only way. I'm your mother. You're the only fruit of my womb...Your father's stooping like an old man though he's barely middle aged. I'm as you see me. But going back

> to prison, giving yourself up to the police this very night is the only way
> to freedom.

The ringing of the telephone, the voice of the outside world, reinforces Dora's argument, but of course Dewi refuses to listen, physically
preventing his mother from picking up the receiver. His childish refusal
raises in our minds the question which his subsequent behaviour is
designed to answer.

Dewi sets out successfully to inhibit his mother's logic and get his
own way. In the process he persuades not only Dora, but the audience
too. There is no way in which they can resist the appeal which he puts
with all the bitter realism he has earned during the few short months
since his arrest. It is ironic that we are probably more prepared to
accept his description of the sexual exploitation involved in prison life
than Dora. She has learned better than to trust Dewi, telling him; "I
don't know this very minute whether you're telling the real reason why
you escaped from prison, or whether the whole thing's a trick to get
me to help you."

We later learn enough to begin to entertain the same doubts, for
Dewi presents us with another quite different explanation at the end
of the Act. However, at this stage Dora has the bitter advantage of
superior experience which sets her apart. Consequently her acceptance
of Dewi's plea is all the more striking. This phase of the action ends
with her complete capitulation, in spite of all that she has urged herself:
"Your room and your bed are just as they were. I'll put a candle on
the little table by the bed. If you draw the curtains and don't put the
light on no one will see as much as your shadow." With these words
Dora becomes an accomplice to Dewi's actions and a criminal herself.
This was the point from which the drama had begun to grow in
Saunders Lewis's mind. As she goes out to prepare food for him Dewi
picks up the phone and calls Bet, asking her to come to see him.
Moments later Dewi's father returns from chapel, quite innocent of
the circumstances. So gradually the consequences of his return spread
to affect others deeply involved with him and the dramatic focus of the
play begins to develop.

The action which follows Dewi's exit and the entrance of his father
delays for a while the development of the movement initiated in the
conversation between Dewi and Dora. The husband and wife discuss
the possibility of his resigning from his ministry and indeed, what
seems to him the impossibility of continuing as a minister now that he

has lost the moral authority on which his rôle as a preacher is assumed to rest. Their conversation develops through three phases which contribute differently to the drama. Firstly it raises questions about the Nonconformist tradition in which they have all been brought up. Dora's argument that her husband should continue in the ministry in spite of his doubts rests on a different, sacramental view of Christian ministry, which she supports by referring to Anglican practice.

In effect she urges that action may have spiritual validity even though it is difficult to justify on moral grounds and this obviously prepares us for the lessons which we are to learn during the two subsequent Acts. Secondly their discussion reveals the instinctive understanding and comfort on which their relationship is based. It is the background against which we learn about the essential isolation of the individual and the privacy and inaccessibility of his or her suffering. Thirdly, as John, so far unaware of Dewi's return, reflects on his condition in the prison, thus increasing his mother's wretchedness, we learn something further of the kind of vicarious suffering which is an inextricable consequence of love. The scene comes to an end in a way which accentuates our ironical awareness. Dora addresses us as it were, directly, over John's head, reflecting on the additional horror of the prisoner's situation, of which he is so far unaware: "I can imagine a worse horror, being locked in all night with someone I was frightened of". Then John, unaware of what lies behind her remark, refers to the possibility of Dewi's being given permission to work outside as an alleviation of his imprisonment: "That could save a lot of people from losing their grip". But not Dewi, as we already know. That very circumstance gave him the chance to comdemn himself to a worse punishment.

At this point their conversation is interrupted by the arrival of the policeman, whose formal reason for coming is to tell them that Dewi has escaped, but who also wants to see how they react to the information and to warn them of the consequences of sheltering the escaped prisoner. By the end of this visit we have learned, with Dora, the way in which Dewi actually got home. Immediately afterwards John goes out to the kitchen, sees the remains of Dewi's meal and guesses what has happened. As he returns husband and wife have an opportunity to take stock of the situation together. In his conversation with the policeman Dewi's father has shown that he has exactly the same attitude to Dewi's escape as Dora had already expressed and she by now has an additional reason for urging him to give himself up. During what remains of the Act, however, they come to accept what he demands of them, in full understanding of what that acceptance implies for him and for themselves. Neither has any illusions as to whether Dewi is capable of telling the truth. They know that he will manipulate their trust quite shamelessly. They also know why he is so inaccessible to them. Remembering, his father says, has no part in Dewi's life because, as Dora comments; "...he's still a child...Today is all that Dewi's got". In spite of this knowledge, they have to go on trusting him "even in his dishonesty", as Dora says, because that is the only way they can relate to him at all. And because of this they are unable to give him up and can only try to persuade him to do this himself.

Dewi himself comes in as they agree that this must be done and in what remains of the Act he strips from them the last shreds of confidence. As earlier with his mother, he is totally aware of what his father will try to do. John's first move is to make some kind of approach to his son and he does this by abandoning his own ground and arguing only on Dewi's own terms. As he does so Dewi quite brutally destroys the ground of his argument by showing that he understands John's motive and aim: "You think your love can save me". This goes so far below the surface to a level of consciousness that John himself has not yet expressed that it leaves him quite helpless. Dora attempts to recover something by insisting herself on the facts of Dewi's situation, but by now Dewi is in complete control. He presents them with another version of his escape which is sufficiently persuasive to provide them with a good excuse for giving him the time he demands. Then, with masterly control, he adopts the terms of their own faith to put himself beyond the reach of their logic. Dewi is an atheist, but he calls for a Bible, and on that he swears he will never return. The way he refers to it, using the terms of a tradition on which he has poured scorn and contempt − "the book of the Covenant" − might be designed to remind them that he is manipulating their response even now. But they can do nothing with that knowledge; as Dora's last action reminds us, they are lost and helpless in their love for him. Dewi breaks down and cries like the child he is and his mother goes to him and comforts him. What else can she do?

A good deal of the first part of Act II is taken up with exposition and explanation of the background to the situation. By means of the conversation between Bet and Dewi we learn about the events which led up to his imprisonment and the reasons for his behaviour. At the ame time the lovers engage in a debate which by now is important to he audience. They respond differently to a situation which they qually recognize as empty of meaning in itself. Bet's Christianity and :oncern for the future of Welsh language and culture rests on the same incertainty as Dewi's deliberate blaggardry.

The difference between them is gradually explained in the way they elate to other people. The scene turns around an exchange which)ewi himself fails to notice, but which is full of meaning for the iudience, "What is left for a man without a nation, without anything o believe in, without anything to be faithful to?" Dewi asks, passing wer Bet's echoing question, "Nothing to be faithful to?" as if he hasn't leard it. The fact is that her need for him doesn't exist for him; his xperience of need is purely subjective.

While this debate forms on the surface of the action there is a :orresponding movement at a deeper level. Only gradually does the iudience become aware of what Dewi is doing. The return home seems o natural in the first instance that they are unlikely to question its notive. Calling on Bet, too, in the first instance might be taken as innocent enough. But Bet knows her lover better than to take his ictions at face value and the question she asks him must force us to ook at him again, "Do you despise me...for coming?" she asks. His esponse is a movement towards her which she stops abruptly: "No.)on't. We've got to talk seriously, not play". The fact is that the greater iart of their love has been play, although for her at least it is also ntensely serious. Had it been so for Dewi too, she would not have teeded to tell him; "You didn't come home to see me". The implied juestion is not answered directly at this point, though we have a clear mough clue to it when Bet tells her lover; "You are disgusting...Because you're so sure of me". What has hurt Bet quite so deeply is her ieing kept in total ignorance of what Dewi was doing and thinking. Ier reproach for this stings him into a curse which tells us more about lim than almost anything else he says: "I never ever deceived you, girl. I could almost say that you're the only one, the only one, I never iurposely deceived. Damn you!"

Bet responds to this curse as Iris responded to her husband's blow n the first Act of *Gymerwch Chi Sigaret?* because she sees it as a proof if love, which indeed, it is. However, it is unlikely to set her mind at est. Dewi goes on to ask her if she still goes to Church and if she does vhether it is for the sake of her father, the Anglican Vicar. This is an ntroduction to a comment on his own history: "When I was on

holidays from college I went to chapel for my mother and father's sake
so as not to hurt them. That's where deceit begins". In Dewi's view of
things either he is right, or Bet: he can't afford compromise — either
he accepts his love for her and abandons everything else, or he destroy
himself in her eyes. Perhaps he comes close to capitulating, but in th
end he is afraid; it is better to die than suffer as she does and as hi
parents do, even though he knows they welcome that suffering.

Another visit from the police breaks across the action shortly afte
this. Dewi has to hide and his father brings the policeman into th
room unaware that Bet is there at all. He is also unaware of the natur
of the relationship between the two and in this case the policemen ha
the advantage of him. Unlike John, he is not at all surprised to see Be
there. The reason he gives for his visit is to inform Dewi's parents tha
the police have found the car he stole and know that he is in the vicinity
The others are quite aware, however, that this is one more attempt to
probe the situation and discover in their reaction how much they know
and what they feel about Dewi's escape.

Throughout *Cymru Fydd* the police represent an attitude to the worl
which all the other characters have abandoned. Their professiona
attitude embodies the assumption that social morality is an absolut
value and their appearances punctuate the process by which Bet, Dor
and John are progressively involved in criminality which eventuall
they cannot even regret.

The end of this visit marks the halfway point in the play, which i
also a point of no return for the audience. The scene which follow
between Bet and John draws them further into sympathy with wha
these characters are going through and into understanding of what tha
implies about life in the inner world represented by the theatre stage
From this point on, Dewi's parents and his lover are drawn farther an
farther into an awareness of the fact that they share Dewi's guilt an
even share a kind of guilt of which he is innocent. This is the guil
involved in taking on emotional responsibility for someone else'
welfare – another name for love. Neither Bet nor John seem to thin
that they have any choice. She tells him openly what she has alread
made clear to Dewi and to us in the preceding scene: "What can I d
Mr. Rhys? What can I do?...If he called me from Hell I'd go". In th
light of this confession he knows that his moral duty is to save her fron
the consequences of her self-abandonment and he does try to do thi
but when she refuses he leaves them together. His hope now is tha
her commitment can save Dewi and persuade him to give himself up

As usual, Dewi is quite aware of what is happening. As his father goes out he laughs and when Bet warns him – "Not a word about your father"– prohibiting his mockery of the implied hypocrisy, he accepts her prohibition quite happily, clearly confident that he can take her on and win the perverted game which he has come home to play.

"Very well, Great Lady..." Dewi accedes and gives her the initiative: "What shall we talk about now?" Her reply, taking up his challenge, is courageous — "About the future, of course". For she knows that she is talking to someone for whom neither the future nor the past exist. In the scene which follows she makes a desperate gamble on a love of which she is dreadfully unconfident. What she does is to offer herself as the reward for accepting the world as it is. The superficial playfulness of their dialogue only partly conceals the deadly earnestness of the combat between them. Bet throws away everything which she might have used to protect herself from Dewi because she knows that he might have used it for the same purpose. In proposing their "ecumenical union" to him she sacrifices every prejudice of class and culture: "Don't be so conventional, so bourgeois, so Welsh!", she tells him and in reply he makes it quite clear to her that she is risking everything else that she has: "Don't tempt me Bet. I've been pretty honourable with you". "If tempting you is saving you, winning you, I'm not ashamed to do it," Bet replies, ignoring the threat in his words. Once again he warns her – "You don't know. I'm a dirty pig". And again she ignores the threat: "I love you, pig and you know it".

The lovers come very close to complete honesty here. Bet confesses her need – "I want children, Dewi, your children". And in answer to her complete self-abandonment Dewi wonders at her courage – "Tell me, are you in your right mind?" But at the last minute honesty fails them. At risk of being swept away to accept what she offers him, Dewi makes a demand which is as good as a statement to her that she has failed. He asks for proof of the future to be delivered in the present – demanding that she give up to him the one thing that she has so far retained. This has nothing to do with morality or convention – she has already told him, "Sacraments aren't conventions". In making this demand he is adopting the same device he had earlier employed in the scene with his parents at the end of Act I. There it was the Bible, which they accepted and he denied, that he used to manipulate their acceptance. Here it is Bet's belief in the sacrament, which is the point at which the spiritual touches the material."I'm an old-fashioned girl, Dewi. It was through the door of the sacrament I always thought to go this way". His reply is precisely that act of deceitfulness which he had come home to commit. "I've only got tonight, Bet. Do you see, I've only got tonight. Tonight is our sacrament". Had anyone else said this, it might have been true, but Dewi adopts these terms only with spiteful irony. So as the Act comes to a close and the two lovers make their mutual pledge we know that they are both in different ways insincere. Bet knows she has lost the gamble, so she takes his hands without a smile; and Dewi has the bitter triumph of reaching the end of the path leading to self-destruction. The audience may intuit this, but as yet they have no means of understanding it completely.

The final Act of *Cymru Fydd* is set early the following morning. it begins with a scene between Dora and John, which gradually reveals to the audience the depth of their understanding of their situation. They are both completely realistic about Dewi's situation and know that there is little hope of saving him from the suicide implied in the oath he earlier took in their presence. Neither has any illusions about his truthfulness or his courage; they know that in the end they will have to take the responsibility of phoning the police and that that is their only chance of saving him. However, they also know that Dewi will consider that as the worst treachery and in considerable measure they share his attitude. From the opening moments of the scene, with rueful humour, they mutually confess their involvement in his crime and its consequences and as it develops we come to understand the full measure of the guilt in which they feel they too are imprisoned.

As Dora tells her husband: "Its impossible not to be unfair". This relates to his treatment of Bet, for they are aware that in leaving her alone with Dewi the night before, John was tacitly shifting the burden of responsibility from his own shoulders to hers. John says again at this point that he will have to leave the ministry and this time Dora fails to contradict him, for his basic attitude to life has changed. Now he can deliberately and willingly put himself in opposition to the law. "If I knew about anything at all I could do to hide him safely," he tells his wife, "I'd do it now". And her reply puts the stamp of approval on what he says: "John you're growing more like a Christian every day".

What has happened to John is that he has come to recognize himself in his son. He sees that Dewi's whole behaviour, including his dishonesty and deceitfulness, follows naturally from the fact that he perceives himself in isolation from a world which is quite empty of meaning. Unable to accept anything which comes from outside himself, and angrily sweeping asides the "shibboleths", Dewi is obliged to create his own criteria of meaningfulness.

His only "crime", John argues, is the imaginative honesty which makes it impossible for him to escape the "unending daily distaste". Christianity offers no alleviation of this sense of failure; as John says; "You have to be exceptionally scatterbrained to enjoy daily bread". Dewi's worst offences are not the result of an evil will, but the inevitable, unplanned consequences of his attitude to a world he has no ability to change. John has found the source of Dewi's guilt inside himself, for he has imagined, and imaginatively consented to, his son's escape through suicide:

Wyt ti'n gweld pam na fedra'i mo'i gondemnio fo? Os ydy'r bachgen yn lleidr ac yn taro dyn yn hanner marw ar y ffordd fawr, rydw innau sy'n dad iddo yn medru dychmygu ei dranc o. Rydw i fy hunan yn llofrudd. Mae o'n deffro pethau yn fy niymwybod i sy'n peri na fedra i ddim edrych arno heb euogrwydd a dychryn.

Do you see why I can't condemn him? If the boy's a thief and has half-killed a man on the road, as his father I can imagine his destruction. I'm a murderer myself. He awakens things in my unconscious which make it impossible for me to look at him without guilt and horror.

Because of this it is impossible for John to betray Dewi. That would be to bring the show which his son has been playing out for himself to a sudden end and would make him then quite literally a murderer. Dora accepts this, and with it accepts the responsibility of phoning the police herself: "I'm his mother. Love has to gamble too".

These words conclude the first movement of this Act and also introduce the next, for as Dora leaves the stage Bet enters, to phone the police in Dora's name. Then when Dora returns the two women have an opportunity to share their love and offer what comfort they can to each other before the inevitable conclusion. For the audience this must be an important scene. In the first instance it continues our education in the matter of love, but most important of all, it shows us how it is possible to live with it, in a way which Dewi is afraid to contemplate. Neither Bet nor Dora are anything but realistic regarding Dewi's courage; both are in the grip of fear and panic, and yet they persist in the attempt to make their love real and secure in the world. "Love's a dangerous thing", Bet says; both know that she is giving everything she has and putting her peace of mind, confidence, her ability to hope and believe in anything at risk in the vain hope of saving her lover. All that she could have won in return for this is Dewi's love, but Dora at least knows quite certainly that what she will actually achieve is his bitter hatred. She tells Bet, "There's no reward for love. You've given him everything he is capable of receiving...He's had his thrill". And though Bet tries to dissociate herself from this knowledge, she can't do it. "He gave me his word...", she protests, but she has no defence against Dora's reply: "He'll never forgive you". Nor has she any answer to the words with which Dora closes their conversation, which implicitly confirm what her husband has already said — it would be better for Dewi to be dead!

With John's re-entry all three share the knowledge that the police are on the way from town to collect Dewi and that they have very few minutes to decide how best to act. Not to tell him the police are coming but to leave them to wake him would be the bitterest betrayal of all. But to wake him before they come would be to give him the time he needs to carry out his threat. The dilemma of the parents is cruel. Seeing him as a child, they know it is their duty to protect him from himself; but as parents they have the stronger duty to protect him from the world outside. There is no way to escape the suffering which results from the fact that it is impossible to achieve even either one of these ends. Bet refuses the bitter knowledge which their behaviour implies and frantically protests the promise that Dewi has made to her against their suggestion that only the worst form of betrayal will save Dewi's life: "Save his life? No one here's threatening his life. He's my lover. I've just risen from his embrace". Dora's reply to this is dreadfully cruel – "To call the Philistines to him"– because only cruelty offers the remotest hope of saving Bet from herself. Only sharing their bitter knowledge can strengthen her in preparation for the inevitable end. "You're spitting on my love", she protests again; "You're killing Dewi in my heart". But of course his parents know that it is infinitely better that they should do that than to wait for Dewi to do it himself. "That's what I would do if I could," John tells Bet, "that's my duty. Before he wakes". Still defiant, Bet moves to wake him herself. Ironically their cruelty has strengthened her. "I'll go and wake him now", she tells John, "To prove my faith in him". Before calling the police was the time to do that, John tells her, but only now does she have the courage to do it: "I didn't dare. I do now". They have said nothing to increase her confidence in Dewi; indeed, she must know now that Dewi is going to die; but of course, he won't die in her heart – confident in that knowledge, she can dare even the dreadful suffering of his denial.

Bet is saved from doing this by the arrival of the police and from this moment the pace and tone of the play change. As the action speeds up it could be said that the drama is at an end, because in what remains the focus of our attention is separate from the focus of sympathy. The police represent what by now we have come to realise is the absolute dishonesty which Dewi challenges; his challenge, on the other hand, is self- destructive and childish. Between them is the middle ground of suffering. The rôle of the Police Inspector is not an enviable one. Beneath his superficial politeness and respectability he is a blaggard – a very ordinary man, perhaps, but a blaggard for all his ordinariness because he will destroy anything about him in defence of his own complacency. By contrast Dewi is honest and straightfoward. We have to accept the truthfulness of much that he says in these last moments. Nor can we fail to understand the element of desperation that motivates his final, savage attempt to destroy himself in Bet's eyes. We learn that she is safe from the violence of his attack when we see her defending herself against the Inspector, showing that she has heard and understood Dora's warning her about the necessity of maintaining her self-respect. This is a guarantee for the future, in much the same way as Dora's closing words. Her last comment as the policemen come in carrying Dewi's body is bitter – "He's had his last thrill" – but this is the bitterness of someone who has learned to live without seeking a refuge from suffering. That perhaps is the worst weakness and the worst betrayal, which refuses love because it is painful and refuses life because it is inconsistent and absurd.

Conclusion

Dewi Rhys has much in common with the heroes of other important post-War European and American plays. He is something of the Existential hero and a good deal of the Angry Young Man. However. although he is very much the central character of *Cymru Fydd*, the action of the play does not centre on him as the action of Sartre's *Les Mains Sales* (1948) does centre on Hugo or that of Osbourne's *Look Back in Anger* (1957) on Jimmy Porter. Dewi is fully involved in the action of *Cymru Fydd* only while he is in the process of deciding his own fate. That is so even during the struggle with Bet in the latter part of the second Act. Thereafter, even when he comes down to face the policemen, the centre of the drama is elsewhere, in the relationship between his father and mother and Bet, as they struggle to come to terms with their own awareness of responsibility and their bitter resentment of his cowardice.

The effect of this is to correct the imbalance between the tragic hero and the social world which had been introduced in the heroic drama of the later Seventeenth Century and accentuated through the Romantic period into the middle of the nineteenth century. Ibsen's development from his early Romantic drama to the quasi-tragic struggles dramatised in his mature plays reflects a changing view of the relationship between the individual and his world. The series of plays which begins with *The Wild Duck* (1884) and ends with *John Gabriel Borkman* (1896) is increasingly dominated by an ironical sense that it was ultimately impossible for man to be at once himself and at one with his world. This irony is clearly apparent in early plays, dominating the ending of *An Enemy of the People* (1882), for example. At the ending of *Hedda Gabler* (1890), in *Rosmersholm* (1886) and at the climax of *The Master Builder* (1896) it is brutally clear in the disparity between the motivating cause and the destructive effect. The structural differences between these reflect a continuing attempt to relate processes of internal change and development to the social world from which they arise on the level of action. However, in his last play, *When We Dead Awake* (1899), Ibsen seems to have given himself over to the developing irony completely. There it undermines the integrity of character and experience and as a result the action of the play breaks up into a series of self-contemplative gestures.

Peter Szondi thought that the crisis initiated in modern drama when Ibsen substituted psychological analysis for inter-personal action was resolved with Arthur Miller's *Death of a Salesman* (1949). Miller gave a double definition to his playing space, which was at once the immediate social world of Willy Loman and inside the Salesman's head. So the action of the play could be at one and the same time inter-personal and intra-personal and the psychological analysis was dramatically presented within the structure of the hero's experience.[1] By this means Miller combined objective and subjective viewpoints and brought his drama to a close with a poignant sense of loss which is at least seemingly tragic. With Willy's suicide the playing area is re-defined in terms of his absence so that the audience quite literally share the experience of Willy's wife as she laments over his grave.

The tragic element in *Death of a Salesman* is increased precisely because our awareness is greater than Linda's. There are in fact two aspects to it, for we combine the knowledge of Willy's inner struggle against the sense of failure with objective understanding of the suffering his cowardice has caused in the world about him. However, in the final analysis we would have to concede that the play falls short of tragedy to the extent that Miller fails to generalize his subject. His achievement, in fact, was less than Szondi argued. Although he had internalized the analysis of Willy's condition, he had not succeeded in formally defining some of the main thematic issues. So there have always been arguments about the degree to which the commercial world to which Willy has tried to conform is responsible for his downfall. Clearly there is a sense in which this is true. Miller's stage directions ensure that we remain aware of the way in which Willy's increasingly urban environment threatens him and distorts his perception of himself. Nor does Miller settle the question of personal responsibility. The ending of the play leaves us with several important questions unanswered: and indeed, the play as a whole leaves them unasked. What share of guilt does Linda bear for what happens to her husband, whom she has persistently humoured, thereby thrusting him back into insecurity and egocentricity? What accounts for the dramatic differences between Biff and Happy's attitude to their father and to life in general? To what extent is Willy's attitude a legitimate protest against a world in which relatedness is impossible?

Even in strictly formal terms Miller's success depends on compromise. If, as Szondi argued, he dramatised the central process of change in his hero, he failed to confront the wider challenge implicit in his own vision of the subject. Instead he fell back on a symbolic gesture reminiscent of similar devices in the plays of Ibsen or Chekov. From the opening moments of the play and at many important points, we are aware of the nostalgic flute music which symbolises Willy's father, whose desertion of his family is clearly a part of Miller's analysis of his hero's fate. By means of this device Miller locks the action of his play into a longer time scale, and implies a wider action which he is unable to present.

There is in fact every reason to suggest that far from resolving the crisis of modern drama Arthur Miller's play actually marks what is, at least for American and English drama, a more acute phase. His daring formal innovation cannot for long distract attention from the fact that his plays reflect fundamental uncertainties about the relationship between the individual and the social world and even about the definition of human character itself, which audiences must perceive eventually as inhibiting tension.

Further formal experiment in Anglo-American drama has done little to resolve these uncertainties, which are deeply rooted in the culture of the contemporary English speaking world. Another aspect of this crisis may be seen particularly clearly in a play which preceded *Death of a Salesman* by only four years, J.B.Priestley's *The Inspector Calls* (1945). The on-stage action of the play concerns the process by which Priestley's Inspector brings each of the other four characters in turn to acknowledge their involvement in the life of the working-class girl whose suicide he claims to be investigating. Priestley's main point here is that we all share responsibility for social evils in so far as we only tacitly support and profit from the social and economic system. The play exemplifies that dramatic indirectness which we have already noticed in Ibsen. The real action concerns past events, when the lives of the characters came into contact with that of the dead girl. What is presented on stage is no more than a vehicle for this past action and when it is complete the play comes to an end. Nothing results from what happens on stage. Indeed, towards the end, the characters discover that the Inspector was not in fact a real Inspector and begin to wrap themselves in the folds of indifference which he had painstakingly stripped from them.

Priestly brings the drama to a close with a device calculated to suggest that reality may not be quite impervious. The announcement of another Inspector suggests that the characters may yet be forced from their self-protective isolation. However, this is no more than a formalistic trick, suggesting an endless repetition of self enclosed actions which lead nowhere. The inevitable comparison with the ending of Nicolai Gogol's *The Government Inspector* (1836), when it is announced after the departure of the false Inspector that his real life counterpart has arrived to terrorize the corrupt town officials, is very much to Priestley's disadvantage. In Gogol's world a false Inspector might well be considered a worse evil than a real representative of the Government, for only the latter can bring to an end the otherwise eternal misery of chaos, corruption and guilt, which his play presents directly to us. In Priestley's drama, on the other hand, the one Inspector is no more capable than the other of actually influencing the world in which the characters live and which the ending of the play leaves the audience quite free to inhabit again a world — in which, as the play itself acknowledges, it is only too easy to bury responsiblility beneath indifference and in which there are no mechanisms which actually work towards social justice.

A harsh critic might be moved to suggest that the function of Priestley's theatre was to substitute awareness for action, thereby making it possible for a middle-class audience to live comfortably with social injustice. Yet it would be fairer to acknowledge that this might be the consequence, without being a part of the dramatist's motivation. Clearly Priestley's intention was to engage seriously with the problem he saw. His problem as a dramatist followed from the fact that he was trying to devise an action which could not possibly exist. Social responsibility existed in his world only as a moral idea, which by definition could arise only in the sensibility of the individual. The social and economic structures governing relationships in the world at large were based on the assumption that individuals are isolated from one another except in so far as they voluntarily relate within a confined relationship. He could imagine a series of interpersonal collisions taking place even in this world, but he could not imagine an action which would dramatise the essential connectedness between them.

In contrast to the brilliantly innovative American writer, of course, J.B.Priestly must have seemed a rather old-fashioned dramatist even

in 1945, when he was little more than half-way through his career. At
this distance, however, the comparison between them may suggest that
they both faced problems which were characteristic of the post-war
period. In 1956, just a short time before Priestley's last play appeared
in London, John Osborne's *Look Back in Anger* was produced at the
Royal Court and critics hailed the beginning of a new epoch. No doubt
Jimmy Porter's strident anger was something new in the theatre;
equally certainly the play's frankness and lack of technical pretentious-
ness seemed challenging and refreshing. Now that the dust has long
since settled, however, we can see that Osborne was confronting
problems similar to those which undermined the effectiveness of *The
InspectorCalls*.

Look Back in Anger presents a phase in a relationship between
working class Jimmy Porter and his middle-class wife, Alison. It begins
with a scene which introduces us to the relationship at a point of strain
which threatens imminent collapse. A third character, Jimmy's friend,
Cliff, who lodges with them, is introduced so as to give us a means of
gauging the tension within the relationship objectively. During this
first scene there is a crisis, when Jimmy deliberately brings about an
accident when Alison burns her arm, followed by a release of tension
and the suggestion, with Alison's anouncement to Cliff that she is
pregnant, that the emotional problems that beset the couple may be
resolved. The end of the scene, however, following the announcement
that Alison's friend Helena is coming to stay, marks a new high point
of tension, as Jimmy, still ignorant of Alison's condition, viciously
wishes on her the miscarriage which does in fact, later occur: "If you
could have a child, and it would die...Please if only I could watch you
face that..."

The play comes to an end when Jimmy's wish has been fulfilled and
Alison returns to him. By now she has learnt the lesson that her
husband referred to. "I was in pain", she tells him, "and all I could
think of was you, and what I'd lost...I'm in the mud at last! I'm
grovelling!..." Jimmy's response is the gesture of reconciliation which
brings the action to an end: "He stands, frozen for a moment, then he
bends down and takes her shaking body in his arms... Don't. Please
don't...I can't..." The wheel of their mutual suffering has some full
circle. Now for the first time they are consciously in the same place
and whatever future they may have together or apart will require a new
beginning.

The problem is that the play does not actually present the process of change and development which is suggested here. Jimmy, in fact, has undergone no change — the restoration of their relationship depends on Alison's accepting the lesson that he is constantly preaching but is quite unable to realize himself, namely that pain and suffering must be willingly accepted if love is to function in any way other than destructively. However, Alison disappears from the play at the very point when she begins the process of adjustment, in defiance and rejection of Jimmy's hatefulness. At this point Helena comes in, firstly as a catalyst, permitting the change in Alison to begin, then as a distraction, filling the stage with her relationship with Jimmy while her friend goes off, loses her baby, suffers and decides to return. Alison comes back only at the beginning of the last scene; even then Helena keeps the stage. Keeping faith with Alison's inarticulateness and Jimmy's childishness requires that Osborne shift the responsibility for action clearly onto Helena's shoulders in this last scene so, seeing Alison suddenly appear at the door, she has a convenient return of middle class morality which convinces her that her happiness with Jimmy is immoral and that she must remove herself from the scene.

What Osborne was facing here, of course, was the old Ibsenian problem of dramatising a process of internal change. What is striking is the fact that he failed to notice that there was a problem. The history of the relationship between Jimmy and Alison was in fact no more than a peg on which he could hang his fascination with Jimmy's heroical protest. This is the real substance of the play and his aim as a dramatist is to persuade us to accept it — that is Alison's real dramatic function in *Look Back in Anger* — she is no more than a device employed to a rhetorical effect.

Jimmy's case is a sad one. Outraged by his father's long-drawn out and early death and by his mother's indifference to it, Jimmy has strong emotional needs which he is unable to acknowledge or satisfy. No change in Alison is actually going to help him unless he can match it with a corresponding change in himself. Osborne, however, writes as if he is satisfied with Jimmy as he is and considers his hysteria an appropriate response to the world in which he lives. He seems on the verge at times of making his hero into a figure similar to the hero of Camus's *Caligula* (1946), who protests against the meaninglessness of human suffering and the complacency with which men protect themselves from reality. Helena's attitude certainly strengthens this suggestion, for the ease with which she slips from one self-protective pose to another is strongly in contrast to Jimmy's honest aggressiveness. However, the action which would develop this awareness never takes shape; the play remains within the false framework of the relationship.

It is difficult to explain this confusion except in terms of Osborne's fascination with his hero. It is quite certain that he was unwilling to let go of Jimmy's anger or to allow him actively to compromise his vision. Clearly, like Dewi Rhys, he was unable to go beyond that original, subjective experience of pain and accept another person as himself. Jimmy's railing may distract himself from this selfishness, but it should not have distracted Osborne, any more than it is likely, at this distance, to distract an audience.

Even while London audiences were reeling in shock at Jimmy Porter's daring verbal assaults on middle class commonplaces there were other developments in European theatre, much more in line with Arthur Miller's work, which were soon to make Osborne's work seem almost perversely old fashioned. In 1956 Freidrich Durrenmatt had already published *The Visitation of the Old Lady*; this was followed in 1958 by Max Frisch's *Biedermeier and the Fireraisers*. These plays combine dramatic conventions derived from different theatres with structural freedom and a flexible attitude to the definition of stage space. The result was a theatre in which the dramatic focus fell on the point of contact between the individual sensibility and the larger social and political mechanisms which determined historical process. They aimed to explore precisely that area of experience from which Osborne had turned away.

Almost immediately this new theatre made itself felt in England, though in a distinctively British version, with John Arden's *Serjeant Musgrave's Dance,* which followed *Look Back in Anger* at the Royal Court in October 1959. Arden employed a dramatic technique similar to that of Durrenmatt to develop a similar theme. His starting point was the typical cycle of colonial repression and terrorist outrage which by now we associate with Northern Ireland, but which at that time resulted from the British Army's attempt to hold on to Cyprus and Aden. However, he set the play in a deliberately vague historical past. Black Jack Musgrave, he said, could have been a serjeant in Cromwell's army; his soldiers wore the uniform of the Imperial period, from 1860-1890; the Constable, on the other hand, was a typical 'Peeler' from earlier decades; and the action took place in a Northern English town the population of which was in the grip of an industrial conflict more typical of the early decades of the Twentieth Century.

The play, Arden said, was realistic but not naturalistic, the action interspersed with songs sung to a variety of folk tunes — a kind of a historical fairy tale, which it might well be true to say could not ever have taken place and which yet must have played itself out in some form or another in the imagination of any honest soldier shocked at the situations of gratuitous violence involved in the 'peace keeping' missions of post-war Colonial armies. His central character, driven mad by the sudden reversal of a world based on Justice and Duty, returns to England and to this winter-bound Northern town to confront its inhabitants with the skeleton of a local lad whose murder in an unnamed colonial town had sparked off a brutal military reprisal against a defenceless civilian population. Musgrave's crazy idea is to bring home the reality of violence by turning it on the civilian population in whose name it is perpetrated through the world. However, the 'logic' on which he bases his endeavour is deficient, in fact madness, as one of the female characters, who bear much of Arden's authority, tells him at the end. So he fails and at the close of the play awaits the time to perform his final dance at the end of a rope, together with his pacifist comrade, Attercliffe, whose final song holds out some sort of crooked promise: "They're going to hang us up a length higher nor most appletrees grow, Serjeant. D'you reckon we can start an orchard?"

In fact, however, as contemporary audiences must be aware, no orchard is to grow from the corpses soon to be planted, as the obvious contemporary reference makes plain. The ending of *Serjeant Musgrave's Dance* in fact represents a compromise not only of the Serjeant's, but of the author's own critical vision. Even more than Durrenmatt's and Frisch's work, this play has a very direct political reference, deriving from the Labour movement's failure to develop the anti-Imperialist critique which had been an integral part of its pre-war programme. Arden makes this plain, though hardly explicit, by setting Musgrave's adventure in the context of the classic social conflict from which the ideology and the mythology of the Labour movement was derived. Musgrave himself is more explicit: he appeals directly to the miners' leader to recognize that the ultimate responsibility for the colonial adventure lies with his own class enemies, but in vain. To accept this appeal would be to take the road to revolution — precisely the road taken by many working class leaders before the beginnings of the Labour movement as we now know it. Historically, however, that road had led to defeat, the memory of which had conditioned the development of the Labour Party and its ultimate failure to fulfil its programme, with which Arden, like other English intellectuals, was trying to come to terms.

In the final analysis he was unable to do this — at least by the means he had adopted in *Serjeant Musgrave's Dance* — because he shared the middle class individualism which the Labour movement had adopted along with the strategy of working within the framework of the Imperialist State. This is why he made his working-class leader reject Musgrave's Logic — a gesture which was historically innaccurate but ideologically accurate in terms of the contemporary situation to which he was actually referring. Having done that he tried to suggest an a-historical source for this rejection in the Polly Garterish sentiment of the female characters. They turn Sparky's accidental death conveniently into a reason for persuading the miners against violent revolt. But having arrived at that point, Arden had to confront another problem. Musgrave's 'madness' had to be resolved unheroically, without a violent confrontation with the authorities which would have validated his rebellion. How then to resolve the action?

Arden found a handy answer to this question in the character of the Bargee, who fulfils a highly symbolic function in the play. Hunchbacked Joe Bludgeon is politically quite independent, motivated only by a gleeful mischievousness associated with the goblins of fairy tale legend. What can he represent, except a wilful, twisted, reductive element in human nature which might be shared by the representatives of all social classes without being the responsibility of any? It is crooked Joe who thrusts the rifle into Musgrave's back and thereby permits the play to splutter to a close. The beer-laden dance which brings the action to an end is also Joe's responsibility. The very last scene, in which Musgrave seals his repentance with Mrs Hitchcock's port and lemon, is no more than an attempt to manipulate the audience's response after the play has finished. It actually comes to an end when crooked Joe takes the weight of the whole social world on to his humped back. Doing that, he absolves his creator of the responsibility he took on in writing the play.

Absolution was also the end point of Harold Pinter's first substantial play, *The Birthday Party*, which preceded Sergeant Musgrave's dance at the Royal Court by only seventeen months — but absolution of the audience rather than the author. If Arden's work represents the characteristically English version of the drama of Durrenmatt and Frisch, then it may equally fairly be said that Pinter's early plays represent an English version of the deconstructive theatre of Beckett and Ionesco. In both cases the difference is similar, blunting the cutting edge of formalistic innovation.

The Birthday Party is a three Act play set in a seedy sea-side boarding house where Stanley, an unemployed pianist, is lodging, apparently at the expense of his landlady, who combines the characteristics of a doting mother and a simple-minded, superannuated siren. The action of the play is initiated by the arrival of two men whom we quickly sense have come to the lodging house only in order to make some kind of approach to Stanley. Gradually their presence defines itself more clearly in his and in our awareness as a threat and from then on, until the central part of the play, the action concerns his clumsy and ineffective attempts to repulse them. The climax of the action comes during a party arranged by the visitors to celebrate Stanley's birthday, regardless of the fact that it may not in fact be his birthday when, under the combined influence of noise, alchohol and darkness, Stanley breaks down. From that point on he is inequivocably in their power. During what remains of the night he is consigned to the care of the Irishman McCann. The senior partner, who presents himself as a Jew, variously Nat, Simey or Benny Goldberg, spends the time seducing Lulu, whose rather vague role in the play until that point had seemed to be based on her potential as a stimulus to Stanley. In the morning Stanley is brought down, washed and newly shaven, but quite helpless, and taken away in a large car by Goldberg and MacCann, to a vague destination, in spite of the protests of Meg's husband, Petey, who was absent from the party and has no real understanding of what is happening. As his impotent appeal to Stanley — "Stan, don't let them tell you what to do!" — goes unanswered and we hear the sounds of the car driving away, the situation drifts back to the excruciating banality of the beginning.

This banality is Pinter's starting point. The ordinary world of human relations as he presents it is totally empty of meaning and potential. Action arises from deeper levels and is quite irrational and unmotivated in ordinary terms. What happens in *The Birthday Party* makes no real sense. Neither Goldberg nor McCann have any recognisable place or function in the social world. They are uncertain of themselves and even unstable as characters. The possibility exists, of course, of interpreting them as messengers from another world, either above or below, but apart from the fact that we have no means of reaching certainty in the matter, their behaviour would remain inconsistent and irrational in human terms.

What is important in *The Birthday Party* is that we construe the action sensibly in spite of its irrationality. The central event is the party and within the party the game of blind man's buff which culminates in Stanley's breakdown. We have no difficulty in understanding this as a theatrical event which has its own logic, derived from the pattern of responses organized around the game. The emotions involved in the childish game which we have all played are real emotions, often stronger than any we experience in 'real' situations. When the game is transposed into a theatrical situation, which is in itself a 'game', supposedly cut off from reality, we find no difficulty in interpreting the 'real' world represented on the stage in terms of the emotions released in the game and the relations acted out within it.

Our experience of the game gives us something around which we can organize our responses to the action as a whole, creating sense out of nonsense. As Stanley takes on the role of the blinded hunter McCann literally blinds him by snapping his glasses. As he stumbles in the darkness Stanley's weakness becomes a door through which the deeper violent instincts of his nature find release. As his hands close around Meg's throat Goldberg and McCann throw him off, but as they do so the lights fuse and we are all cast into Stanley's darkness together. Now, in the darkness which we share, his violence becomes more threatening, outside the control of his persecutors. When they find the torch and shine it on him we find him bent over Lulu, spead-eagled on the table. As the light hits him his violence evaporates and he is reduced to giggling helplessness, but by that time we have seen enough to accept, at least passively, the unexpected culmination of the 'real' game in which Goldberg and McCann have been engaged since the beginning of the play.

The audience of *The Birthday Party* are implicated in the action of the play by virtue of their ability to construe it sensibly. This is very clear during the long verbal exchanges between Goldberg and McCann on the one hand and Stanley on the other, which make no sense in terms of continuous and consistent dialogue, but which are easily understood as a coherent series of gestures. It is on this level that *The Birthday Party* is to be understood as a parable of transgression and guilt in which we are all involved by virtue of our humanity.

However, it is also, though indirectly, a contribution to the debate which was currently being conducted elsewhere in English drama. The function of the play is actually to absolve its audiences from precisely that anxiety concerning the relationship between the individual and society at large that we have seen Arden more directly addressing in *Serjeant Musgrave's Dance.* Pinter's play concerns the social world directly. It's starting point is the audience's aprehension of an empty, jejune, normality, in which language is reduced to a series of incomplete and egocentric gestures — a world of isolation and banality. From among the meaningless scraps of commonplace experience a coherent action begins to take place, which develops as it draws energy from habitual patterns of response which lie beyond the control of the conscious mind. Experiencing the play obliges us to concede that the whole dimension of inter-personal, social experience, far from reflecting a logic derived from our objective awareness of each other and the world, is actually organized in terms of sub-rational impulses and inchoate energies. At this level individuality itself and even subjectivity are undermined and with this knowledge the audience are released into a world in which they may only live by accepting their inablity to alter it.

The contrast between Pinter's theatre and that of Saunders Lewis is very marked. At the end of the *Cymru Fydd* the audience are released into a world where they must live with an enhanced sense of responsibility, understanding that suffering, so far from reducing human dignity, is the only means by which it may be sustained. Though his drama has nothing to say directly about the individual's social responsibility, it is nevertheless implicit in the view which the audience have gained of themselves. The irritating contrast between the individual's enhanced awareness of himself and his uncertainty in relation to the objective world, which stimulated and frustrated contemporary English writers, simply did not exist for Saunders Lewis. The whole drive of his thinking from the earliest years had been towards a view of the human situation which reconciled acceptance of the conditionality of subjective experience with the individual's freedom to act in an objective world. This is precisely the reconciliation which Ibsen had been unable to achieve because he was unwilling to relinquish the Romantic demand that individual integrity should reflect the integrity of the created universe. Having achieved this reconciliation, Saunders Lewis was free to explore the traditional field of the drama, which is also the dimension in which our living is actually conducted, that is the field of inter-personal relations, where we learn what we are and what we have to do, day by day, and on that basis to create a distinctive form of modern tragedy.

This dramatic achievement is in no way a model, even for imitation by Welsh writers, not only because it was based on a series of private intellectual battles, but also because it is rooted in a distant and inaccessible past. The tradition which he mastered and to which he contributed, may actually by now also be inaccessible, because it depended on certain assumptions about human character which could be progressively revalidated as the world changed by means of a clearly identified group of theatrical conventions and gestures. One of the things that Saunders Lewis's drama has to teach a wider audience inside and outside Wales, however, is that the formalistic and thematic developments of recent English drama do not denote a new departure. Against the background of his theatre they may rather be seen as a series of devices designed to mediate an illusory reconciliation of ideas and feelings which English society is unwilling to relate on the level of substance. It could well be that at the point when a radical adjustment is made in Britain, regarding the way in which individuality is felt and experienced, the traditional theatre of Europe may once again become available, a new common ground between the artist and the audience.

Notes

Introduction

1. Perhaps more than most terms used in connection with the Theatre, Naturalism requires careful definition. The characteristics I associate with 'Naturalist' drama have already been referred to in the text — preoccupation with the material world, its laws and characteristics and the effect they have on human life; the attempt to represent this world directly in the theatre and the consequent tendency to distract the audience from the essential conventionality of Theatre by an appearance of reality; a dependence on actions drawn from the immediate social world, combined with an attempt to assimilate literary to social structure. There is a striking coincidence between Naturalist drama and the Neo-Classic drama of Seventeenth Century France in respect of the dependance on dialogue and faithfulness to unity of time and action, which makes for a constrictive definition of the stage, in contrast to the flexibility and openness of Romantic drama.

2. Peter Szondi, *Theory of the Modern Drama* (1965), tr. M. Hays (1987).

3. Gerhart Hauptmann (1862-1946) began a series of Naturalistic plays with *Before Dawn* (1889). Maxim Gorky (1868-1936) has had wide influence as a dramatist outside his native Russia, with *Lower Depths* (1902).

4. Maurice Maeterlink (1862-1949), Belgian dramatist, among whose most important plays are *La Princess Maleine* (1889), *La Morte de Tintagiles* (1899) and *L'oiseau bleu* (1909). W.B.Yeats's activity as a dramatist began with *The Land of Heart's Desire* (1894). His was the most immediate and perhaps the most lasting influence on Saunders Lewis.

5. The title *The Four Branches of the Mabiniogi* refers to a cycle of four loosely related prose tales composed some time around 1100. Saunders Lewis borrowed from the second and the fourth branch for the material of *Blodeuwedd* (1947) and *Branwen* (1971) and less directly from the third for his comedy, *Eisteddfod Bodran* (1952).

6. The plays which, by implication I have labelled as minor include:*Eisteddfod Bodran* (1952); *Gan Bwyll* (1952); *Serch yw'r Doctor* (1960); *Yn y Trên* (1965); *Problemau'r Prifysgol* (1968); *Y Cyrnol Chabert* (1968) *Branwen* (1975); *Dwy Briodas Ann* (1975); *Cell y Grog* (1975); *1938* (1978) *Excelsior* (1980). Some of these are very interesting and considerable plays, but I have not considered them in this study because they do not seem to me to fall within the compass of the distinctive type of Theatre with which it is concerned.

7. Modernism, though widely recognised as a twentieth century literary and artistic movement, would be differently defined by different critics. The important point here is to recognize that Saunders Lewis may be categorized together with writers like T.S.Eliot, the Anglo-Welsh poet and artist, David Jones, the novelist's William Faulkner and Ford Madox Ford, in that he shared their preoccupation with exploring the integrity of experience and their confidence in the artist's ability to deconstruct experience or to render it down

to its component parts by deconstructing literary forms and linguistic structures. What is unique about Saunders Lewis is that he built his literary work around the assumption that human experience was in essence social and spiritual.

Part I

1. Edward Gordon Craig (1872-1966), theorist, theatrical practitioner, famous by 1921 for his work in London, Florence and Moscow and for his ideas regarding setting and stage design and acting. His *On the Art of the Theatre* had been published in 1911, followed by *Towards a New Theatre* (1913), and *The Theatre Advancing* (1921).
2. "A counted number of pulses only is given to us of a variegated, dramatic life. How may we see in them all that is to be seen in them by the finest sense? How can we pass most swiftly from point to point, and be present always at the focus where the greatest number of vital forces unite in their purest energy? To burn always with this hard gem-like flame, to maintain this ecstasy, is success in life." Walter Pater (1839-94), Conclusion to *The Renaissance* (1873); first published in *Westminster Review*, November 1868.
3. "Maurice Barrès. Prif Lenor Ffrainc. Cysylltiad Dyn a'i Genedl", *Baner ac Amserau Cymru*, Ionawr 24, 1924.
4. Maurice Barrès (1862-1923), unfortunately remembered recently for his jingoistic response to the First World War, remains one of the most important French writers of the nineteenth century. The three novels which made up his trilogy were *Sous l'oeil des barbares* (1888), *Un homme libre* (1889) and *Le Jardin de Bérénice* (1891).
5. *Loc. cit.* uchod.
6. *Ibid.*
7. 'By Way of Apology', *Dock Leaves*, Winter 1955, 12..
8. *Ibid.*
9. Lascelles Abercrombie (1881-1938) and Gordon Bottomley (1874-1948), poets and dramatists, contributed to the revival of the poetic drama and developed many of the themes and manerisms which had emerged in contemporary Anglo Irish drama. Abercrombie had taught Saunders Lewis at Liverpool University and the two men had been close friends at that time.
10. 'Nodyn ar Ibsen', *Y Darian*, Rhagfyr 23, 1920.
11. 'Celf Drama. 1 —Sut i Drefnu Llwyfan', *Y Darian*, Mai 20, 1920.
12. 'Celfyddyd y Drama', *Y Darian*, Tachwedd 25, 1920.
13. Jacques Copeau (1879-1949), actor producer, whose work at Les Vieux Colombiers initiated a new movement in French and European theatre, introducing new standards, a freer, more symbolic approach to setting and performance. Gémier (1865-1933), famous as an actor, producer and teacher, worked in the same direction, training a number of the actors and producers who have contributed most to the development of modern French theatre.
14. 'Y Drama yn Ffrainc', *Y Darian*, Gorffenaf 7, 1921.
15. *Loc. cit.*, 'Nodyn ar Ibsen', *Y Darian*, Rhagfyr 23, 1920.
16. 'Recent Anglo-Celtic Drama', *The Welsh Outlook* (1922), 64.

17. The Abbey Theatre, Dublin, a cooperative venture by W.B.Yeats, Lady Gregory and others, opened in December 1904, had established itself with productions of their plays and those of J.M.Synge. The first presentation of his *Playboy of the Western World* in January 1907 had been a particularly notorious event. In the early 1920's the theatre attracted new attention on the occasion of the presentation of O'Casey's first plays.

18. 'Recent Anglo-Celtic Drama', *Loc. cit*.

19. J.M.Synge, *The Playboy of the Western World* (1907), Preface.

20. 'Recent Anglo-Celtic Drama', *op. cit*., 63.

21. 'Mudandod y Môr', *Baner ac Amserau Cymru*, Medi 29, 1943.

22. *The Eve of St John* (1921), Foreword.

23. Thomas Edwards, 'Twm o'r Nant' (1738-1810), author of a number of dramatic interludes, satiral, moralistic and humourous, played on a semi-professional basis in makeshift conditions in the later Eighteenth Century.

Part II

1. For the background to this most important event, see *Presenting Saunders Lewis* (1973), ed. A.R.Jones and G. Thomas.

2. The Welsh Calvinist Methodist Church grew out of the Evangelical Revival of the Eighteenth Century, when leaders of the Methodist congregations in 1811 took a decision to ordain their own ministers. Throughout the nineteenth century it had grown in strength and authority, imposing many of its attitudes and practices on other Non Conformist Churches in Wales and eventually assuming a dominant position in Welsh life. The social and devotional conservatism of Calvinistic Methodism, combined with its increasing spiritual aridity, led to what has been termed the 'Chapelism', which hindered and in some measure perhaps continues to hinder, social and religious development in Wales. At the same time it has to be said that Calvinistic Methodism has contributed immeasurably to the development of Welsh culture and still has access to a rich spiritual tradition which its theologians and hymn writers have made distinctively Welsh. While many Welsh writers consider an attack on Calvinism to be a guarantee of their progressive tendencies, Calvinism as it was understood by men like William Williams, Pantycelyn, offers a framework within which we may yet experience the fullest intellectual and spiritual life.

3. Most notably, Jean Louis Barrault (b. 1910), who produced *Le Soulier de Satin* (1919-24) at the Comédie Francaise in 1943 and went on to present many of Claudel's other plays in France and abroad during the 1950's.

4. Rather ironically Pelagius was a Brythonic Celt who taught in Rome in the late fourth and early fifth century, whereas Garmon, as his name implies, was a German. The main point of the Pelagian heresy was the assertion that man could initiate the process of salvation without the intervention of Divine Grace.

5. For a thorough and sensible treatment of the origins and development of this story, see J. Bédier, *Les Légendes Épiques*,II (1908), 170 196. A fifteenth century Welsh version of the story, as told in the twelfth century Latin Vita

Amici et Amelii carissimorum, was copied into the Red Book of Hergest, the main repository of Medieval Welsh literary texts.

6. Freely translated from *Kymdeithas Amlyn ac Amic*, ed. J. Gwenogvryn Evans (1909), 24-25.

7. The play 'Cain and Abel', part of the Towneley Cycle of Corpus Christi plays is one of the plays attributed to the fourteenth century Wakefield Master.

8. 'Ave Maria, Gratia Plena...'; 'Hail Mary, full of Grace, the Lord is with thee. Blessed art thou among women and blesed is the fruit of thy womb, Jesus. Holy Mary, Mother of God, pray for us sinners now and at the hour of our death.'

9. 'Lord have mercy, Christ have mercy', a prayer which has been inserted at the beginning of the Roman Mass since the Sixth Century.

Part III

1. 'Drama ar gyfer Gwyl Ddewi', *Radio Times*, February 22,1957, p.9. I owe this reference to Professor Bedwyr Lewis Jones.

2. 'Cwrs y Byd', *Baner ac Amserau Cymru*, Hydref 11, 1947.

3. 'Difyr dychwelyd' is Saunders Lewis's phrase (*loc.cit.*); I have allowed myself a little freedom in translating it.

4. 'Cwrs y Byd', *Baner ac Amserau Cymru*, Hydref 11, 1947, 8.

5. 'Cwrs y Byd', *Baner ac Amserau Cymru*, Rhagfyr 28, 1949 and Ionawr 4, 1950.

6. *Le Cid*, III,4; V,1.7.

7. Saunders Lewis wrote in 1955: "I remember being overwhelmed by young Miss Sybil Thorndike's performance in the Gilbert Murray translation of *Medea*. I thought on and off for some years about that revelation of Euripides. It was Miss Thorndike's Medea that gave me my first idea of a kindred character in Welsh legend; later on I wrote the first two acts of my own play *Blodeuwedd* in the hope that some day and some where there might be a Welsh-speaking Sybil Thorndike." 'By Way of Apology', *Dock Leaves*, Winter 1955, 10. Sybil Thorndike appeared in *Medea* under her husband's direction at the Holborn Empire in 1920, before the composition of *The Eve of St John*!

8. 'Cwrs y Byd', *Y Faner*, Mawrth 14, 1951, 8.

9. 'Penteulu' may be translated as 'Steward', but literally it means 'Head of family', or household. Modern English has no exact equivalent because, of course, the Medieval idea of 'family' has long ago disappeared.

10. *Antony and Cleopatra*, II,2.

11. *The Tempest*, I,2; *Much Ado About Nothing*, IV,1.

12. 'Mintai' is another difficult word to translate. The dictionary gives 'troop or company', but this fails to suggest the very personal relationship implied by the Medieval term.

13. A year of Sundays spent in this manner would clearly prevent attendance at Mass and leave Llew's killer in a state of mortal sin.

14. Letter to Dr. Gwenan Jones, 14,10,49. I am grateful to Ms Nerys Ann Jones of the Canolfan Uwchefrydiau Cymreig a Cheltaidd, Aberystwyth, for drawing my attention to this letter. See also *Taliesin*, December 1988.

15. 'Cwrs y Byd', *Baner ac Amserau Cymru*, Tachwedd 26, 1947.
16. Sir John Edward Lloyd, *History of Wales from the earliest times to the Edwardian Conquest* (London, New York, Toronto,3rd ed, 1939), II, 693.
17.'Cwrs y Byd', *Baner ac Amserau Cymru,* Tachwedd 26, 1947.
18. *Richard II,* V,5.
19. 'Saunders Lewis yn trafod...', *Baner ac Amserau Cymru*, Mawrth 14, 1951.
20. 'Cwrs y Byd', *Baner ac Amserau Cymru*, Mawrth 23, 1949.
21. *Phédre,* V,6, 1498-1570.
22. Twelfth century authoress of a number of 'lais', which are among the earliest texts assimilating the manners of Courtly Love with material drawn from Welsh and Irish legends. For Saunders Lewis her work exemplifies the way in which the different cultures of Norman Wales met and enriched each other and, in subsequent centuries, Europe generally.

Part IV

1. 'Cariad Pur', *Radio Times*, October 14, 1965.
2. *Antigone*, I,1; see *The Theban Plays*, trans. E.F.Watling (Penguin Books, London, 1988), 128.
3. *Troilus and Criseyde*, 1818-27.
4. *Othello,* III,3.
5. Blaise Pascal (1623-62), author of *Pensés*(1670), like Racine, was associated with the Jansenist movement in France. Pascal's thought has been widely influential in the twentieth century. Starting from the assumption that, in Housman's phrase, "Life...is nothing much to lose", Pascal argues that the leap to Christian faith and observance is essentially a reasonable act, even though the existence of God may not be susceptible of rational proof.
6. 'Cwrs y Byd', *Baner ac Amserau Cymru*, Gorffenaf 5, 1939.
7. 'Cwrs y Byd', *Baner ac Amsserau Cymru*, Hydref 11, 1939.
8. *Ibid.*
9. 'Cwrs y Byd', *Baner ac Amserau Cymru*, Mawrth 6, 1940.
10. The Hebrew version of Esther's story probably dates back to somewhere around 300 BC. The Greek version, which was sent to Egypt to authenticate the feast of Purim, was in existence before 160 BC.
11. J. Racine, *Esther* (1689), I,3,226-7.
12. The Jerusalem Bible (1966), 363.
13. *Loc. cit.*,II, 6, 630-31.
14. *Cynghanedd* is the complex system of alliteration and assonance which appears in the earliest Welsh poetry and developed during the Medieval period to become its most characteristic and persistent feature. For Saunders Lewis the Medieval system of *cynghanedd* exemplified the harmonmious, integrated vision of the universe on which he based his definition of what he called the Welsh aesthetic.
15. *Barnaby Rudge*, chapter 77.
16. *Esther,* III,7, 1177-78.
17. Cymru Fydd, the 'Young Wales' movement, founded in imitation of the Young Ireland movement, to advance the cause of Home Rule, was eventually

absorbed into the Liberal movement in Wales. Its emasculation and total collapse was one of the main factors behind the founding of the Welsh Party in 1925.

18. Capel Celyn lies under the waters of the reservoir which drowned the village of Tryweryn, in order to supplement the water supply of Liverpool. The drowning of Tryweryn, in spite of a widespread campaign and universal opposition in Wales, demonstrated that an English corporation could ride roughshod over all considerations of national feeling. It has done much to embitter political feelings in Wales and to undermine national self-respect. In much the same way rural Wales as a whole is presently being drowned under a wave of monolingual English immigrants and the subsequent bitter experience of helplessness is the most important single component of Dewi's nihilism and the vandalism and drunkenness which are its common counterparts in less sophisticated minds.

Conclusion

1. Peter Szondi, *Theory of the Modern Drama* (1965), tr. M. Hays (1987), 91-5

Select Bibliography

An indispensible book for the English reader is *Presenting Saunders Lewis* (1973), eds. Alun R. Jones and Gwyn Thomas, University of Wales Press. This contains several translations, including *Blodeuwedd*, *Siwan* and *Treason (Brad)*, together with a short list of articles in English on different aspects of the author's work.

The Oxford Companion to the Literature of Wales (1986) has an excellent general article on Saunders Lewis and many shorter pieces on his plays and other relevant topics.

There is a booklet in the 'Writers of Wales' series by Bruce Griffiths (1979 and 1989), University of Wales Press.

Translations of many of Saunders Lewis's plays have been published in the four volume collection by Joseph P. Clancy (1985), Christopher Davies Publishers, as follows: I, *The Vow, The Woman Made of Flowers, The King of England's Daughter;* II, *Have a Cigarette?, Treason, Esther;* III, *Excelsior, Academic Affairs, Tomorrow's Wales, On the Train;* IV, *The Daughter of Gwern Hywel, The Condemned Cell, The Two Marriages of Anne Thomas.*

Another volume of interest is Saunders Lewis, by H. Pritchard Jones (1990), Templegate Press, Illimois, which contains translations of a number of poems, essays and other material, including extracts from *Blodeuwedd, Siwan, Amis and Amig* [sic], *Buchedd Garmon* and *Esther.*

Appendix

Gwaed Yr Uchelwyr.............Noble Blood
Buchedd Garmon.................The Life of St. Germanus
Amlyn ac Amig....................Amlyn and Amig
Blodeuwedd.........................'Flowerface'
Siwan...................................Joan
Gymerwch Chi Sigaret? ....Have a Cigarette?
Brad.....................................Treason
Cymru Fydd.........................The Wales to Be

Index